BEYOND SURVIVAL
HOW FINANCIAL INSTITUTIONS CAN THRIVE IN THE 1990s

Michael T. Higgins

Dow Jones-Irwin
Homewood, Illinois 60430

Sponsoring editor: Jim Childs
Project editor: Joan A. Hopkins
Production manager: Diane Palmer
Jacket design: Mike Finkelman
Compositor: Editing, Design & Production, Inc.
Typeface: 11/13 Times Roman
Printer: Arcata Graphics/Kingsport

Library of Congress Cataloging-in-Publication Data

Higgins, Michael T.
Beyond survival: how financial institutions can thrive in the 1990s / Michael T. Higgins.
p. cm.
Includes index.
ISBN 1-55623-210-1
1. Financial institutions—United States—Management. 2. Bank management—United States. 3. Financial services industry—United States—Deregulation. I. Title.
HG2491.H52 1990
332.1'068—dc20 89-11920
CIP

Printed in the United States of America
1 2 3 4 5 6 7 8 9 0 K 6 5 4 3 2 1 0 9

I dedicate this book with an old Irish prayer to those who understand the banking industry's real needs.

Let them that understand us, spread the word . . .
Let them that do not understand us, hear the word.
And for those who do not understand after they hear the word . . .
may the Lord attend to them to turn their hearts.
And if He cannot turn their hearts, let Him turn their ankles . . .
so we will know them by their limping.

FOREWORD

As bankers look ahead to the increasingly competitive, economically uncertain, and politically unpredictable world of the 90s, there is one compelling reality that cannot be ignored: there simply will not be enough quality business to go around. As a result, not everyone will survive.

Banking as a deregulated marketplace is no more immune to the forces of change than any other industry. As users and providers of funds take advantage of sophisticated telecommunications and funds-transfer technologies, direct-marketing strategies, and a more liberal legislative environment in order to deal with each other directly, the traditional role of banks as financial intermediaries is being systematically eroded. Every generic product offered by banks can now be obtained elsewhere, quite often at a more attractive price from lower cost providers.

It should, therefore, come as no surprise that the financial markets are demanding that banks perform better in order to compensate shareholders for the greater risk associated with owning bank equities. Returns that might have been acceptable in the past will no longer be tolerated in the 90s. There will be no place for bank leadership that fails, for whatever reason, to maximize its potential in creating long-term shareholder value.

In response to these unprecedented challenges, enlightened CEOs in banks and in bank holding companies of all sizes have recognized the need to accept the forces of change as neither good nor bad, but simply inevitable. Because change is the one enduring constant, it is not change itself that threatens an organization's existence but rather the failure of its leadership to adapt strategically to the uncomfortable and unfamiliar new realities that challenge the prevailing common sense of the industry. More and more it is becoming clear that not only must banks change, but that the change which must be undertaken to survive and prosper go far beyond mere refinements to traditional and outdated ways of doing things. Radical transformations, however painful they may be, are needed in virtually every area. Traditional leadersip styles and priorities, organizational structures, corporate cultures, and market orientations are no longer appropriate in the new environment. Even the very ways in which a bank defines its business must be reconceptualized.

Astute bankers are now viewing strategic planning not as an annual "event" but as being synonymous with mastering the management of change. It is the process by which an organization moves from today's reality, whatever that might be, to tomorrow's strategic vision. It is the successful design and realization of that vision that this book is all about.

As a highly successful community bank president, a dynamic and effective president of the Bank Marketing Association's Council, and one of the most respected and sought after consultants to the financial services industry, Mike Higgins has long been an outspoken and persuasive advocate of the need for bankers to adapt strategically in order to survive the revolutionary changes affecting their industry. Now, in *Beyond Survival,* Mike presents a comprehensive and systematic process by which any bank, regardless of its size or location, can seize the unlimited opportunities that change inevitably creates by mastering the transition to a strategically focused, sales-driven financial institution. Building upon the nine key essential disciplines needed to become a high performer in the 90s, and stressing the critically important role of the CEO as a catalyst for strategic change, *Beyond Survival* provides specific examples of successful change management, as well as step-by-step implementation guidelines to managing the change process successfully.

This is an important book that should be read by every bank manager and director whose strategic vision goes *Beyond Survival.*

Cass Bettinger
Bettinger Isom and Associates
Salt Lake City, Utah
1989

PREFACE

It is becoming increasingly difficult for traditional banking companies to provide financial services while continuing to achieve real growth in assets and profit. Economic vulnerability has become particularly acute in the 1980s; competition is severe and is growing dramatically. The increased competition is resulting in downward profit pressures. Furthermore, the environment holds a great deal of uncertainty.

The most accurate conclusion that can be made about this decade is that it is not significantly different from any other period in this great nation's series of economic cycles. But the most consistent characteristic of this decade when compared with all previous decades is the unrelenting pressures and urgency for change. A deregulated, viable, and free economic environment demands it. Second, and equally important, the only time there is opportunity—real opportunity—is in an environment in which the demand for change is constant.

The financial services industry has held a unique position in the free enterprise system since the mid-1930s. Regulation was imposed following the Depression. The long period of regulation since then resulted in a generation of senior management in a majority of banks that learned how to do things successfully in a protected business environment. Not surprisingly, this background provided few of the skills needed to compete and survive in today's deregulated, competitive, and unpredictable environment.

Deregulation has had a substantially greater impact on banking than on other deregulated industries. The airline industry, for the most part, still competes only with other airlines. In contrast, banking deregulation has created a new industry called *financial services.*

No longer are there the neat, compartmentalized, and protected "fiefdoms" of commercial banking, mortgage banking, brokerage houses, real estate companies, and insurance providers. Today, a single and overcrowded arena of financial services exists, with the contestants all chasing the same customers with increasingly common product and service offerings.

This new environment creates an opportunity and an urgency that cannot be ignored. The competitive environment will be very unforgiving for laggards. If banks competed only with other banks, the industry could wait for a new generation of management with a more competitive orientation and new skills. But the luxury of time does not exist. The nonbank brokerage houses, credit card and debit card organizations, insurance and investment houses, and retail stores are all hungry. They see tremendous opportunities because commercial banks and thrifts no longer have a unique advantage in the financial services marketplace. Furthermore, in most instances, the nonbank competitors have cultural histories that are far more market-driven than those of banks and thrifts. In addition, many possess economies of scale and national marketing skills not available in banks other than the regional and money center banks.

To overcome these challenges and take advantage of the unlimited opportunities provided by a deregulated marketplace, every bank and thrift executive must have an explicitly defined corporate strategy.

Not all financial organizations will survive. However, each financial institution has within its grasp the *ability* to survive.

In a sense, the rise of the new financial service powers has centered around nonbanks and the regional and money-center banks. In this new age of competition, which will stretch long into the twenty-first century, those institutions competing with the nonbanks and the regional and money-center banks have unique advantages. They have, by far, the largest market, the most trained managers, and the best access to capital. They also have the greatest body of applied scientific and technological expertise available, both internally and through specialized entrepreneurs.

If you, as a manager of a financial institution competing with banks and nonbanks, have the market, the management, the money, the materials, and the magic, how can you lose? For any financial institution, as for any individual, the answer is simple. You lose, even when you have all the cards, by playing them poorly. The loss begins by not knowing what the future can bring. It begins by not defining what the future will bring because management has not established the institution's long-term business purpose. Too often, management is unable to come to grips with the complexities of dealing successfully in an ever-changing environment because it has not previously had to deal with those considerations.

In a recent survey conducted by this author, a group of consultants and senior management teams from throughout the country were interviewed relative to the most critical challenges facing the financial services industry. The response to that research resulted in the formulation of this strategic time line to maximize their potential for success, *Beyond Survival.*

All of the consultants surveyed responded with a consistent set of priorities. Their priorities provide an overriding message:

> The prerequisites for competing successfully in a deregulated environment are to first *focus* and *organize,* and then to truly *commit.* The challenges are people, not products and systems, and the people challenges to be resolved pertain to management, not staff.

In contrast, the banking CEOs identified products and systems as the most critical issues, and they pointed to staff, not management, as the source of people challenges. Significantly, the other banking officers—senior officers from the same banks as the CEOs—did not concur with their bosses, but with the consultants. Moreover, they expanded on their most critical concern: their concept of commitment to marketing, training, sales cultures, and change. Senior officers desperately want to see commitment from their CEOs. Their CEOs, however, do not perceive commitment as an issue.

As traditionally organized financial institutions prepare to do battle in an entirely new competitive environment, there are significant differences of opinion on where to begin, what to do, and how to go about doing it. It appears that CEOs as the ultimate decision-makers are looking outward for external strategies, whereas those who are responsible for implementation recognize a greater priority for internal strategies. Their priority on internal strategies confirms the need to reorganize and to reinforce a commitment to change.

The issue is not who is right and who is wrong; both internal and external strategies are needed. The challenge lies in finding comprehensive and timely solutions. A traditional approach to strategic thinking, that is, limiting the institution's focus on external opportunities, is not valid. Those competing with money-center and regional banks and nonbanks need and deserve to understand how to develop chronological internal strategies in addition to a more refined focus on external strategies, priorities, and options.

Beyond Survival provides that comprehensive plan of action. It gives management teams the power to maximize their unlimited potential and to compete successfully with nonbanks as well as regional and money center banks.

ACKNOWLEDGMENTS

It was about the time I joined the banking industry that banks and thrifts began to think seriously about preparing to compete successfully in a deregulated marketplace. The experience I brought to the industry in 1973 was gained from the exceptional role models I was fortunate enough to work with in industries that were never regulated. Their commitment to professional selling and what I now refer to as managerial leadership proved invaluable. I am indebted to

Harry Hausen, Seventh Avenue, New York City, New York

Morris Fonda, A.O. Smith Harvestor, Chicago, Illinois

Earl Gadbery, Aluminum Company of America, Pittsburgh, Pennsylvania

However, our competitive "truths" were not applicable to the financial services world. Great visionaries in that industry helped me mold the critical issues and applicable methodology through test and challenge. These people also made a significant contribution to this book.

- Glen Johnson, President of Federated Investors, Pittsburgh, Pennsylvania, shares Federated's great success in chapter 1, as does Jan Carlzon of Scandinavian Airlines.
- Daryl O'Conner and Warren Smith of ODR, Atlanta, Georgia, share their change management methodology in Chapter 2.
- C. W. "Bill" Ress and Bill Huckabee of the Crescent Group, Columbus, Ohio, offer their ingenious and creative approach to identifying the real value of customer needs in Chapter 10.

- Cass Bettinger of Bettinger Isom Associates, Salt Lake City, Utah, has questioned, challenged, clarified, and contributed as well as supported me before and since we began this critically important project.

I am very grateful.

CONTENTS

PART 4
UNLIMITED OPPORTUNITIES

PART 1

PLANNING FOR SUCCESS

Banks and thrifts have traditionally learned from each other by sharing successful programs and techniques. Today, however, we can learn very little from each other. In a truly competitive marketplace, strategic positioning must focus on the long-term, and we have little experience to share.

We must look outside of our industry to study the disciplines required to be successful in a deregulated environment. There are many successful companies and entire industries to emulate, because leadership skills and management disciplines are identical in all successful organizations. These are the themes of this text.

1. Each and every financial institution in America currently has the resources to compete successfully.
2. It will take a *total commitment* to implement the comprehensive set of nine disciplines necessary for success.
3. However, the only difference between those institutions who will achieve beyond survival and those who will not is the CEO's decision that the issue is important enough to do something about it.
4. The only reason the issue will become so important is because the cost of not making the commitment is too great.

The initial four chapters clarify the nine prerequisites for success with emphasis on the planning activities necessary to maximize the unlimited opportunity resulting from deregulation.

CHAPTER 1

SUCCESS

> It's not the critic who counts. . . . The credit belongs to the man who strives valiantly . . . who at the best knows in the end the triumph of high achievement; and who at the worst, if he fails, at least fails while daring greatly; so that his place shall never be with those cold timid souls who know neither victory or defeat.
>
> —*Theodore Roosevelt*

Business success is easier to achieve with role models. Those who have gone before and succeeded brilliantly can inspire us to new levels of business achievement. The particular industry they operate in or the specific problems they tackle matter less than the fact that they have applied techniques and disciplines that will prove to be prerequisites for success in any competitive business environment.

The success stories in this chapter are intended to serve as examples and motivate those of us in the banking industry who are determined to reach beyond survival and achieve long-term prosperity under difficult circumstances. The stories of Glen Johnson of Federated Investors and Jan Carlzon of Scandinavian Airlines (SAS) illustrate the consistent combination of ingredients necessary to make a competitive enterprise successful.

GLEN JOHNSON AND THE PURSUIT OF A MARKET NICHE

The story of Federated Investors, Pittsburgh, Pennsylvania, serves as a model for banks and thrifts in their quest to compete successfully in a deregulated, highly competitive environment. In less than 18 years, the company grew from a storefront office to become the nation's fourth largest investment firm with approximately $40 billion in managed assets. Today, Federated has business relationships with more than 2,500 financial institutions nationwide.

Federated's brilliant business strategy employed every discipline that bank management teams must master to take their organizations beyond survival.

Federated Investors, founded in 1955, made a business of developing investment products for brokerage firms to market to the public. The company experienced modest success during the subsequent 15 years. By 1970, it managed $200 million in assets. During the next three years, the company continued to succeed, but it became apparent there were opportunities to evaluate and new market segments to serve. In 1973, Federated decided to create a new service: a money market fund for savers, allowing them to achieve money market rates of return for their short-term or savings deposits.

The company believed in the potential of this new service, but it was a first and one whose success would be achieved only through unparalleled persistence.

This new direction began in 1970 when Jack Donahue, chairman and founder of Federated Investors, hired Glen Johnson to be the company's marketing director. At the time, the company had less than 30 employees.

Three years after Johnson's arrival, Donahue and Johnson had a vision: to create a fund to be invested in short-term bank certificates of deposit (CDs), providing an 8 to 11 percent return and marketed directly to consumers or through bank trust departments. If marketed through bank trust departments, the instrument would allow financial institutions to achieve a market rate of return on short-term deposits for their trust clients, would deliver daily dividends, and would have no principal fluctuation. More specifically, the instrument would

- Significantly improve customers' returns on their trust savings (most trust departments' idle funds were not invested because the instruments available provided only a minimum return to the client and resulted in very high administrative overhead expenses for the bank).
- Eliminate the bank's bookkeeping expenses, which typically exceeded their own spread.

- Provide an adequate fee for the bank.
- Offset Federated's operational overhead expenses.
- Return a good profit to Federated.

To clarify, the return on previously uninvested cash (once it was placed with Federated) was credited to the bank client's account. The bank receives no part of the spread. The fiduciary customer is entitled to the total return. Because the client is already paying the bank a fee for managing the assets, the bank's advantage is that the trust department can perform more effectively with their trust client receiving the revenue benefits.

Potential Markets

The most advantageous route to acquiring customers for this new and innovative product was through banks' trust departments. The challenge was that no bank had ever used such an instrument. At the time, bankers regarded mutual funds with suspicion. In particular, funds with variable net asset value were not looked upon favorably by bank decision-makers.

Because banks were not a sure target, Federated considered marketing its new instrument through brokers. Brokers had dealt with the implications of variable net asset values and had contact with investors. However, investors and savers were two different financial customers, and there were a lot more savers than investors to be served.

Another alternative was to direct Federated's efforts toward attracting the consuming public directly, without going through either banks or brokerage houses. But Federated did not have the distribution system, sales force, or the capital resources to approach that option successfully.

The decision was made to market to banks. Johnson and his wife departed by car from Pittsburgh and stopped in every city that had a bank trust department en route to Florida, Arkansas, and back home again. Johnson would walk in unannounced and proclaim, "Hey, I'm Glen Johnson from Federated and I've got this great idea to manage your surplus, uninvested cash." He consistently received one of three responses: he would be thrown out; he would be told that mutual funds were not worth talking about; or he would hear, "Wow, what a great idea! Who else is using it?"

The follow-up to the latter response was always the same. "Nobody is using it? Well, let me know when someone decides to try it!"

Unsuccessful in every attempt, Glen Johnson drove back to Pittsburgh, determined to concentrate on Federated's immediate market area. There the response was different. Pittsburgh bankers had only two retorts: they either gave Glen blank stares or they asked, "Who else is using it?"

Persistence

It did not get better for a long time. Along the way, there were many examples of how success is achieved. One was Johnson's persistence in landing the first account. Glen Johnson made business calls on over 400 different banks before the first trust department chose to do business with Federated Investors. Bankers just would not respond.

Therefore, taking another approach, Federated promoted the identical product directly through small newspaper ads. Interestingly, the public's response was overwhelming. The first small ad resulted in 800 inquiries. A follow-up ad resulted in 1,200 inquiries. Soon, people started walking into Federated's offices. The fund grew to $40 million with walk-in and call-in business from individual consumers alone. Still, banks did not respond.

Although the market had obviously caught on, Federated did not have the capital resources to take advantage of the demand. It could not advertise in every newspaper, nor could it afford a sales force. The key selling point for its fund was that banks were still paying 5 percent at a time when the money market fund of bank CDs was paying 11 percent. The public was going nuts! Yet Johnson continued to call on banks with no success. Could it be that banks could not relate to the opportunity because they just could not conceive of paying more than 5 percent on "savings accounts"?

Federated had created a way for banks to make the same income for their trust customers and to do so without the overhead expense. The important fact to keep in perspective was that this savings instrument was not competing with the banks' savings accounts. Regulations prohibited that. The instrument was strictly for the investment of trust customers' "idle" cash.

Interestingly, there was no regulation to prevent the banks from using Federated's fund. The problem was that banks did not have the mind-set to change or to understand that very attractive rates could be paid on consumer deposits. They did not see a way to do it. Some wanted to, but they were waiting for someone else to do it first. The reticence of banks was all the more unfortunate when you consider the earnings potential for their customers, which was astronomical. The Federal Deposit Insurance Corporation (FDIC) reports revealed that there was over $30 billion in uninvested cash waiting to be placed in the new instrument.

The irony of the situation was particularly evident at one bank Johnson called on, where 30 people were employed who did nothing but post trust savings balances in more than 25 outside institutions. Pure clerical posting was their full-time job. The funds were often uninvested. If they were invested, the funds cost more for clerical support than they produced in interest.

However, the banks would not listen. In contrast, money was pouring in from individuals. Every day, checks were coming in the mail, and new customers were walking in the door. Still, the banks would not budge. Johnson began to think that the direct approach was the only way to maximize the instrument's potential.

Another Federated executive, Dick Fisher, suggested that Federated use a Boston public relations firm. Perhaps a PR firm could get the word out through various media to generate a still greater response with direct marketing. At the time Federated approached the public relations firm, it still had not been able to sell one bank account. The public relations specialist scheduled hundreds of talk shows on radio and television and many newspaper interviews. Every call-in talk show in the country was talking about Federated's great new enterprise. The public relations program was a smashing success, and money kept pouring in. A Boston interview resulted in 3,000 leads. An interview in St. Louis resulted in 5,000 people requesting more information about this new savings instrument. A Wall Street Week public television interview resulted in 8,000 leads; banks were not among them.

Glen Johnson did seven live television shows in one day. After every show, the switchboard lit up with more inquiries than those stations had ever had about any other program. Federated had so many responses to the public relations program that everyone, including spouses, had to work nearly around the clock to respond to all the inquiries. In 1974, over 350 individual stories were told in various media throughout the United States. Those stories resulted in over 90,000 leads, inquiries from individual consumers wanting and needing the service.

In the meantime, Johnson never gave up on the banking industry. He persisted because he knew banks were the better vehicle for offering this great new service to the public. Johnson *persisted* because he had *belief*.

Tapping the Market

Johnson created very innovative material to communicate to bank trust managers the features and benefits of his product. Some days after the mailing, Johnson got a call from the head of the trust department of a bank in Martinsville, Virginia. The banker said he had just reviewed the information about Federated, and he thought it was a fabulous idea. He asked when he could come to Pittsburgh to learn more about it. Soon thereafter, he visited Federated's meager offices. After spending time with everyone on the staff, he went back to Virginia as Federated's first bank client.

Having landed his first bank customer, Johnson called every bank who had told him they would be interested if someone else tried the product first. Before the dust settled, Federated had an additional 22 bank customers and $50 million in assets.

Six weeks later, the Virginia banker called and told Johnson the bank's president had found out what he did. "And now I have to undo it," he said. He took the $1 million out of Federated and put it back in the bank's savings accounts. Federated had lost its first client. It was unfortunate, because the Virginia banker had recognized something that few other trust managers at the time could see. Federated could not only invest the idle funds, but it could manage its clients' bookkeeping and reporting, pay their customers a significant return on their short-term savings, and greatly enhance the bank's performance. The concept was so simple, yet so different from the traditional way of doing business. In the regulated banking environment there was no significant reason to differentiate from competitors.

Three years later the Virginia bank returned to become a multimillion dollar client, but only after the president died.

Even bankers who were converted saw the new instrument only as an opportunity to improve bookkeeping and reporting. When Johnson sold the first account in Boston, the client reduced its staff by 30 people. The operational efficiency, more than the return on client's savings, was what had sold the client.

In a very short period of time, most of the banks that were waiting not to be first jumped on the bandwagon. Banks from New York to California and from Minnesota to Texas soon captured the opportunity.

Not too long thereafter, the regulators started to put pressure on trust departments to invest their idle cash. One big West Coast bank had $30 million in cash that was not invested. This was precisely the opportunity that was driving Johnson. He began to see things happen, and he knew that he was the catalyst.

By 1975, Federated's individual accounts and its banking relationships grew astronomically to $450 million. Then, interest rates dropped, and the return on idle savings decreased from a high of 11.5 percent to an all time low of 4.15 percent.

Interestingly, the banks that were clients primarily because of the bookkeeping and operational support had a reason for staying, despite the 4.15 percent rate. The funds had not been invested previously anyway, and the banks had been relieved of a tremendous amount of operational expense. Therefore, when interest rates fell, the banks stayed, but Federated's personal account relationships left.

The light was on; the market segment had been identified. In January 1976, a major decision was made. Federated started a new 45-basis-point "wholesale" fund invested in government securities. The fund was purely institutional—no individual could get into it. The company had decided never again to advertise for a consumer account. The market niche that Federated could best serve was banks, and Johnson and other Federated managers agreed never again to compete with the clientele that had been consistently loyal in the retail world.

In bankers' eyes, the perceived value of Federated's fund was that it reduced administrative detail and bookkeeping overhead.

Their positive response to the product line had little to do with client needs or customer service because bankers were not required to think that way. They were driven by operational priorities, not customer priorities. This, unfortunately, is the very challenge the industry still faces today. Operational priorities too often have priority over customer service.

Glen Johnson did not rest, even after he had a respectable list of bank clients. Once, he recalls, he had a meeting at one of Pittsburgh's largest banks. Federated was doing business with a few banks in town, but it had not really penetrated its local market yet. Arriving promptly 5 minutes ahead of schedule, Johnson was ushered into a meeting room in which sat 11 lieutenants without their decision-maker. Precisely, 15 minutes after the meeting was scheduled to begin, the decision-maker appeared.

Halfway through the presentation, the decision-maker interrupted, "Mr. Johnson, as you know, our bank is one of the largest and one of the most successful banking organizations in the state of Pennsylvania. It would be very difficult for us to justify a decision to do business with a company the [meager] size of Federated Investors." The meeting was adjourned. The decision-maker departed abruptly. His lieutenants followed.

The ending to the story occurred 6 years later when Glen Johnson made another appointment at the same Pittsburgh bank. He arrived promptly 5 minutes before the scheduled meeting. Again, on time, the 11 lieutenants appeared and placed themselves quietly around the conference table. Precisely 15 minutes later, the decision-maker appeared. Glen Johnson's opening began with, "Thank you for this opportunity. Now that Federated Investors is the largest financial organization in Pennsylvania, I know that your organization is anxious to learn how we can help you help yourself and help your clientele."

Another interesting challenge for Federated was the resistance it encountered from banker prospects who managed cash. These individuals would perceive Federated as being there for the sole purpose of taking away their jobs. For example, Johnson remembers making arrangements for a hospitality suite for a regional meeting in Mobile, Alabama. As usual, Johnson was busy lining up the food and refreshments and coordinating the hotel staff. A client banker who was helping Johnson make arrangements came in and said, "I want you to meet the piano player I hired for your hospitality suite. He used to manage our cash. After Federated came in, we didn't have a need for him anymore, so now he is playing the piano." Johnson thought to himself, "Oh, no! He's the last guy in the world I want to meet." The incident brought home how careful he had to be as he pursued the potential of the marketplace.

In living up to his commitment to have someone in the bank within 24 hours if a problem could not be resolved by telephone, Johnson dispatched a "problem solver" to an Iowa bank that just simply could not seem to balance Federated's numbers and theirs. When the Federated employee arrived, the person in charge took her aside and confided that she purposely mixed up the numbers so that the system would not work. No one else ever knew. That particular bank went on to be an outstanding client and still is today.

Differentiation: Quality Service

If you use the one-word response test with a client of Federated Investors' services, the response to describe the company would consistently be "quality." The commitment to quality service began early in Federated's service to the banking industry. That commitment began with the very first meeting with its very first client. That client was met at the Pittsburgh airport in a limousine. Symbols like these became the introduction for all future relationships.

In 1976, Federated Investors decided to sponsor a hospitality room for the American Bankers Association National Trust Conference at the Peachtree Plaza in Atlanta. Johnson knew the visiting bankers would have dozens of other hospitality suites to visit, including those of all the regional banks. Bankers had more places to go for drinks and hors d'oeuvres than they had time to make the visits. Johnson realized he had to *differentiate* if he was going to entice bankers to visit his hospitality room.

At the very last moment, Johnson persuaded the hotel manager to allow Federated to use half of the entire top of the Peachtree Plaza. Having found a place, he still had to attract the bankers. Johnson did not have a staff. He had no one to help him develop the invitations, and the local printers did not have time to work on the invitation. So Glen reached back into his first career as a small town newspaper owner. He remembered how he used to sit in a dirty old print shop setting type. He did it again. Right then and there, he devised the wording and set the type:

COME SEE ATLANTA FROM THE TOP
OF THE PEACHTREE PLAZA
WITH CRAB LEGS AND CHAMPAGNE
COMPLIMENTS OF FEDERATED

Johnson then personally addressed all the invitations.

His effort and ingenuity paid off. Over 500 people came to eat crab legs and see Atlanta. And before they left, Johnson had sold them on Federated Investors. Johnson had cracked his niche, and it was all due to differentiation. The extravaganza at the Peachtree Plaza set the tone for all of Federated's subsequent promotional activities.

Another extravaganza came a couple of years later at the National Trust Conference in Los Angeles. By then, Federated had a staff, but Johnson himself was still creating the environment, negotiating with the caterers, and following up on the necessary transportation requirements. Again, he contemplated how Federated could be different. Everyone was providing entertainment to get the attention of the trust manager decision-makers. Johnson's answer to the question of how to differentiate was obvious: Quality! "Our feast must be fit for a king! What if we rent a castle?"

And he did. Berwinshire Castle on top of a mountain in Beverly Hills would set the stage for Federated's promotional activities for decades. What an opportunity!

Johnson hired actors and actresses dressed in medieval costumes to serve refreshments at a medieval banquet. He rented limousines to pick up over 400 trust managers and their spouses and bring them to the castle. Upon arrival, each guest was met by a cadre of medieval horn blowers, the horns forming an arch over a red carpeted entrance to the gala. No one who attended ever forgot Federated.

The company had been expanding so rapidly that cash flow became a significant problem. Prior to the Los Angeles Trust Conference, Chairman Jack Donahue got word that Johnson had decided to throw another party. He desperately tried to call him, time and time again, to confirm his greatest fear. It was not until after the party that Johnson returned his call.

"What is this I heard about you spending $25,000 for a party?" demanded Donahue. Johnson reassured him, saying, "Jack, that just isn't true." He then went on to describe the gala and the great response. "The party was a tremendous success!! Over 400 bankers and their spouses came and over $800 million in new business was brought in. And, by the way, Jack, the party didn't *cost* $25,000. We *invested* $88,000."

Federated had established itself. Incomparable social events replaced advertising. This approach was much more effective and much more efficient.

The company started hiring salespeople and scheduling regional seminars for the purpose of inviting users from all over the country to become a part of its successful future.

Looking back, why did Federated achieve such success? The key was not the extravagant social events and parties but rather the commitment to effectively serving its customers and overwhelming them with service beyond their expectations. VIP service was Federated's symbol of quality, and it set the company apart from the competition. Moreover, Federated committed to reinforcing that symbol with attentive service before, during, and after the sale.

Quality Service with Commitment

The point to be understood about its promotional events is that Federated was not attempting to be "good old boys." Instead, the company wanted to demonstrate that it stood for quality—quality beyond anything any other company would dare commit to. The demonstration was visual, and the commitment was real.

Glen made a personal commitment to each and every user that, if there was a question or a problem, it would be answered or resolved within 24 hours. If necessary, someone from Federated would be there. He or she would be on the first airplane out, even if Federated lost money, because the company could be perpetuated only by making good on its commitment to serve unquestionably and beyond anyone's expectations.

By 1978, Federated was on a roll. It grew $1 billion in one 16-

day period. It was not long after that it grew another billion in a 13-day period and then another billion in a 10-day period. In one hectic month, Federated added 100 new bank clients to its user list.

The challenge now was not in getting new accounts and building assets. Success created a new challenge: how to support the operational demands of managing billions of dollars.

I asked Glen Johnson what the one secret was for Federated's success. We had discussed the product innovation, persistence, differentiation, the commitment to quality, and the extravaganzas. All of those were important, but none was the most important. According to Johnson, the reason Federated was so successful was that Johnson *listened* to the people in the marketplace. The implications were twofold: one internal, one external.

Internal Listening: Be with Your People

Early on, Johnson made a commitment to listen to his people. This required him to be with his people in the user regional meetings, the conventions, and the seminars; to be with his people at the extravaganzas and at the sales meetings; to be with his people when they had challenges; and to be accessible to their ideas. *"If you accept the role of president of a competitive organization, you accept the role of sales manager,"* said Johnson. Managing successful sales organizations in a competitive environment requires a very personalized approach to the business. That begins with creating pride.

The excitement and loyalty engendered at Federated are a result of pride the staff now creates for themselves. Just establishing a place to work for someone will not work anymore! You are competing with teams of people who believe in their organization and its purpose. It is *belief* that sets one organization apart from another, not merely commitment to making a profit. Profit comes from the ability to create belief, which springs from enthusiasm for the organization and its services. Profit is the result of a vision, and the ideas of an energetic management team give life to that vision.

Federated differentiated itself by staying years ahead of the competition. Building internal quality through belief was important in nurturing staff loyalty and enthusiasm and building a satisfied client base. But how did Federated stay ahead of the competition? External listening is the key.

External Listening: Be with Your Clients

Glen Johnson devotes 60 days each year to listen to his clients. He schedules informal client group meetings throughout the United States. His usual posture is to sit in the middle of the room with his coat off and ask critical questions:

- "What can we do to make you more successful?"
- "How can we better serve you?"
- "What products need to be developed or enhanced?"
- "How can we assist you with regulatory information?"
- "How can we help you reach your customers?"

Johnson takes everything he gathers back to Pittsburgh, and Federated responds. It responds by creating more information systems, enhancing products, and establishing new product lines. Furthermore, it communicates its response to every client who made a suggestion, reinforcing the importance of the client's feedback.

The key is that Federated recognizes that the trust officer is the client. The client is the most important person in the world. "We remind them of it often," Johnson confirms, "and we remind ourselves of it every single day."

Listening and responding is the hook. That is the essence of identifying customer need. Listening and responding is what keeps Federated ahead of the competition. Listening and responding is the prerequisite to differentiation!

Another lesson can be learned from Federated's success. The nature of a successful business in a competitive marketplace demands that management avoid the temptation of thinking that the company can be all things to all people. This observation is confirmed by Glen Johnson when he explains why Federated does not branch out once again beyond the banking industry and sell directly to consumers. "We certainly have the resources now to compete for the individual consumer. But if people call us and want us to put money into a money market fund," he replies, "I send them to their local bank."

Federated's founder and chairman, Jack Donahue, recently reflected on the company's past and future. "We don't accept the norm. If we are going to stay on top in serving our clients, we must continually challenge ourselves not to accept where we are. We see change for what it is. Change has never been a challenge for Federated. Change and managing change is managing opportunity."

The Federated experience serves as an example to bank management because it reveals the critical disciplines that underpin success in a competitive environment. These disciplines are exhibited in any successful operation, as demonstrated in our next model success story.

JAN CARLZON AND THE CUSTOMER-DRIVEN ORGANIZATION

Jan Carlzon is the president and CEO of Scandinavian Airlines (SAS). He was the prime mover in a success story that is relevant to the deregulated financial services industry. He took an airline company that was losing $20 million in 1981, and, in one year, turned it around to earn $54 million. He did it by capitalizing on what he calls the "moments of truth."

Moments of truth are the times when customers come into contact with a company's staff. In a regulated environment, where there is little or no competition, customer contact is not a significant competitive experience. However, in a deregulated, very highly competitive environment, each moment of truth—each contact with a customer—is the most important moment in the life of a service business if it is to reach beyond survival.

The key to Carlzon's success was finding out what customers wanted and then delivering it. To find out what they wanted, he turned the company's traditional organization chart upside down. He delegated responsibility and authority to employees who dealt directly with the customers. He challenged his people to determine what it was the customer really wanted.

He reoriented the entire company to become a customer-driven organization. Carlzon recognized that a company's most important assets were not just its people, as many of us advocate. Rather, the most important assets were its people and its satisfied customers, all of whom expect and deserve to be treated as individuals. In addition, he surmised, people would seek out an airline that would make that commitment and live up to it.

Carlzon knew he would achieve differentiation when he created a truly market-driven, customer-oriented organization. When his customers talked about the positive experiences they had with the pilots, flight attendants, reservations personnel, and ticket agents, he knew he was succeeding.

In defining his strategy, Carlzon observed that each of the airline's 10 million customers came in direct contact with approximately five employees. Each average contact lasted less than 15 seconds. Those 10 million customers making five employee contacts resulted in what Carlzon refers to as the 50 million "moments of truth." Those moments, he perceived, would ultimately determine whether SAS would succeed or fail. The "moments" would demonstrate to customers that SAS was not only the best alternative but the only alternative if one was seeking customer-oriented, market-driven service.

To ensure a positive outcome from each moment of truth, Carlzon did not want his employees to have to go up the organizational ladder to get an answer to a customer's request. If the employee had to go up the organizational chain of command for a decision, then the company would lose that moment as an opportunity to earn another loyal customer.

The key to decentralizing the customer response mechanism is to recruit and train people to be able to respond intelligently. The traditional corporate structure, which resembles a pyramid, had to be inverted. The pinnacle was redirected to permit decision-making in the marketplace.

Prior to coming to SAS, Carlzon turned around another airline, Linjeflyg, which had been a classic product-oriented company. Ninety-five percent of its passengers were business travelers whose companies were resigned to paying for air fares as they were determined by the airline's expenses rather than by the demands of the travelers or the perceived value of the service. The expenses were primarily a result of the number of aircraft in service, which was determined by a self-imposed requirement that *all* the cities in the market area would be the origination point for a flight into Stockholm before 9:00 A.M. every weekday morning. This commitment caused fares to be high.

Unfortunately, Linjeflyg had a conflict of objectives. While early accessibility to Stockholm was one objective, profit certainly was another. The conflict was between profits and trying to be everything to everyone. If nothing was done to counteract the effects of the conflict, Linjeflyg would soon be bankrupt. To resolve the conflict, Carlzon established four overall business strategies:

- Use fixed assets more effectively.
- Become the world's "best airline" in terms of passenger service.
- Spread responsibility among more people in the organization.
- Streamline administrative resources.

Three strategies were internal management activities, whereas the fourth one involved a commitment to the company's customer base. Of course, saying that the company would become the world's best airline and making that happen were two different things. Good service meant offering convenient timetables, frequent departures, and lower prices—not serving fancy foods and fine wines. Linjeflyg was about to move against the tradition of the industry. For that reason, there was a significant improvement in morale and a palpable excitement among the staff members who participated in the new challenge for reaching beyond survival.

Carlzon credits the reshaping of the organizational structure of a company as the Number One prerequisite for success. The approach Carlzon advocates is to let the market tell the company what services are needed. Then, the marketing department tells the operations department what to produce. "In this way, we have turned the traditional organization on its head," says Carlzon.[1]

For most airlines, operational considerations determine an aircraft's schedule. Instead of cutting services to cut expenses, as operations-driven management had suggested, Carlzon's new marketing-oriented management team vowed to maximize the company's potential by increasing revenue.

Prior to introducing the new strategy to the public, Carlzon gathered his entire company in two shifts in a huge aircraft hangar to present the company's plans. He described in detail the new business strategy, including the organizational responsibilities, the ways customer responsiveness would be ensured, the new timetables and fares, and examples of the advertising campaign that would support

---

[1]Jan Carlzon, *Moments of Truth* (Cambridge: Ballinger Publishing Company, 1987), p. 14.

the new program. As Carlzon blasted the campaign's theme music over the loud speakers, everyone became very excited about the new challenge. A wave of *enthusiasm* formed, driven by the leader who had communicated his vision to each and every staff member directly.

Then, it was up to the staff to implement the new plan, and Carlzon made himself available to bolster their efforts.

One of the key moves in Carlzon's business strategy was to reduce the price of every flight. To do that, the company had to reduce some of the other costs. Accordingly, the first thing they evaluated was the wisdom of serving free meals that no one enjoyed. Carlzon's team decided to offer exceptional but modest meals at half the price available on competing train systems. Research proved that not everyone wanted a full breakfast, but those who did would pay for it.

One employee came up with the recommendation that the staff create other money-making ideas. Soon the airline was selling chocolates, perfumes, and other kinds of gifts. The flight attendants were allowed to receive significant commissions for their sales. This resulted in the airline making millions. Why? Because it dared to *break with tradition* and because Carlzon challenged his company not to accept where it was. The customers were better served at an overall lower price, and they purchased what they chose at a price they were willing to pay. The company made a fortune because it was *customer-driven* not product-, or operations-, or profit-driven. Almost from the day the concept was introduced, the number of passenger miles booked exceeded every expectation.

Carlzon went on to turn around SAS and one other company. In each situation, *the demands were different and the strategies were different, but the disciplines were the same.* Some people attributed Carlzon's success to marketing gimmicks, but the truth was that he solved problems by reorienting each company toward the specific needs of a specific marketplace, that is, the market niche that could best be served by that specific company. He was able to open up each new company by looking at specific market-oriented possibilities and then creating an energy and willingness among the employees to be responsive to customers. Carlzon's ideas on how to deliver quality service do not sound new, but they were.

When Carlzon began at SAS, the company had lost a significant amount of money over a prolonged period of time. The commercial airline market had stagnated. The current SAS executives assumed that there was no way they could overcome the market and improve revenues. As a result, they concentrated on cutting costs. They used the fairly traditional, noncompetitive technique of cutting costs across the board, an ill-advised method of resource allocation that is unrelated to market priorities. The retrenchment eliminated many services customers needed and wanted, while retaining others of little interest to the marketplace. Furthermore, across-the-board cost-cutting typically has a traumatic impact on the staff. Because priorities are not served (or even identified), staff members rarely take the initiative on anything. As a result, no one really feels responsible for controlling or maintaining costs because decision-making becomes arbitrary and lacks priorities.

Carlzon's approach to improving revenues was much more creative. He responded to the demands of the marketplace. His overall strategy was to provide the best service in the marketplace for the company's primary market niche, thereby increasing the market share in an otherwise stagnate environment. His strategy was not centered on profits. Rather, the focus was on quality service, which would result in a fair profit. There is a significant difference between the two approaches.

Carlzon began developing a strategy by first gaining a clear picture of the outside world and recognizing where the company had positioned itself. Next, he had to establish a goal and determine how to reach it. This process of creating a business strategy has nothing to do with cutting costs. It has nothing to do with becoming more profitable. A business strategy has to do *only* with meeting the demands of the marketplace. Meeting the demands of the marketplace is the only critical responsibility of a contemporary management team seeking to prosper in a competitive environment. Profit must be a part of every major consideration, but profit is never the driving force in a highly competitive environment.

After careful intuitive analysis, Carlzon founded the company's business strategy. SAS would not only become the best airline in the world, it would become the best airline in the world for its target market: the frequent business traveler. To accomplish this goal, SAS needed to determine the special needs of business travelers. By identifying the unique services sought by business travelers, the airline would be able to attract loyal, full-fare customers. Service came first; profit would follow.

The trick was to recognize that expenses were not necessarily an evil. To continue to curtail expenses would minimize the ability of SAS to respond to market needs. Without being able to respond to market needs, it could not improve its competitiveness by differentiating itself from its competitors. Increased expenditures, by managed line item, would give SAS a competitive edge if, and only if, the company reallocated expenses to priority activities that would contribute to serving the explicit needs of its market niche.

In allocating resources, Carlzon implemented the marketing strategist's golden rule: Every organization, no matter how large or small, no matter how successful, has limited resources. The only way an organization can maximize its potential in a competitive environment is to reallocate resources to ensure that they are employed explicitly to serve targeted market segments. Carlzon saw to it that if a budgeted value was not employed to serve the business frequent flyer, the SAS expenditure was not allocated. Moreover, Carlzon asked the board of directors to support a unique strategy for turning the airline around. Rather than cutting costs, Carlzon proposed to invest an additional $45 million on 147 projects to serve the specific needs of the frequent business flyer. It was an enormous risk. There was no guarantee that the additional expenses would generate more revenue, but Carlzon understood the proven marketing principle that calls for identifying explicit market segments and allocating all resources to serve the needs of those targeted market segments.

Carlzon's strategy reinforced another part of the golden rule. By allocating and investing over $45 million in areas of priority to serve a distinct market segment, a number of significant projects recognized as lesser priorities were scrapped. This decision resulted in a reduction of some $40 million in operating expenses. Once having identified the goal of concentrating on the frequent business traveler, the cuts were easy to identify and none of them would hurt SAS. For example, Carlzon knew that the frequent business travelers were not interested in the airline maintaining a tourism department, even though commercial airlines typically had tourism departments.

A side effect of the marketing strategy was that the airline was able to streamline its staff because fewer professionals were required to concentrate on a more explicit market segment. Oh, the lessons to be learned by the banking industry!

As in traditional banking, the airline's executives had previously dealt only with investments, management, and administration. Service was of secondary importance to them. The people who dealt one-on-one with the clients were at the bottom of the company. After implementing Carlzon's strategy, however, the entire organization—from the baggage handlers to the executive team, from the pilots to the ground crews, and from the flight attendants to the reservation and ticket clerks—was focused on service. Equally important, all employees received special training in providing attentive service.

Carlzon recognized that training is required to support a corporate vision. The attention given to each individual via the training programs was even more important. Everyone recognized the company was interested enough to invest what was, at the time, its very limited financial resources in improving the ability of employees to implement the strategy. Previously, people felt unappreciated. They felt that airplanes and financial reports were the focal points of the organization. As Carlzon's strategy was being implemented, however, each and every person throughout the entire organization was designated as a carrier of the vision.

In addition, management did more than just train; it reinforced training with a further commitment to the vision. Each employee received a booklet defining the SAS vision in very concise terms. It was the same copy that the board and top management reviewed, endorsed, and incorporated in their own activities. Carlzon could not risk the message becoming distorted, so he put it in writing. His exact message worked its way throughout the entire company.

The strategy caused management to place more demands on everyone, but there was still a new energy at SAS. As a result, each and every employee began striving toward a single, clearly articulated, and very clearly understood purpose.

With its more refined focus, decision-makers throughout the organization began to look for and understand the needs of the frequent business flyer. In evaluating ways to respond to the needs of its targeted market segment, SAS eliminated first-class fares and created a "Euro Class," which offered considerably better service than coach fare, less pretentious service than first-class, but more in line with the needs of the frequent business flyer. SAS became the first airline to offer business class service without a surcharge. Their business class (Euro Class) was priced at the standard coach fare, which motivated, by added value, business travelers to pay coach fare instead of looking for discounts.

SAS also began to advertise more effectively. Gradually, the rest of the world began to understand the SAS competitive difference. To underscore SAS's commitment, the company installed beautifully appointed and comfortable airport lounges especially for the Euro Class passengers. It furnished business travelers with separate check-in counters, telephone and telex services, more comfortable seats, and better food. The special check-in service produced a 40 percent improvement over the check-in time required for tourist-class travelers. In addition, business travelers were allowed to board the plane last and disembark first. They received their meals first and were provided free drinks, newspapers, and magazines. The focus of all these initiatives was not on profitability. The focus was on serving needs. If SAS met its target market's needs, profits would follow.

The results were overwhelming. The initial goal was to increase earnings by $25 million the first year, $40 million the second year, and $50 million the third year. SAS achieved an $80 million earnings improvement in the very first year! During the same time period, the airline industry as a whole was suffering losses in excess of $2 billion.

In August 1983, *Fortune Magazine* named SAS the "best airline for business travelers in the world," and *Air Transport World Magazine* recognized it as the "airline of the year" that same year.

In 12 months, Carlzon had taken an airline that was losing money, market share, and good personnel, and he transformed it into the best airline in the world for frequent business travelers.

Profit was not Carlzon's most cherished accomplishment. His most important achievement was the product of investing in its employees and its customers by identifying and serving the needs of its targeted market segment. The net result—the true bottom line—was that SAS re-established its critical asset, that is, its resources for the future: satisfied customers and enthusiastic employees. The achievement of an almost unbelievable level of profitability was the payoff for that focus.

In summarizing his unique contribution to contemporary management, Carlzon concludes, "I can neither fly a plane nor repair one—and no one at SAS expects me to. A leader today must have much more general qualities: good business sense and a broad understanding of how things fit together—the relationships among individuals and groups inside and outside the company and the interplay among the various elements of the company's operations."

"What is required is strategic planning, a talent for rising above the details to see the lay of the land. The ability to understand and direct change is crucial for effective leadership. Today's business leaders must define clear goals and strategies and then communicate them to employees and train them to take responsibility for reaching those goals. A leader can create a secure working environment that fosters flexibility and innovation. Thus, the new leader is a listener, communicator, and educator—an emotionally expressive and inspiring person who can create the right atmosphere rather than make all the decisions himself."[2]

The secret of Carlzon's success was his ability to delegate, to let go of ego. In a changing business environment, a leader cannot control a business environment from the top of the pyramid. Responsibility must be delegated, and the delegation must be communicated to the right people, who must be recruited and/or trained. Good employees must be rewarded with the authority to make decisions at the point of customer contact. The leader, then, is a person who is oriented to results more than attracted to power.

CONCLUSION

The lessons to be learned from the two success stories presented in this chapter will be reinforced throughout this book. In a competitive environment, each organization's situation is significantly different from that of everyone else, even the competitor across the street. Therefore, each organization's strategies must be tailor-made. Only

---

[2]Jan Carlzon, *Moments of Truth* (Cambridge: Ballinger Publishing Company, 1987), pp. 35–37.

the disciplines required to compete successfully—beyond survival—are the same for all competitors. The disciplines begin with creating a *vision* and developing *focus* through strategies to fulfill that vision. The strategies must direct the organization toward *differentiating* itself from its competitors.

Both Federated Investors and SAS were consistent in mastering the prerequisite disciplines. Each avoided the temptation to become all things to all people. Each recognized the immeasurable value of defining and making a commitment to serve a very explicit *market segment.* This self-limiting focus allowed them to achieve their unlimited potential by employing all available resources toward becoming the very best in a very competitive environment. *Service quality* then could be clearly defined by the needs and expectations of their designated targets, rather than confused by expectations of an all-encompassing marketplace.

Both Johnson and Carlzon recognized the role of a company president trying to compete successfully. Both accepted the role of *sales manager* as their primary function. They knew that the responsibilities of a sales manager are to be available to clients and staff and to *listen.*

Financial institution management's new responsibilities are not limited to managing. Today, *leadership* is required, which involves caring enough to listen in order to learn how to differentiate. Leadership also involves stimulating an enthusiastic *belief* in the service provided, and the belief must exist throughout the organization.

All too few companies involved in strategic business activities experience an acceptable level of successful implementation. The challenge lies in the ability to lead an organization through the changes necessary to compete successfully. This takes *commitment* and *persistence.*

Most bank managers are extremely well-trained in the operational and technical disciplines necessary to run a bank. However, because they were trained in a regulated environment, their experience and understanding of the commitment necessary to compete successfully in a deregulated environment requires a significant change in thinking.

Additionally, the amount of change taking place in the banking industry is unprecedented. Deregulation and increased competition have caused the industry to switch its focus from short-term, product-driven objectives to long-term, market-driven, strategic objectives. This new focus requires a management team to begin to learn about an entirely new discipline: *change management,* the subject of Chapter 2.

CHAPTER 2

MANAGING THE CHANGE TO A MARKET-DRIVEN BANK

> There is nothing more difficult to take in hand, more perilous to conduct, or more uncertain in its outcome, than to take the lead in introducing a new order of things. Because the innovator has for enemies all those who have done well under the old conditions, and lukewarm defenders in those who may do well under the new.
>
> —*Machiavelli*

A re-examination of what it means to be truly "market-driven" has motivated some financial institutions to develop an entirely new structure for banks and entirely new ways for their managers to think. This sales-oriented, service quality culture must be embraced, not just by the CEO but by every customer contact and support person in the organization. Most bankers agree that this is a fact, but for a variety of reasons very few have made the necessary changes for this to become a reality.

Many management teams have purchased new systems and introduced new disciplines. Strategic planning, sales training, and various management programs have been implemented in untold numbers of organizations. But research[1] confirms that all too many experience an unacceptable level of success.

Perhaps making professional selling a priority has not been demonstrated by the CEO. Some managers have been preoccupied by short-term challenges. Or, it could be that most bankers have not understood the need for—and therefore have not incorporated—all of the mechanisms, monitoring processes, and reward systems neces-

---

[1]Michael T. Higgins, "Bank Strategies," *Bank Marketing Magazine,* October 1988, p. 9.

sary to support a sales culture. In any event, it is clear that mere rhetoric will not make the necessary changes happen. Only commitment and action initiated by the CEO will cause the needed changes to occur. Developing a pervasive, functioning sales environment demands an enthusiastic transfer of CEO belief into a level of service that can be seen throughout the organization. This means that the successful senior management teams in the 1990s and beyond must not merely be excellent strategic decision-makers, they must also be able to implement those decisions so that the organization maximizes its potential. They must, in other words, become effective managers of change.

Effective managers of change must understand that change in a business environment parallels personal experiences such as a divorce or losing a loved one. Just as counseling is needed for personal change, professional counseling is often needed for those dealing with managing change in a business environment. Management teams must also understand the necessity of dealing with change as an opportunity rather than a danger.

CHANGE MANAGEMENT DEFINED

A good definition of successful change management is "that participants implement priority action plans and achieve objectives within a scheduled time and agreed upon budget."[2] There are five prerequisites to achieving major organizational change:

1. All participants need to understand the implications of the dangers and opportunities that exist within a time frame so that appropriate action can be taken.
2. Participants, as well as the individual in charge of implementing change, need to understand the tremendous amount of discomfort that will develop as a result of change.
3. Participants must understand how to recognize and remedy the discomfort.

---

[2]Daryl R. Conner, *"Managing Organizational Change, Dangers and Opportunities, Report,"* O.D. Resources, Inc., Atlanta, GA, 1986.

4. Management must continually reinforce, support, and recognize those individuals who are most affected by change.
5. The implementation team should address openly the unique barriers that exist within the organization that might jeopardize the desired results or goals.

CHANGE IS A PROCESS

In approaching most projects, a critical mistake executives often make is to assume change is an event, not a process. The successful manager of change must demonstrate an understanding that change is a process to be carefully orchestrated at each level of the organization. Viewing change as a process can be simply illustrated with the following model (Figure 2–1). To achieve movement from the "present state" on the left to the "desired state" on the right, targets of change must pass through the "transition state," a period of high insecurity and ambiguity in which people are unfrozen from their current ways of doing things and are drawn to a new frame of reference.

What would cause a person or group to be willing to depart from the present state for a transition state of ambiguity and insecurity? Only "pain" will provide the kind of motivation necessary. Substantial change, especially cultural change, must be more than merely "intellectually stimulating" before people will embrace it fully. A significant change will be sustained *only* if it is proved to those affected that the present way of doing things is more expensive than the price for transition. The pain of the status quo is the prime impetus for movement into the future.

There are two kinds of pain powerful enough to motivate change: current pain and anticipated pain. Current pain is generated by problems. Anticipated pain is caused by the possibility of missed opportunities. Current pain is seen when a manager says, "We spent $5 million on a computer system to automate our item processing, and we still don't have what we need. We're in trouble today." This manager is facing current problems and is missing current and future opportunities. A manager who anticipates the future is one who is in pain because the present definition of success will not sustain the organization in the future, and he knows it. For example, in the late

FIGURE 2-1
Change is a Process

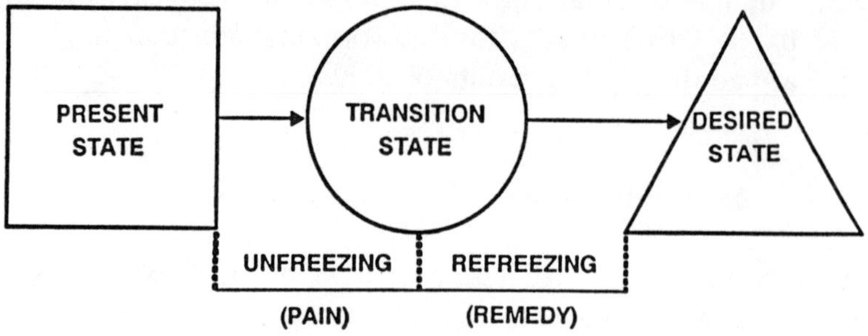

CHARACTERISTICS OF THE TRANSITION STATE:

- Low stability.
- High emotional stress.
- High, often undirected energy.
- Control becomes a major issue.
- Past patterns of behavior become highly valued.
- Conflict increases.

1970s, C&S Bank of Georgia anticipated that deregulation and changes in state banking laws would cause major power shifts in the financial services environment in the South and around the country. C&S anticipated the need to change rather than wait until change was absolutely necessary. By the early 1980s, C&S actually had a Department of Change manager. As a result of this proactive approach to managing change, The Citizens and Southern Corporation is now one of the strongest financial institutions in the nation, with over $20 billion in assets and subsidiaries in Georgia, Florida, and South Carolina.

Often, only the senior executives in an organization are in a position to know the problems their bank may face months or years ahead. These managers must generate pain through the use of education and consequence management. This kind of pain will motivate the kinds of behavior needed to ensure future success. However, whether the situation is one of current or anticipated pain, managers must be aware that the critical task is to generate sufficient pain to motivate change without creating so much pain that yet more problems result. This balancing act is a key skill that managers in financial institutions must demonstrate to successfully implement change in their organizations.

For many people, the concept that only pain will motivate change is a hard one to accept or understand. However, a true, life-threatening incident will illustrate this key concept.

The survivor of a disastrous fire on an off-shore drilling platform in the North Sea was being interviewed by Ted Koppel on *Nightline.* In matter-of-fact terms the man described being awakened in the middle of the night by the explosion and alarms, of running to the edge of the platform, of jumping into the sea below, and of his subsequent rescue.

Mr. Koppel knew, however, that there was more to this story than the man's simple retelling revealed, so he said, "Now, wait a minute. Let me get this straight. There was all manner of debris floating in the water. The water itself was covered with oil and on fire. And yet you awoke from a sound sleep, ran immediately to the edge of the platform, and without hesitation jumped fifteen stories into the water without knowing if you would survive the jump or if you would be rescued if you did survive the jump." Mr. Koppel paused for dramatic effect before asking, "Why in the world would you do that?"

The platform worker did not hesitate even a second: "Because if I did not jump, I was going to fry."

The platform worker undoubtedly knew the risks of making his jump. He knew that death was a possibility. He could also see explosions and roaring flames all around him. When it became clear to him that the possibility of survival—however remote—was better than the certainty of death, he made the jump. The point is clear: a major, potentially cataclysmic change will not occur without pain as a motivator.

Practically speaking, management is really a function of helping key persons in an organization understand the true costs of not changing. Some of these costs include:

- The problem is not solved.
- An opportunity is not exploited.
- Time, money, and people resources are wasted.
- Morale suffers.
- Job security for those involved is threatened.

There are three other very important consequences for senior managers who are unable to fully implement needed changes. If left unattended, these consequences can become devastating to the long-term health of any bank. These consequences are

- People within the organization will learn to ignore strategic directives.
- The organization loses confidence in the leadership because senior officers do not appear to be in control.
- Short-term comfort from status quo is replaced by an inability to survive.

Communicating the high costs of mismanaged change is the key to releasing people from the present state and moving them toward the desired state. However, merely broadcasting the costs of mismanaged change via various "pain messages" is not enough. They must go to the right people. Effective managers of change have a clear understanding of thc kcy roles and relationships involved in a change project, and they use this understanding to initiate change throughout the organization.

KEY ROLES AND RELATIONSHIPS

The strategies used to orchestrate both current and anticipated pain are a function of the ability to manage the various types of relationships between those who participate in change. Participants are identified as sponsors, agents, or targets. Sponsors are those with the organizational power to legitimize a change. Agents have the responsibility for carrying out the change. Targets are those who must actually make the change.

Relationships between sponsors and their agents and targets usually take one of three forms shown in Figure 2–2. The simplest kind of relationship to understand is the linear relationship. In the linear relationship, the target reports directly to the change agent, who has responsibility for making sure that the target makes the desired change. The agent, in turn, reports directly to the sponsor. This kind of target/agent/sponsor relationship may not always be successful in implementing change, but at least it is an easy one to relate to because it is based on hierarchy or chain of command.

The second kind of relationship is triangular in nature. In triangular relationships, both the agent and the target report to the sponsor, but the target does not report to the agent. A classic triangular relationship occurs when the sponsor is senior management, the agent is management information systems (MIS) or the marketing director, and the target is staff. Most triangular relationships are dysfunctional because sponsors attempt to delegate their "legitimization power" to agents by telling them it is their job to get line management to comply with the new computer system or the human resources policy. Effective sponsors know that they cannot delegate sponsorship to change agents. In order to sponsor change in a triangle, one must be willing to turn directly to the target and say unequivocally, "I am the one who wants this change to occur. The agent is here to help you do what I have requested. He is not the person driving this change; I am." This kind of direct, unequivocal sponsorship will significantly lower the change resistance and dysfunction inherent to most triangular relationships.

Another common problem is represented by the square relationship. In this type of relationship, not only does the target of the effort not report to the agent who wants the change, the target does not report to the agent's sponsor either. If the sponsor of the proposed action has any hope of successful implementation, he must convince the target's sponsor that the change is essential. Such persuasion is called "advocacy." Advocates are people who want change but who lack the organizational power to legitimize it themselves.

An understanding of linear, triangular, and square relationships is essential because most large change projects, especially culture change projects, involve numerous sponsors, some of whom may be

FIGURE 2-2
Critical Roles: Three Basic Relationships

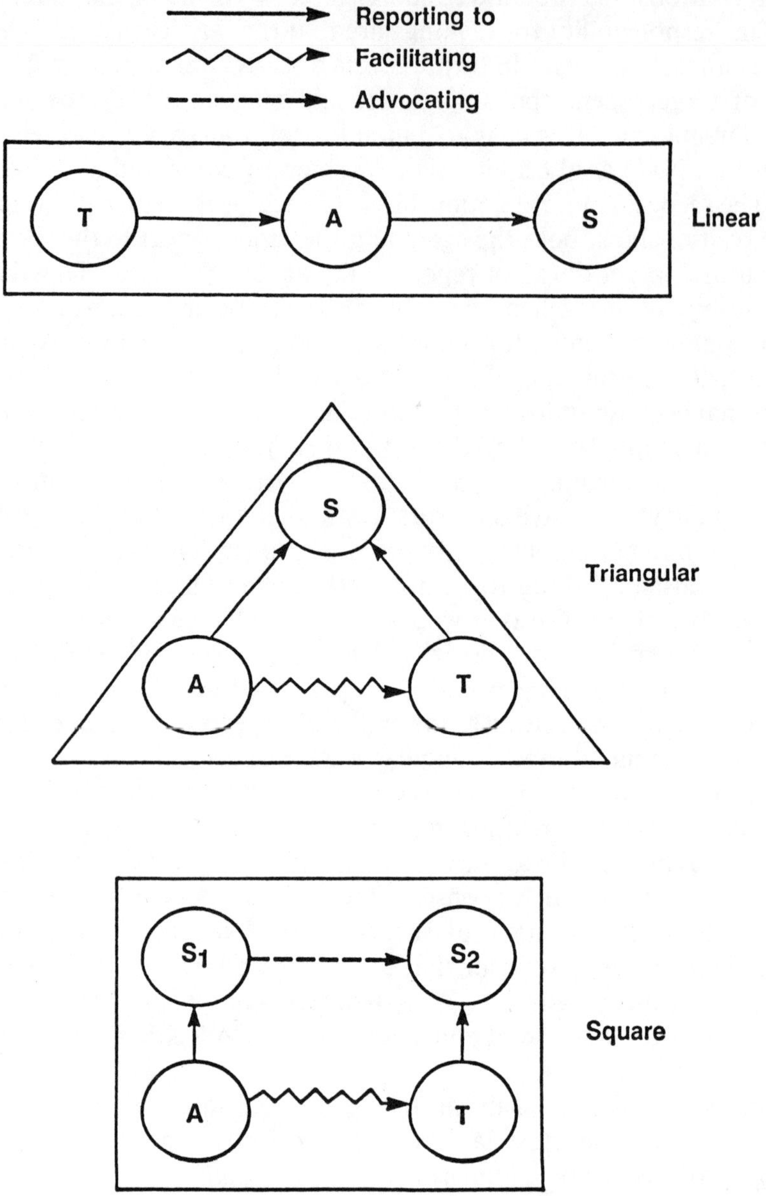

involved in each kind of relationship. An understanding of the critical roles and relationships involved in a change often will allow a skilled agent or sponsor to go directly to the source of the problem and to conserve valuable financial and other resources by dealing with it specifically and prescriptively.

CORPORATE BLACK HOLES

Senior managers sometimes are aggressively committed to effecting a cultural change in their bank, yet they discover that the change does not occur. We refer to this phenomenon as the corporate "black hole." Astrophysicists first coined the term to refer to locations in space where gravity is so strong that all surrounding matter and energy, even light itself, is drawn in and unable to escape.

The ways senior level initiatives are typically disseminated throughout an organization suggest a similar dynamic. Corporate black holes are present in organizations (Figure 2-3) in which a change decision enters but is never heard from again. A black hole occurs when there is enough logistic, economic, or political distance between the sponsors of a change and the targets that strategic deci-

FIGURE 2-3
Typical Ineffective Sponsorship

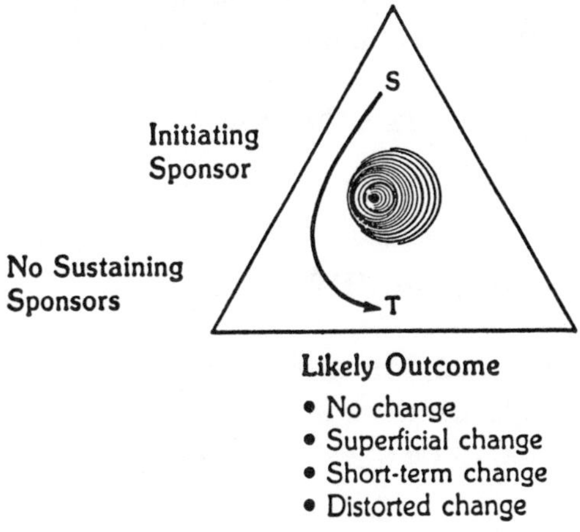

sions are significantly distorted or are totally ignored by the time they reach their ultimate destination in the organization.

The gap between sponsor and target is easy to identify when the bureaucratic layers, individual priorities, geographic distances, and budgetary implications that typically separate management from staff are examined. For example, several years ago a large international bank wanted to change its culture. It gathered its managers from around the world in various key cities and sent out a satellite television broadcast outlining the changes that would occur and the changes that each country's operations would have to make. It was an impressive show, but when it was over the senior manager from Paris turned off the television and told those gathered with him that "Those guys in New York don't understand how things work here. We can't make those changes. Keep doing what you've been doing. How will they know whether we changed or not?" This is a black hole, and an obvious one at that. However, do not be fooled. An organization does not have to have an office in Paris to fall victim to black holes. A close look at most organizations reveals that it takes only a few doors down the hallway to create enough logistic, economic, and political distance for a black hole to develop. Black holes exist in any company in which the top executives can dispense strategic rhetoric but do not have the direct control over day-to-day activities necessary to fully implement their decisions.

In fact, in virtually every organization observed in 15 years of change management research, characteristics of the corporate black hole were evident. Traditional hierarchies are just as susceptible as highly matrixed organization designs. Publicly traded, entrepreneurial, public-sector, and nonprofit organizations are indistinguishable in their capacity to generate the devastating symptoms of the black hole phenomenon.

CASCADING SPONSORSHIP

Only one effective solution to the black hole problem exists. This solution is to build a network of cascading sponsors (Figure 2–4) who are committed to taking strategic directives and driving them at the tactical level.

Most major change projects actually have two kinds of spon-

FIGURE 2-4
Cascading Sponsorship

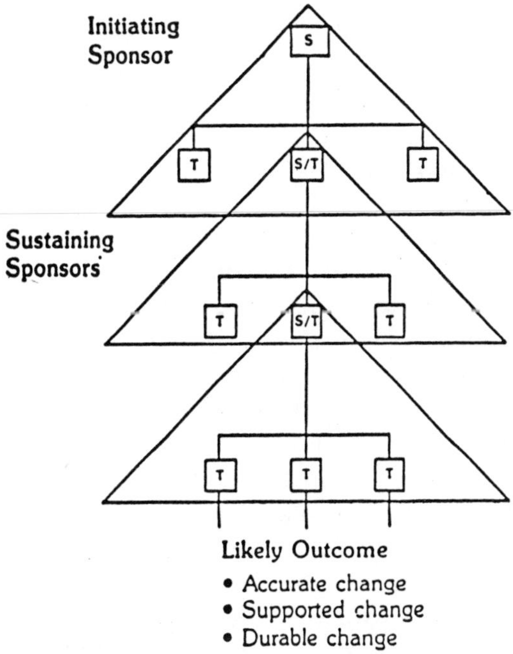

sors. The "initiating" sponsor is the one who first legitimizes the change project. This person has the organizational power to sanction the action. In many cases, the idea for the change did not necessarily originate with the initiating sponsor. In fact, there are many situations in which the initiating sponsor did not even fully understand the change he was approving. What is important is that a sponsor has the power to sanction change and to allocate people and other resources to the effort. Without this legitimization, substantive, durable change will not occur.

Although initiating sponsors are extremely important, major projects require the acceptance of change by people lower in the organization who may not have direct contact with the originating sponsor. When this occurs, initiating sponsors must enlist the support of "sustaining" sponsors. Sustaining sponsors are usually mid-level managers with the power to legitimize change on a more local level. Sustaining sponsors primarily manage consequences to accomplish the specific objectives that must be met in order for the strategic directives of the initiating sponsor to succeed.

Initiating sponsors must, therefore, manifest the necessary commitment to change by applying their personal and organizational powers to ensure that sponsorship cascades to the levels below. They must treat those who would later be sustaining sponsors as targets first, educating them and applying rewards and consequences to build commitment at this level. They are then charged with legitimizing the change with those who report to them. This commitment from both upper and middle management demonstrates to the target audience that there is true support for the change from the top of the organization on down through the mid-level ranks.

An excellent example of how sponsorship can be positively reaffirmed in order to pull a project out of a black hole occurred recently at Maryland State Universities and Colleges (MSUC), which was attempting to integrate 28 VAX minicomputers. The project had stalled because of resistance from the target population: users in eight institutions throughout the state. The managers of the project knew that they were in trouble if they could not get a renewed statement of sponsorship. Therefore, MSUC project managers recommended that the board of trustees reaffirm the original strategy for a centralized, coordinated network. The project managers also analyzed and created a detailed series of steps to resolve all of the concerns of the end users. The original plan and the new recommendations were quickly and publicly approved by the colleges' and universities' council of presidents and by the board of trustees. This combination of substantive and ceremonial actions lowered target resistance, reaffirmed initiating sponsor support for the project, and brought on board sustaining sponsors who now knew that they had the backing necessary to drive the change throughout the organization.

An initiating sponsor who discovers a black hole in the organization faces three potential options:

- Use education and consequences to help those exhibiting poor sustaining sponsorship to see that such behavior is not in the organization's or their best interest.
- Replace uncommitted managers with those who are more supportive of the change effort.

- Prepare to fail the stated change objective within the originally prescribed time and budget constraints.

The implementation of major change on a sustained basis cannot occur without the coordinated efforts of committed initiating and sustaining sponsors.

The building of a cascading network of sustaining sponsors is a time- and energy-consuming process. However, there are no quick cures for the symptoms of poor change management. Sophisticated problems such as black holes require substantial investment. There are no alternatives! Effective managers are those who are willing to work hard at reducing the risk of failure because they know they cannot afford to fail.

MANAGING CHANGE REQUIRES CULTURE CHANGE

The kind of a change that a bank must undergo to become a competitive, market-driven institution (and therefore successful in the 1990s and beyond) is not merely a small, tactical adjustment. It will require a complete shift in culture, because whenever there is a discrepancy between culture and change, culture always wins.[3] This kind of change cannot, of course, be implemented overnight, because a culture shift is a re-definition of what an organization is and how it defines success. The problem is compounded by the fact that even though culture is a very powerful force in a bank's day-to-day operations, most executives think of it as a nebulous, almost mystical entity. Most bank CEOs will acknowledge that corporate culture is a powerful force. However, many think there is nothing that can be done to affect it.

Culture can be understood and managed, but to do so is a difficult process that must be entered into soberly. Understanding the following three principles is important for establishing a common ground for managing culture.

---

[3]Daryl R. Conner, Bryon G. Firman, Ernest E. Clements, "Corporate Culture and Its Impact on Strategic Change in Banking," *Journal of Retail Banking,* Summer 1987, p. 17.

- *Culture has patterns.* Patterns of beliefs, behaviors, and assumptions serve as a predictable guide to appropriate behavior in individuals and at the group level.
- *Culture is shared by members of an organization.* It provides cohesion among people who perform different functions throughout the same bank.
- *Culture is developed over time as a result of past successes.* A bank's existing culture is the product of what has worked in the past. In other words, it is a pattern of beliefs, behaviors, and assumptions that is learned.

On the basis of these principles, culture can therefore be defined as the basic pattern of shared beliefs, behaviors, and assumptions acquired over time by members of an organization.

Culture affects daily business operations in two ways: conscious and unconscious. Conscious ways consist of the intentional, overt, and direct influences on operations. Examples include the stated goals of management, policies and procedures, statements of corporate philosophy, and the formal structure of the organization. Unconscious ways are the unintentional, indirect influences on operations. Examples include informal ground rules, unofficial guidelines, or "the way things are done around here." These influences are very difficult to change because they are often below our level of awareness.

HOW DOES CULTURE DEVELOP?

The successful alignment of culture with a bank's strategic decisions requires the development of beliefs, behaviors, and assumptions that are consistent with the achievement of those decisions. For instance, if a bank wants to increase its cross-sell ratios, a comprehensive program including training, goals, measurement, and compensation might be developed that rewards the development and utilization of successful selling skills. The cultural change in this case is the development of new beliefs about what should be rewarded and, probably, new behaviors when relating to customers. The hoped-for outcome (goals) is an alignment of culture with strategy so that the cultural norm actually drives this key business initiative.

Another characteristic of culture is that it is learned over time, and it is based upon past successes. A behavior is tried in response to a problem or opportunity. If the behavior solves the problem or allows the opportunity to be exploited, it will be applied again whenever a similar situation arises. This "evolutionary" process continues until a complex pattern of assumptions is firmly established.

Years ago, for example, bankers learned that personal contact with clients was important. Some found that if they followed their business calls with handwritten letters, their sales increased. Today, even though word processing systems can provide highly personalized communications and free a manager's time for making yet more sales contacts—and, therefore, more sales—many banks continue using handwritten letters. The old culture is inconsistent with the new sales strategy. The point is not that handwritten letters have no place in an automated business environment but that cultures that developed by evolution often fail to drive new strategies.

Consider, for example, an aluminum manufacturing plant in the Midwest that was undergoing a major retooling and automation process. The technology was superior to the old methods in virtually every way. Still, resistance at the line level was tremendous. Productivity did not improve. It actually fell. Resistance usually manifests itself in such comments as: "The new system takes twice as long and our work is half as good." "Everybody is comfortable with the new system except so-and-so. We decided to wait until everybody was comfortable before we made the switch." "We're in the middle of a job that we have to finish before we can make a change. Give us 90 days."

Resistance reached the point that there was no doubt that the targets were actually feeding false data back to management regarding the performance of the new system.

A survey of line employees revealed that it was, in fact, a personal, not an organizational, issue that affected the employees' acceptance of the changes. They were worried about job security, not their own jobs but the jobs of their sons and daughters. The small town in which most of the employees lived was totally dependent on the plant. Most families had two or three generations working there. Many people believed they possessed a "birthright" to work at this plant.

Once these concerns were uncovered, they were addressed through training programs in the public school system that taught the skills necessary for gainful employment in the upgraded plant. In fact, as a firm demonstration of sponsor commitment to the change, these programs were largely funded by the company that owned the plant. Once these programs were put in place, the systems change went on to enjoy a successful implementation.

Few, if any, banks are "the company" in one-company towns. However, banks are, many times, symbols of community beliefs, behaviors, and assumptions—both to customers and to employees. Not taking these cultural components into account results in change projects that are, at best, "hit-or-miss" propositions.

Similarly, the banking industry's inability to create successful sales cultures is more than disconcerting.[4] The inconsistencies of new initiatives has been a hit-or-miss proposition. Instead of a planned alignment between culture and change, implementation strategies can be better described as "spray and pray": senior officers take a shot in one direction, stand back, and hope for the best. In these situations, strategic decisions are not likely to be successfully implemented, and their results are poor or mixed.

Many community bank holding companies are committed to professional selling. Management allows its acquisitions to keep their individual identities and to continue to operate under their old names. These community banks are treated as individual marketing units, with the bank president serving as the chief marketing and sales executive. This executive's role, managing sales, will be reflected in part by the fewer number of persons who report to him. The bank president will have directly reporting to him only the managers of commercial services, consumer services, and other specialized services, such as trust services. These managers will be charged with generating profitable new business and will be evaluated almostentirely on that basis. Data processing, cost accounting, auditing, human resources, deposit services, item processing, and training—while still vital—will be performed at the holding company level, where specialists can exercise economies of scale, improved service delivery, and tight accountability.

---

[4]Michael T. Higgins, "A View from the Field: Managing Change," *ABA Banking Journal*, November 1988.

This kind of change does not require an "evolutionary" development. Rather, it deserves an "architectural" development, which involves changing the very definition of success in an organization. Architecturally designed culture changes are the proactive development and maintenance of the beliefs, behaviors, and assumptions of an organization. In this process, the culture is carefully planned and implemented to achieve success as it is defined by top management.

The first step toward architecturally shifting a bank's culture is the development of a clear statement of

- Vision ("Why are we here?").
- Mission ("What are we going to do?").
- Strategy ("How are we going to do it?").

The redefining of vision, mission, and strategy sometimes creates entirely new definitions of what "success" means within an organization. Such was the case at the Norfolk, Virginia–based Sovran Bank, a $20-billion "super-regional" that wanted to redefine the mission of the 135 auditors who worked there.

"We had a top-notch professional organization," said Corporate General Auditor Jimmy Jarvis. "But we were performing the traditional audit functions: evaluate controls and give a historical snapshot of the auditee. We wanted to change our role so that we were helping the auditee anticipate problems before they develop." Sovran therefore implemented the "proactive audit."

"Twenty years ago auditors were pencil-pushers, people who showed up occasionally to count the beans," Mr. Jarvis said. "Today, the audit function in banks should be used more as a decision-support tool by senior management. These changes mean that we have to have a different view of ourselves and our clients." This redefinition of vision will require vastly different systems and skills for the auditor at Sovran. It will be a transition that this bank and others will need to manage carefully.

The second step is to assess the degree of consistency between the existing culture and the kind of culture needed to drive the plan. Both of these vital issues are covered in subsequent chapters. For now, it is enough to say that you must know where you want to go and you must architecturally build a culture that takes you there. These two are fundamental to business success, especially as the changes facing your organization come more and more rapidly.

IMPLEMENTING CULTURAL CHANGE

Typically in an organization experiencing change, one-third of the participants will readily accept a new focus. One-third will likely be concerned and look for clarification of the implications. The final third of the organization will dig in their heels and fight change.[5] The key is not to criticize or challenge the resistance, because open resistance is critical to achieving success. The challenge is to identify covert resistance. Covert resistance results in all types of red flags. How to deal with this challenge is critically important in order to be successful.

A series of management prerogatives and/or alternatives should be examined. Considerations should include:

- Redefining **organizational culture** to be more supportive of corporate business objectives.
- **Restructuring** the organization to achieve a competitive advantage.
- Increasing output capacity through the installation of **productivity improvement programs.**
- Establishing **new products and markets.**
- Adjusting to the **changing profile and needs of today's employees.**
- Increasing the use of **computerized information systems and office automation technology.**
- Integrating new personnel through **expansions, mergers, or acquisitions.**
- Incorporating new **procedures** that result from technological breakthroughs.
- Adapting to fluctuations in the economy by **down-sizing.**
- Initiating major **reorganization** plans.

In addition, a methodology should be created for any one or a combination of the following:

- **Establishing the overall organizational parameters** within which to make change decisions.

---

[5]Daryl R. Conner, *Cultural Audit Workbook: Corporate Culture and Its Impact on Organizational Change* (Atlanta: O.D. Resources, Inc., 1987).

- **Assessing the implementation risk** of major strategic actions before decisions are made.
- **Planning the implementation process** to minimize resistance and maximize support from those expected to change their skills, attitudes, or behavior.
- **Executing implementation plans** with a skill base that increases the likelihood of success.

This methodology, when applied in an organizational setting, will

- Significantly increase the likelihood that a change will **achieve its human/technical goals on time and within budget.**
- Develop the implementation architecture that **generates high degrees of commitment and diminished resistance** from those affected by a change.
- Teach key people a **systematic procedure for implementing change.** The procedure can then be applied to specific projects on an isolated basis, or it can be institutionalized throughout an organization and used to implement all key management directives requiring major organizational change.

Organizations seem to put all of their time, effort, and resources into identifying the need to create change and setting goals that will be achieved by change. However, minimal effort or resources[6] are applied to manage implementation and to ensure successful execution. Change management is the issue; therefore, a commitment to create a change management methodology often is the most efficient resolution.

The specific, prescriptive changes that a bank should make in order to thrive in the 1990s and beyond are covered in detail in subsequent chapters of this book. The purpose of this chapter is not to go into detail about what you should change, but rather to point out key issues that will be relevant no matter what changes your organization must eventually make. Therefore, the following are a few of the characteristics that successful organizations have displayed in the

---

[6]Michael T. Higgins, "Stale Structures Impede Marketing Change," *Bank Marketing Magazine,* March, 1988, pp. 38–42.

process of a culture change. In effective organizations, the process was

- *Initiated and legitimized by top management.* Without sponsorship from the very top of the organization, no sustainable change will occur. Change initiatives without top-level, highly visible sponsorship will be perceived as another meaningless announcement that will never have any real effect. The CEO and executive management must embrace marketing as a vehicle for obtaining the desired success in the marketplace, or the success will not occur.
- *An integral part of achieving business goals.* Bank managers must believe that the continued competitiveness and even the very survival of the bank depends upon its ability to make the shift from a product to a market orientation. In order to ensure a strong link to business objectives, the bank's senior officers should ask: "What market are we trying to dominate?" The second question should be: "What kind of company do we need to be to achieve dominance in this market?" This contextual framework will help the bank manager define the beliefs, behaviors, and assumptions necessary for future success.
- *Measurable, with meaningful, tangible objectives.* Progress should not be measured by activity alone.
- *Implemented bank-wide.* Everyone in the organization must understand his relationship to the ultimate goal of becoming a market-driven bank.
- *The responsibility of line managers, with support staff playing a supportive role.* Culture change cannot be sponsored by support staff, such as human resources or strategic planning. Cultural change must be legitimized by line managers with the authority and power to initiate and sustain the process.
- *Publicized in a gradual manner, primarily focusing on tangible results, not slick slogans and fancy brochures.* "Hype" should be avoided. It is more realistic and beneficial to wait and report on the achievement of a few concrete objectives later in the process than to publicize activity that may or may not lead to accomplishment.

This business of managing major change is, as you can see, not a simple process. There are no quick fixes when it comes to changing an organization's culture. Therefore, culture shifts should be avoided if organizational changes can be made to conform to the existing culture. However, managing the shift from a product-driven to a market-driven environment is not a minor tactical change. It is a fundamental redefinition of the corporate vision and master strategies, it's about the way business is going to be done. Managers cannot afford to fail at dealing with such change.

CHAPTER 3

VISION, MASTER STRATEGIES, AND THE DRIVING FORCE

> If you do not look at things on a large scale first, it will be difficult for you to master any strategy.
>
> —*Miyamoto Musashi*–1643 A.D.

The purpose of developing strategies is to give focus. Initially, the focus must define what the organization will become. The purpose of strategic planning is not to define the future external and competitive environment. Rather, the focus must define what kind of business the organization will be, regardless of what external influences develop.

The prerequisites are, first, creating long-range vision; second, identifying the organization's master strategy; and third, confirming the organization's driving force. These are not participatory management decisions. The creation of the overall corporate vision, the definition of the master strategy, and the confirmation of the company's driving force are the responsibilities of the institution's owners and possibly a very limited number of senior officers. The strategic planning process, in other words, is ultimately the responsibility of the organization's top leadership. During subsequent phases of the process, participatory management activities that encourage discussion and understanding by all other players in the organization are appropriate.

In most organizations, the management and staff are doing many things right. Too often, however, they are not concentrating on doing the right things. Without an understanding of the ultimate vision, master strategy, and driving force, individuals, teams, and departments will go off in diverse directions and undertake a variety of activities because they do not understand the organization's ultimate focus. During the initial planning process, defining explicit strategic focus allows organizations to understand and, therefore, to concentrate on doing the right things right, that is, undertaking the most important activities first. By doing so, companies achieve the organizational and service priorities necessary to maximize their potential. It begins by creating a corporate vision.

VISION

Jan Carlzon feels very strongly about the need to create and reinforce a corporate vision. He concludes, "Successful executives will give all employees an opportunity to understand the company's guiding vision. Only then can they really pitch in and give all they've got. Only then can each and every one assume the full responsibility for his own share of the overall goal. Only then can you unleash the mighty energy generated by a group of enthusiastic people."[1]

In the previous regulated, considerably less competitive environment, traditional banking institutions could afford the luxury of defining the purpose of their business as simply to make money. The only strategy necessary for increasing profit was to increase volume. This approach is no longer valid.

Bankers have every good reason to take comfort in the past. They were successful. They made a significant contribution to their communities and to their marketplace. They consistently concentrated on the right things, and they did things right to serve in a regulated environment. Regulation ensured survival. Now all of that has changed.

Deregulation demands that bankers consistently do the right things right in order to survive. Change becomes the norm. Anticipating, planning for, and managing change is essential in today's competitive banking industry. Managing change and combatting resistance to change will separate prosperous organizations from those

---

[1]Jan Carlzon, *Moments of Truth* (Massachusetts: Ballinger Publishing Company, 1987), p. 27.

that will not survive. Resistance to change occurs because people are comfortable with the past. The challenge is to become comfortable with the present and to focus on the future.

When top management has reached a consensus about a reasonably clear definition of the institution's future, vision is present. Vision does not come easily. It is a product of structured, as well as not-so-structured, activities and an unflinching commitment to maximizing the organization's potential. Moreover, vision must continually be shaped, reshaped, and clarified. Throughout the strategic planning process, vision is the undying catalyst planted in the minds of every participant.

Therefore, vision must be established very early in the process. It will evolve and expand. Not to be confused with forecasting, vision is not a statistical or empirical science. Instead, vision springs from an intuitive process and is a product of disciplined, creative thinking.

The financial services industry deserves and desperately needs creative thinkers. Officers and staff desperately want to understand their work purpose beyond a method to earn a wage and improve shareholder value. They want to contribute, and they want to contribute to something meaningful. A properly defined vision will serve as the very foundation from which bankers can become enthusiastic about that all-important responsibility to their bank and their customers.

The bank's leadership must come to recognize that imaginativeness is an attitude as well as a style of thinking. It involves a commitment of time and effort and a readiness to consider more possibilities, to search more widely, and to consider every alternative, even those that seem to carry a low probability of implementation. In the visionary world, there is no such thing as a dumb idea.

More often than not, the most successful companies exhibit this kind of dedication and vision. They differentiate themselves from their competitors by bringing to market novel and unusual ideas. Management's commitment to the creative thinking process always pays off.

We know enough about the conditions that nurture creative thinking to believe that it can be taught and learned. Similarly, our considerable knowledge about how personal value systems form and evolve prove that if we choose to be committed we can clarify our own values and then encourage the development of similar values in others. We also know a good deal about the situational conditions that increase people's determination. Therefore, there are many opportunities for effective change.

The Challenge

Bankers must expand their management skills. The previously regulated financial services environment allowed bankers to concentrate on developing operational and administrative skills. Today and in the future, those skills will continue to be important. However, additional skills must be developed, with visionary skills having priority. Chapter 6 and Appendix B elaborate on other skill implications.

Leaders in the industry must demonstrate a respect for the past while forging a redefinition of the future. One change they should embrace is ceasing to be "all things to all people." Unlimited opportunities can open up to bankers who recognize the need to define business parameters, allowing them to concentrate on those things the organization does best and thereby to differentiate themselves from their competitors. This will take creative leadership.

The essential element of every successful strategy is differentiation, because it places all other competitors at a distinct disadvantage. This means that any corporate vision that is no different from others in the industry is not really a vision.

Don Mengedoth, Chairman of Community First Bankshares, a midwestern holding company, is a visionary. He is an excellent manager and an exceptional leader because he not only achieves what he sets out to do, he knows how to lead and how to get others to lead others in getting caught up in his vision.

In facilitating the last two strategic planning retreats of Community First Bankshares, I experienced a unique patience and a perseverance to instill a true force of power among Don's management team. Afterwards, I observed, "Don, the time we spent reinforcing your vision was the most productive experience I have ever participated in, and the value of that experience was in your belief and commitment." I then asked, "Why is vision so important to you?" He replied, "Vision is the glue. It is my statement of perception about how we will bring all of our stakeholders to a common understanding. Every stakeholder—our employees, our stockholders, our customers, and our regulators—must have a common understanding about our purpose, how we will set our company apart from our competition, what we stand for, and where we are going. I can't believe an organization can function without it!"

That is why vision is so important. The cultivation of visionary ability has become the traditional banker's greatest challenge. Previously, banking leaders in the regulated environment achieved their level of success by seeking out and sharing ideas with their peers. That was appropriate. However, in a deregulated, highly competitive environment, organizations will not excel if peer consensus is the only leadership resource. Mirror images create mediocrity. Differentiation demands excellence. Differentiation requires vision, and vision requires creative thinking.

Therefore, the first step in strategic planning is for the organization's leaders to create their own distinctive vision of what their company will become. How much they differentiate from their competitors will determine their level of success.

Defining Business Purpose

Theodore Levit, in *The Marketing Imagination,* wrote, "Financial institutions will no longer be in the loan and deposit business. Rather, they will be in the business of creating and keeping customers."[2]

In a regulated, comparatively noncompetitive environment, banking organizations assumed that the purpose of their business was to make loans and, by doing so, to make money. At the time, the only effort required to make more money was to increase volume.

In a deregulated, competitive environment, the need to make money still holds. In fact, the need to make money in any business is prerequisite to survival. That is, without profits, business stops. Making money, however, is not the purpose of the business. *The purpose of the business in a competitive environment is to get and keep customers.* It is important for management teams not to confuse the purpose of their business with the requisites of that business.

---

[2]Theodore Levit, *The Marketing Imagination* (New York: The Free Press, 1983), p. 5.

The purpose is to satisfy customers; the prerequisites are to manage assets and liabilities. The difference is very significant.

The purpose of the business should be creative and serve as a rallying cry, in response to which the staff can become enthusiastically supportive. They must believe in a purpose that will become the very foundation for their belief in the service and the organization they represent.

Equally important, a cogent and clearly articulated business purpose makes customers enthusiastic about doing business with a particular organization. This takes vision, and it takes creative thinking to create vision.

Profitability goals alone will not serve as a rallying point. The only people who will get enthusiastic about profitability are the directors, shareholders, and the limited number of senior managers who will benefit significantly from improved profits.

Satisfying customers is the purpose of every competitive business. This purpose will force management to figure out what clients really want and what they really value. Then, uniquely catering to those wants and values through differentiation becomes the essence of the organization's market-driven environment. It will again be helpful to look to other companies in other industries to reinforce the importance of differentiation in a competitive marketplace.

Differentiation

McDonalds' founder, Ray Kroc, differentiated his hamburger stand from all the rest in the country by concentrating on his target market: children. The strategy was to create a "good time" environment for the target market. Kroc's secondary target market were the adults who brought their children to his restaurant.

Through research, he differentiated his hamburger service from all others by (1) picking exceptional locations and (2) demanding consistency in both product quality and the cleanliness and attractiveness of the environment.

In contrast, small, specialized restaurants and diners prior to McDonalds did not try to attract children, and there was little emphasis on consistency in cleanliness or product quality. No wonder McDonalds surged ahead of its competitors.

Vision, Differentiation, and How to Dominate

All successful companies experience and require visionary strategic thinking. Examples in our contemporary high-tech world abound. *USA Today*'s goal is to become the Number One second newspaper in every household and business place. Its approach is to combine text and color graphics in an appealing new format.

The visionary analyzes the competition—its strengths and vulnerabilities—and then differentiates. The original Nissan Z sports car was designed to compete with the Chevrolet Corvette by providing an equally contemporary-looking automobile with better mileage and lower maintenance costs for half the price. The demographics supporting this visionary concept were overwhelming. There were vast numbers of buyers who could afford a Z but never thought of buying a Corvette. There are many other similar examples in the contemporary auto industry: Mazda successfully marketed the RX7 as a lower-cost alternative to the German Porsche. Honda's vision was to differentiate from the Volkswagon. The result: the Civic destroyed the Beetle.

Leaders in the financial services industry can also learn from visionary heroes whose influence has endured for generations, for example, Henry Ford, John D. Rockefeller, William Kellogg, Harley Proctor, and others who established some of the major businesses in America. The entrepreneurial spirit of the country fostered them, and they, in turn, became symbols of that spirit.

Entrepreneuralism lives today. A new breed of entrepreneurs is making a significant contribution to American business. In fact, the majority of new and successful businesses represent the ongoing entrepreneurial spirit in this country. The entrepreneurs driving these companies will also become symbols of the future.

The success of visionaries consists not only of having built an organization but also of having established an institution that survives them and adds their personal sense of values to the world. The financial services industry can learn from visionaries to change the way it does business. Bankers need not emulate other leaders. However, they can gain invaluable perspective by studying the leadership at institutions like General Electric, Proctor and Gamble, and IBM where employees today share the values of their founders as well as their shareholders. These heroes have great symbolic value within the cultures of their companies. They can serve equally effectively as symbolic values for people striving to provide visionary leadership in deregulated industries such as banking.

A good example is Thomas Watson, the builder of IBM. Watson had reached the top in another company when he was suddenly fired at the age of 39. He was newly married and out of work for eight or nine months when he finally landed a job with a relatively small record company. For his first six years there, Watson had to play to the whims of the chairman of the board, a financial man who founded the company. Watson carried out his decisions, but he never lost sight of what the company could become. Only when the founder grew old and Watson had won his trust was he able to gain a free hand in managing the organization and to proceed with turning the company into IBM.

Today many people assume that IBM reached its present market position through superior computer technology. Yet General Electric, Univac, and RCA were the computer technology leaders when IBM entered the market.

The fact is that IBM became the leader through vision and by focusing market-driven planning strategies. While competitors were refining and selling products, IBM focused on how to differentiate itself from its bigger and more resilient competitors. To ensure significant differentiation from its competitors, IBM concentrated on the four basic marketing axioms:

- Define who the customers are (market segmentation).
- Find out what customers value (perceived value).
- Determine what customers need (needs analysis).
- Learn how customers buy (decision-maker characteristics).

IBM's research found that a business's decision to buy a computer was based on the input of many individuals, including the client's technicians, accounting and financial managers, operational managers, marketing specialists, and so on. Therefore, IBM designed a marketing plan that reached and "sold" each employee who influenced the buying decision.

IBM's ability to surpass its competition provides an excellent example of the power of marketing through differentiation. Yet too many financial institutions allow their planning efforts to become preoccupied with budgeting, forecasting, and controlling costs.

Managers may speak in vague terms about planning objectives, such as increasing sales and developing new markets, but the amount of time spent on these areas too often is negligible in relation to the entire corporate planning effort. Yet one fact remains: the purpose of a business is to satisfy customers; this is what IBM did, with spectacular results.

Characteristics of Visionaries

Visionary heroes share several characteristics that guarantee their survival as legends within their institutions, and they become standards of behavior for others to follow. The most apparent characteristics are that they

1. Set time aside to be creative, enabling them to reach the depths of their intuitive potential.
2. Were right about a new way to do business, which gave them the handle for differentiating themselves from their competitors.
3. Recognized opportunity. They could define a better way to get and keep customers.
4. Were persistent. Indeed, they were virtually obsessed with seeing their visions become reality, even though their ideas often ran counter to conventional wisdom.
5. Had a sense of personal responsibility for the continuing success of their business. Thomas Watson once said, "You have to put your heart in the business and the business in your heart." This is more than the testimony of a workaholic. It is the counsel of an individual who strove to build a business that was not only prosperous but important in terms of what it represented.
6. Recognized the need for making the business strong by treating people well and instilling in them a lasting sense of values.

These characteristics distinguish visionaries from less illustrious managers. The values of these heroes live on in the companies they create, and those values touch each employee in a very personal way.

We need not look only to the past for visionary heroes. Even in today's world, visionaries are still making the ultimate commitment to their companies, and they exhibit the same characteristics as the heroes of earlier times. Visionaries today continue to build institutions and occasionally even new industries, driven by the unlimited opportunities presented by the demand for change in our high-technology world.

The financial services industry needs visionaries more than ever before, not only to recapture market presence but also to stimulate better ways to accomplish goals. The industry's leadership must demand that any new idea is worthwhile only if it results in creating new customers or increases customer satisfaction. The leadership should emulate the likes of Integra in Pennsylvania and Community First Bankshares in the Midwest, who are breathing a new sense of value, purpose, and worth throughout their great organizations.

Visionaries in business, as in any other part of life, are not a rare breed. Every day, in every town and city throughout this great country, people with vision appear when they are most needed. The function of the visionary within an organization is so important, yet some companies with strong cultures often decide to leave little to chance. In that environment, the visionary will struggle, challenge the status quo, and then, if not allowed to work creatively, move on to become a competitor. This, of course, wastes the talent that financial institutions so desperately need. Instead, financial institutions should actively preserve and nurture their creative people and the potential visionaries within their ranks. This is a very critical consideration, which will be expanded upon in subsequent chapters dealing with expectations, measuring performance, and reward.

MASTER STRATEGIES

Once the corporate vision has been created, a limited number of senior management should gather to define their *master strategy*. The master strategy is the organization's ultimate or priority objective and plan of action for an agreed upon period of time.

Gaining that critically important, preeminent position needed to make the bank competitive begins with what can be called a CEO's perspective. The CEO is accountable to the shareholders and therefore has a primary role to maximize long-term shareholder value. There are four primary master strategies available for consideration in accomplishing this task.

Growth

The first master strategy is to increase the earnings base through market presence. This is a pure growth strategy that responds to market opportunities and, if necessary, permits sacrificing profitability in the short-term. Since long-term devotion to this strategy could adversely affect asset quality, strain capital, and weaken earnings, the bank, as a result, might become undervalued and vulnerable to aggressive predators. Therefore, a pure growth master strategy should be viewed as temporary. In pursuing such a strategy, profit-enhancement opportunities that do not violate the master strategy itself can be actively pursued.

Profit

A second master strategy focuses exclusively on profit enhancement. The result of this strategy may actually be to shrink the bank. As such, this master strategy may be appropriate when market conditions are extremely depressed or when there is a serious capital constraint. Because long-term devotion to this master strategy will result in reduced return on equity and declining market share and because it will not maximize long-term shareholder value, it too should be viewed as a temporary strategy.

Balance of Growth and Profit

A third master strategy calls for growth *and* enhanced profitability. It is the most difficult, yet potentially rewarding, of the four master strategies. It depends for its success on the creation of value-added benefits that transcend price, making it a marketing-driven strategy.

Sell

A fourth master strategy calls for selling the bank to an outside organization. This strategy is often selected when management can clearly establish that selling is the best short-term and long-term way to maximize shareholder value.

Once consensus has been reached on a master strategy, the appropriate operational and marketing strategies become much more clear. Therefore, in refining the CEO's perspective, one of the first things that bank leadership must do is develop an in-depth understanding of the bank's master strategy and how it will influence the development of the related corporate strategies. The master strategy then must be communicated throughout the organization. Otherwise, all subsequent strategies formulated by the various departmental groups are sure to be inconsistent and, often, counterproductive.

Surprisingly, the process of defining a master strategy is not evident in most financial institutions. Even when a master strategy is confirmed, it is rarely communicated throughout the organization to achieve a thorough understanding by all levels of staff. Therein lies one cause for a lack of management credibility. For everyone in the organization to carry out his or her responsibilities, the master perspective must be communicated and understood. Upon gaining a clear grasp of that perspective, managers and staff members can harmonize their activities with the master strategy, as well as prioritize their responsibilities for the present and subsequent strategies.

A series of recent decisions within the United Airlines management group exemplifies the importance of consensus. It began with a visionary, Richard Ferris, then Chairman of United Airlines, Inc., and its parent company, Allegis. His vision was to create a vertical travel services company that could serve the needs of a well-defined number of market segments. His master strategy was to pursue growth through market presence, respond to market opportunities, and sacrifice profitability in the short run.

His vision led to the creation of Allegis, a travel conglomerate that reinvested United Airlines' earnings in the acquisition of travel companies that would complement the global air carrier. The conglomerate quickly grew to include Hertz rental cars and the Westin, Vista International, and Hilton hotels.

The strategy was market-driven, targeted to serve the comprehensive needs of frequent travelers via a "one-stop" shopping service company. Subsequent strategies centered around improving service quality, offering service options, and pricing a total travel relationship for the company's captive audience.

The vision, the master strategy, and the subsequent strategies were brilliantly progressive and all-conclusive, save one major consideration: consensus. The architect for Allegis failed to secure consensus among those who would prefer an exclusive focus on a profit-enhancement master strategy. Shareholders and various employee groups, including the pilots' association, soon revolted. The board followed. Their priority was short-term profit. The CEO was replaced, the subsidiary companies are in the process of being sold off, and earnings are being redirected to pay off borrowings, increase dividends, and add to employee benefit and pension programs.

The vision was lost because consensus was not achieved. Since then, the company's priorities have been revised. It has chosen not to differentiate itself as a vertical travel service company and has reverted back to a traditional air travel company.

As this example illustrates, reaching a consensus is critical to defining and understanding the organization's "driving force."

DRIVING FORCE

To effectively exercise strategic decision-making responsibilities, managers must be conscious of which decisions are key. Identifying the driving force is one such decision. The driving force gives managers a central ideal or concept that they use to "see" into the future of their organization and to assess the product and market decisions that will get them where they want to go.

Having identified the organization's driving force and its underlying momentum, managers can perceive its nature and direction. This perception is the key to effective decision-making. Without a clear, explicit understanding of the driving force, managing key decisions becomes difficult, and managers are unable to make choices relative to opportunity and potential. Rather, decisions are made solely on the basis of operational considerations such as profitability, buying price, available management capability, and the like. Furthermore, all subsequent decision-making is likely to be inconsistent.

Alternatives

Eight basic driving forces provide the momentum for an organization's business activities. The driving forces are different in regulated and deregulated environments. All successful organizations address all of the following disciplines to one degree or another. However, every successful organization is driven by only one.

Products Offered as the Driving Force

A product-driven organization has a concept that its existing products are key to the future markets it serves. The organization will continue to produce and deliver products similar to those it has previously delivered, no matter what external influences evolve. Rather than refine or enhance its products for its existing markets, the organization will seek new geographic markets and market segments where there may be a need for its products. Agricultural producers are typical of a product-driven business group. They produce the same or similar products and rarely change feature or design. When their existing markets become saturated, farmers seek new (export) market areas.

Obviously the deregulated banking industry cannot compete with a product-oriented driving force. It is not a wise alternative to pursue. Competition from the nonbank financial institutions has already created an overabundance of products in the marketplace.

Market Needs as the Driving Force

The market-driven organization provides a range of products and services to fill current and emerging needs in the market segments or customer groups it serves. It constantly looks for alternate ways to fill the needs of a very specific market and constantly searches for new or emerging needs in the market segments it serves.

For the organization driven by market needs, significant resources must be directed to needs analysis, market research, and similar functions. This is a viable alternative strategy that the banking industry can look to as its driving force. Using market needs is a way that banks can capitalize upon their existing products and delivery systems rather than investing in the creation of more products to offer the consumer. Apple Computer is an excellent example of a market-driven company. McDonalds is another. Both companies create products to serve the specifically identified needs of targeted market segments.

Production Capability as the Driving Force

An organization that is driven by production capability offers only those products or services that can be made or developed using its production know-how, processes, systems, and equipment. The focus is on increasing the production capacity of existing products without significant consideration to market needs. The American automobile industry was an example of a production capacity-driven industry during 1946 to 1980. There was very little (global) competition for their product. Therefore, the industry was content on producing more products, with little attention to innovation, cost control, or meeting customer needs. Intense competition will force a *production*-driven company out of business or will force them to become *market*-driven.

Size or Growth as the Driving Force

The size or growth of an organization is defined as its overall asset size or rate of growth as measured by the most appropriate indexes. An organization whose driving force is size or growth determines the scope of the products or services it offers, the markets it serves, and its geographic scope relative to its desire to become larger or smaller.

In the past, most regulated banking institutions were driven by growth considerations because that emphasis allowed them to maximize all other goals and priorities. Banking organizations with a priority to increase capital would also be considered size- or growth-driven because they may have to "shrink" the bank to meet capital requirements.

Profit as the Driving Force

Profit is the primary financial result of an organization's effort. An organization that is profit-driven defines the scope of its products and markets based on its desire to maximize profit. Profit-driven companies usually emphasize short-term gains and the distribution of earnings. They typically do not invest in the future. The U.S. steel industry from 1946 to 1980 is an example of a profit-driven industry. They had the technology and resources to reinvest in a more viable future. Instead, they chose the short-term route to reward current players, management, labor, and shareholders for a market presence created by World War II.

Price or Rate as the Driving Force

An organization that is driven by pricing decisions determines the products or services it provides, the markets it enters, and its geographic scope primarily on the basis of the ultimate cost to the customer and its competitive price position. Discount super stores are good examples of price- or rate-driven companies that can be successful in regulated or deregulated environments. In order to survive, a price- or rate-driven company must reduce personal or professional service, convenience, and decor, and the company must focus on volume.

Method of Distribution as the Driving Force

An organization that is driven by method of distribution bases its decisions about its services, its customers, and its geographic scope according to the capabilities of its established distribution channels. Method of distribution is a self-limiting alternative. The U.S. Postal Service was limited in its method of distribution and is typical of an organization that is not particularly creative or efficient. A lack of imagination in satisfying customer needs, even in a monopolistic organization, will stimulate competitive enterprise (for example Federal Express).

Quality Service as the Driving Force

An organization that is driven by quality service demands that all decisions be based on its ability to maintain a certain level of service to each customer, no matter what the implications of those decisions are. The product, pricing, service, and geographic scope decisions depend totally on the organization's ability to maintain or improve its service and thereby to improve its position in the marketplace. IBM's driving force is quality service. They have not defined their future by being innovative to serve customer needs. Rather, IBM's strategy has been to follow consistently its competitors' innovative leadership. IBM's strength and uniqueness is being an exceptional service company. When things do not go as well as their customers expect, the challenge becomes IBM's problem, and it is never returned to the client until it is resolved.

Not all banks in a deregulated environment have the same driving force. Furthermore, an institution's driving force changes as different priorities or challenges are identified. However, one, and only one, driving force can be in place during a strategic and tactical implementation period. Once the management team reaches agreement on the organization's driving force, it can use that driving force to build the strategic framework as a basis for all future planning and decision-making.

Choosing a driving force is not a matter of making a moral judgment. It is a tough, practical choice that weighs such factors as an organization's strengths and vulnerabilities, its competitive position, its basic beliefs, and the external/environmental events that are likely to affect the organization.

It is also important to remember that once the driving force is identified, it is not etched in stone. Given the impact of both internal and external change, a new driving force may be considered at any time. Overall strategy will be quite different, depending on the driving force set, the kinds of products offered, and the markets served.

As a strategy-setting tool, the selection of a driving force presents an opportunity for flushing out different points of view and for consolidating those divergent viewpoints into specific statements of strategy. The concept of the driving force allows managers to develop and evaluate alternative future strategies for the organization. It also provides a mechanism for surfacing differences in directional thinking among managers and then for reconciling those differences without compromising the clarity and usefulness of the final statement of strategy.

Some executive teams may find that grappling with vision, the master strategy, and driving force requires a willingness to acknowledge that they were previously inconsistent and sometimes unclear in their understanding of the very nature of their organization. This is not true, and, therefore, it is not a relevant concern. Vision, master strategy, and driving force were not necessary considerations in a regulated, volume-driven environment. However, today, when leadership consensus is sharply defined, the strategy statement that emerges will be clear and specific and will allow the organization to prioritize and refine all subsequent strategies to maximize its potential in a very competitive marketplace.

CHAPTER 4

THE STRATEGIC PLANNING PROCESS

> If you know the enemy and know yourself, you need not fear the results of a hundred battles. If you know yourself but not the enemy, for every victory gained, you will also suffer a defeat. If you don't know the enemy nor yourself, you will succumb in every battle.
>
> —*Sun Tzu* (500 B.C.)

The importance of strategic planning was underscored in an interview with John Bookout, Chief Executive Officer of Shell Oil Company, the nation's fifth largest petroleum company.

When asked how he saved Shell from the blunders many other oil companies experienced, he did not cite the company's number one position in gasoline marketing, nor its decision to replace crude oil reserves while its competitors were liquidating, nor its enviable technology, nor the rebound in its chemical operations. Instead, he said, "as difficult as it is to bring life to it, it has been the implementation of our strategic planning process. Our vision and strategic plan is firmly in place. We don't just put it on the shelf. It stays in our minds, on our tables every day of the week, in every business meeting."[1] John Bookout is committed to strategic planning as a process, not an event.

In order to ensure that strategic planning becomes an integral part of the corporate mindset, we must first discuss the broad implications of the process. Then, we will be prepared to deal more effec-

[1]Caleb Solomon, "Shell Oil's John Bookout to Step Down," *Wall Street Journal,* March 1989.

tively with the tactical considerations and alternatives. This discourse will reinforce the difference between winners and survivors.

Winners function strategically to sustain successful results over an extended period of time. Winners require a very specific, balanced strategy because, without balance, there will be no continuity, and without continuity there will be no longevity of the strategic purpose or of the strategic process.

OVERVIEW

Strategic planning is different from all other types of business planning. The difference is that business strategy deals with competitive advantage. The only reason to engage in strategic planning is to gain, as efficiently as possible, a sustainable edge over competitors. Without competition, there would be no need for strategy.

There is formidable competition in today's rapidly changing financial services industry. The realities are that

- The number of competitors is increasing.
- Many of the new competitors are more aggressive, highly focused, more market-driven, and more sophisticated than the competition banks have historically faced.
- In *any* market, there is a very limited supply of quality businesses.
- Few markets are experiencing impressive growth, and those that are cannot expect to do so indefinitely.
- Consumers and businesses are becoming far more sophisticated, discriminating, and demanding relative to their choice of financial service providers.

The inescapable conclusion is that there is not enough good business to go around! Banks must develop a coherent and proprietary market-positioning strategy, or they will find it extremely difficult, if not impossible, to compete.

The quality clients that banks want to attract are not wandering the streets looking for a home. Quality clients already have a home. It is management's responsibility to find ways to lure quality business away from competitors and to do so in ways that will contribute to the bank's objective of maximizing long-term shareholder value.

I have worked with over 250 banking organizations. Some have become significantly more successful in becoming more competitive with banks and nonbanks.

Success among banking institutions is always the result of strategic thinking and commitment to implementation. Success has never been attributable to regulatory protection and proprietary products because all banks have equal regulator protection and literally identical product line availability. Yet, many banks have become significantly more successful by becoming more competitive among their peers.

The reasons for the wide disparity in performance among different financial institutions is that those institutions that have sustained a competitive advantage owe their success to the quality of their strategic plans and more importantly to implementation by orchestrating the strategic planning process among all managers and employees. Everyone is focused on employing every available resource to only those activities that have the greatest priority.

Strategic planning and a commitment to successful implementation are the keys to success in the financial services marketplace. Furthermore, product or service differentiation is consistently present to a greater extent in companies that are committed to strategic planning and implementation.

As the competitive nature of the financial services industry continues to evolve, strategies will provide the means to reach business objectives. The implementation of the most important of these strategies becomes the critical link between an institution's business goals, as defined by management, and the reputation the organization earns in the marketplace. An acceptable level of profitability results only if appropriate strategies are focused toward the desired reputation. In other words, *positioning priorities must precede priorities for profitability.*

The purpose of strategic planning, then, is to focus on what the organization will become. The purpose is not to define the future external environment. Rather, strategic planning defines what kind of business the organization will be in no matter what external influences develop. The emphasis is on making things happen, not letting things happen.

The primary role of strategic planning is to define what business the organization should be in. These are concerns and decisions that cannot be quantified or programmed for a computer. Quantification has very little to do with strategic planning. Rather, the most important questions in strategic planning are answered in terms of direction, priorities, activity, responsibility, and implementation schedules.

DEFINITION: WHAT STRATEGIC PLANNING IS NOT

According to Peter Drucker,[2] it is important to understand what strategic planning is *not.*

- *Strategic planning is not quantifiable.* Strategic planning is not the application of quantitative techniques and models to business decisions. Although it may incorporate some of these tools, the basis for strategic planning is intuitive. It deals with creative thinking about how to allocate limited resources most effectively toward an overall focus and with the commitment to priorities and specific action.
- *Strategic planning does not forecast.* The future is unpredictable, and attempting to forecast the future discredits the strategic planning process. In fact, the reason strategic planning is so essential is because no one can forecast the future with certainty.
- *Strategic planning does not deal with future decisions.* Strategic planning deals with decisions made today that will affect a company's future position in an uncertain marketplace. It deals only with current decisions. The question that faces the strategic decision-maker is not what the organization should do tomorrow but rather "What do we have to do today to be ready for an uncertain tomorrow?"
- *Strategic planning does not eliminate or minimize risk.* Rather, strategic planning helps to transform uncertainty by allowing management to evaluate risk against various alterna-

---

[2]P. Drucker, *Management Tasks, Responsibilities, and Practices* (New York: Harper and Row, 1974), pp. 123–125.

tives. The ultimate product of successful strategic planning must be the organization's ability to assume greater risk. To expand this ability, it is important to understand the implications of those risks.

THE HISTORIC FAILURE OF STRATEGIC PLANNING

Strategic planning was once a time-consuming, awkward series of events. To formalize strategic planning, a major effort was made to instill it throughout the organization, then to construct budgets and link it all back to the plan. This created an enormous bureaucracy bent on creating paperwork to justify some people's decisions and other people's existence.

In the late seventies, professionals dedicated to a more practical strategic planning process set out to eliminate the inefficiencies. As a result, contemporary strategic planning is now a simplified procedure.

In a highly competitive deregulated environment, no one can afford to attend endless meetings to discuss the various implications that impact ultimate decision-making. Management teams are still setting business objectives and orchestrating critical action plans in order to achieve those objectives, but the formality and the structure that was characteristic in the 1960s and the early 1970s have now evolved into a very practical and effective process.

Even today, however, strategic planning fails to live up to expectations. When strategic planning falls short, it often stems from

- *Measuring the validity of the plan by its weight.* If the plan is all inclusive, no one will be able to remember what the commitment is. In addition, because the plan is so unnecessarily voluminous, no one can find anything, even if the plan is remembered. The most effective strategic plans are less than 20 pages in length, including the implementation schedule and action plans.
- *Lack of vision.* Planning is too often directed inward rather than focused outward toward the organization's competitive environment.

- *Lack of consensus among all stakeholders on the organization's master strategy and driving force.* Stakeholders include stockholders, directors, management, and staff.
- *Confusion between quantitative goals, objectives, and strategies.* Budgeting and quantitative objective-setting is too often confused with strategic planning. Inconsistency or a lack of an underlying corporate culture causes strategic planning to be statistics-driven instead of people- and action-oriented. Then, when quantitative numbers are established, methods for accomplishing those goals remain vague. In other words, specific action plans are not established to make things happen.
- *An inability to identify or maximize the organization's competitive advantage.*
- *An inability to creatively exploit competitive vulnerabilities.*
- *Lack of delegation.* There is no participatory management for creating action plans and goal-setting once management has established the overall corporate focus.
- *Lack of awareness of the implications of change and of middle management and staff's ability to respond to the force of change.*
- *Lack of awareness of change management methodology.*
- *Failure to create the appropriate implementation tools to monitor, anticipate, and adapt to ever-changing external influences.*
- *Lack of commitment for implementation and the absence of a "take charge" approach by the CEO.* There is inadequate accountability or responsibility for action plans to be implemented.
- *Individual implementation performance not being linked to compensation.*
- *The misallocation of time and resources.* Too many management teams dedicate 95 percent of their planning activity to preparation and budgeting, less than 3 percent of their time to creative thinking, and less than 2 percent of their time to follow-up on implementation. The lack of creative thinking in action planning and structured follow-up is the primary cause for unsuccessful implementation.
- *The misconception that strategic planning is an event.* It is not an event; it is a process.

THE BENEFITS OF STRATEGIC PLANNING

Those who advocate the strategic planning process recognize that all organizations, no matter how large or small, have limited resources. Successful strategic planning and implementation ensure that limited financial, physical, and personnel resources are concentrated on those priority activities that will maximize the organization's potential. Planning also improves internal communications, and it defines explicit responsibilities and fosters accountability. Finally, planning helps coordinate management and staff in working toward the organization's primary purpose and priorities.

In most organizations, people are doing many things right. However, too often, they are not concentrating on doing the right things. Strategic planning directs everyone to concentrate on doing the right things right—the most important things first—in order to achieve priorities.

As the competitive nature of a deregulated industry evolves, one of the critical factors governing profitability is corporate strategy. There is a direct and critical link between creating business strategies and the ability of management to communicate those strategies throughout the organization. To take advantage of the unlimited opportunities in a deregulated marketplace, every bank and thrift management team must not only define their corporate strategies, they must communicate those strategies clearly and consistently so that each participant understands the strategies and their implications. Also, management teams must work diligently to ensure that strategic planning becomes a process rather than an event. A financial institution that relies solely on an annual strategic planning session is almost certain to suffer from constant expansion and contraction because it lacks a long-term perspective. However, when strategic planning and market planning are integrated into a corporate strategy, there is long-term vision and year-by-year progress toward goals. By engaging in market planning as an on-going process, a financial organization is much less likely to over-react to external fluctuations. Rather than expanding at the first sight of a profit or growth opportunity and retrenching at the first economic downturn, the institution, like any other successful company, can confidently pursue a long-term strategy of managed growth and profitability.

Today, successful planning is a concise, intuitive process that consists of reinforcing a corporate mission with objectives that are based on an assessment of the competitive environment. An operational plan of action is created that has explicit implementation schedules and responsibility assignments. This provides the follow-up and review tools critical to successful implementation. The key to successful planning is the process, which includes structured follow-up on a never-ending series of implementation activities.

RESISTANCE TO THE PLANNING PROCESS

By nature, the strategic planning process is comprehensive. However, it need not be complicated or complex. Nonetheless, while most financial institutions have initiated elements of the planning process, few have made a total commitment to develop a strategic plan, which would allow them to experience the simplicity and, therefore, the real benefits of a more comprehensive process. Resistance to comprehensive planning is often the result of misunderstandings, which can be summarized by six typical excuses:

1. *Skill.* "I do not know or my management team does not know enough about strategic planning to be effective."
2. *Unknown Future.* "No one can forecast the future. Things are changing too fast for us to waste time planning for the unknown."
3. *Security.* "I don't want my staff or my board to really understand what I am trying to do at the bank. I am trying to position to sell my bank in the next three years, and I cannot afford to allow that to be known."
4. *Don't Fix It.* "We've been successful before without planning. There is no need to fix what isn't broken."
5. *Time.* "There isn't enough time for me and my officers to serve our customers and set time aside for planning meetings."
6. *Expense.* "Strategic planning is too costly in wasted effort. The plans always end up on the shelf anyway."

Let's look at each of these six excuses:

1. *Skill.* Strategic planning skills are mastered the minute a participant recognizes that planning is an on-going process. Suc-

cessful planning, like a business, should begin small and continually evolve into bigger and better things. To ensure that strategic planning becomes a process, a systematic approach must be developed that enables management to separate the process into manageable phases with objectives that can be achieved within a reasonable time frame.

Learning how to incorporate the more comprehensive and complex planning skills is part of the process. The techniques used initially are much less sophisticated. As time passes, each participant improves in his or her skill, knowledge, awareness, and, finally, support for the strategic planning process.

2. *Unknown Future.* Strategic planning has nothing to do with defining the future. Decisions exist only in the present. The critical decision-making process deals with defining what needs to be done today to be ready for an uncertain tomorrow. As the senior management team becomes more skilled in planning, the participants begin to realize how futile it is to try to project the future.

   An uncertain future is no excuse not to plan; rather, it argues for the need to plan. Initially, one of the great benefits of comprehensive strategic planning is the communication created throughout the management team. For the first time, members begin to understand how each other thinks, and they start to perceive priorities and the need for better coordination among their individual responsibilities.

   Comparisons of activity against projected priorities also enable the management team to modify future plans and add perspective to the planning process. And management's accountability for making plans happen—that is, implementation—becomes the most important next step in improving the planning process.

   Finally, an uncertain future is the justification for a phase of planning called contingency planning. Contingency planning is nothing more than an organized, pre-arranged method of changing the direction of a business in the event it exceeds or does not achieve desired goals. The strategic planning process provides a tool for interpreting uncertainty and directing corrective action.

3. *Security.* A reluctance to inform officers and staff about an intent to sell a business very often is an expression of a deep-seated apprehension about individual management skills. In weighing whether to inform the staff of management's intent, vision, strategy, and driving force, it is important to understand that
   - A staff will both interpret and misinterpret management's failure to communicate. Also, the failure to communicate seriously strains management's credibility and will result in reduced productivity.
   - Management must depend on the staff to maximize the organization's potential. Anything less than keeping people fully informed results in the organization not realizing the opportunities presented.
   - The plan should be communicated so that the organization functions as a cohesive unit working together toward the same goals. Equally important, communication ensures that the organization does not work counterproductively.
   - Both officers and staff have much at stake—for example, income, pension plan, and favorable working conditions. It is not only fair, it is ethical to keep the various options above board.

   The latter point is very important. If, in fact, the decision is to position the bank to sell, or position it to sell as a contingency, then the options acceptable to management should be communicated. Otherwise, the rationale comes full cycle, in which case, see the first bullet point above.
4. *Don't Fix It.* Although some financial organizations have been successful in the past without formulating a comprehensive strategic plan, few will survive in the future without one. Without a strategic plan, the number of failures will far surpass the number that succeed. Second, in a competitive environment in which change is the one constant prerequisite for opportunity, management must continually reflect on its status relative to each critical action plan.

   Strategic planning provides the vehicle for identifying and utilizing the essential managerial skills required for a successful operation. It identifies strengths, weaknesses, opportunities, and vulnerabilities. Responding to those critical considerations as part of the planning process results in a stronger management team that is more capable of surviving and prospering in today's environment.

Another more obvious reason to begin strategic planning—even if prior success has been experienced without it—is that all financial institutions are facing ever-changing environments. What worked in the past to promote growth or any other achievable goal has nothing to do with what will work in the future. The automobile, steel, and airline industries are all proven examples. It is not prudent to rely on past success to predict future success. Conditions change and, therefore, management must change if it is to compete successfully in a more competitive marketplace.

5. *Time.* Strategic planning does take time. However, contemporary strategic planning techniques have reduced the time requirement significantly. All personnel who participate in implementation should also participate in development. The challenge becomes managing the time spent on participation.

   Not all team members need to participate in the planning process at all times. To limit actual time spent in planning, the key is to hold a planning retreat for only decision-makers—the most informed people—to deal with the most critical issues. The planning retreat should not be used as a "briefing" session for middle management.

   There is no best or worst time for an annual planning retreat. Since planning is a process, it can be incorporated and introduced into a management scheme at any time. Some companies find that a strategic planning retreat is best scheduled a month before the budgeting process. Others find that the months following the fiscal and budgeting process are much more critical and timely. Others find mid-year most effective.

6. *Expense.* A contemporary management team can ill-afford not to plan effectively. The very essence of management is to maximize potential, which requires planning. A successful planning process eliminates low priority activity and directs all resources toward the activities having the greatest priority.

STRATEGIC PLANNING TEAMS

The strategic planning process incorporates the perspectives of as many people within the organization as possible. Anyone who has something to contribute should participate in the process. However, each participant will likely contribute in a different way and at different times during the process. The prerequisite is to ensure that the process involves small, manageable teams, with the most effective teams having 6 to 10 people. In some situations, there should be fewer than six members.

The teams should be grouped by responsibility to include:

1. The CEO Focus Team (One to three officers)
Responsibilities are to control and

- Create a written vision statement.
- Draft a written mission statement.
- Confirm the organization's master strategy and driving force.
- Set the parameters and climate for the strategic planning process.
- Develop a preliminary set of objectives.
- Identify planning participants and assignment of responsibilities.
- Confirm the planning process time frame.
- Monitor the planning process to ensure that plans are completed as scheduled.

2. The Strategic Planning Committee (6 to 10 people)
This group includes those involved in the CEO Focus Team function and other senior management members. Typically, the challenge lies in limiting the planning committee to 6 to 10 participants. The issues are contribution, decision-making, and influence. This planning committee should not be used to inform participants nor for middle management to witness the process. Rather, the committee should include a limited number of participants who have senior management decision-making responsibilities. In a typical financial institution, this committee might include the:

- Chairman.
- Chief executive officer.
- Chief financial officer.

- Senior operations officer.
- Marketing director.
- Senior commercial services officer.
- Senior consumer services officer.
- Senior trust officer.
- Subsidiary CEOs/managers.
- Holding company representatives.
- Human resources manager.
- Outside strategic planning facilitator.

The primary responsibilities of the Strategic Planning Committee are to create and review the bankwide strategic plan and implementation status. Reviews should be at least quarterly. At least once a year, the committee should meet off premises for a minimum of two days to

- Review and update: (1) vision, mission, master strategy, and driving force; (2) performance and achievement of previous objectives; (3) market opportunities; (4) market potential and behavior; (5) competitive presence and behavior; (6) external influencing factors; (7) internal strengths and weaknesses; (8) competitive advantage.
- Formulate departmental business unit objectives.
- Create: (1) action plans to make things happen; (2) a strategic implementation time table.

The committee's ongoing activities are to

- Review, revise, and ratify the proposed strategic plan with management and board.
- Implement the formal strategic planning implementation schedule.
- Assign explicit responsibilities for each action plan and action step.
- Review, revise, and ratify final budget and resource allocation with the board.
- Establish formal departmental business unit subcommittees for implementation.
- Formalize subcommittee orientation session to discuss objectives and responsibilities.
- Schedule status and progress meeting with all key committees and personnel.

- Review monthly the strategic planning status and progress meeting with the management team and board.

3. Departmental Planning Teams
Responsibilities are to implement and

- Duplicate the strategic planning committee's role within individual departments to support the overall bank-wide plan.
- Periodically communicate status of the implementation of departmental responsibilities.
- Provide functional guide to departmental staff.
- Ensure that the implementation of a plan at each departmental level reports planning progress and status.

4. Board of Directors
Responsibilities are to monitor and

- Confirm corporate philosophy and policies with CEO focus groups.
- Review, revise, and ratify the proposed business definition, vision, and mission.
- Review, revise, and ratify the strategy objectives and goals.
- Review, revise, and ratify the completed strategic plan.
- Audit the process and implementation status.
- Introduce necessary corrections as required.

FUTURE SUCCESS: PREPARATION

A properly orchestrated strategic planning retreat should take a limited amount of the participants' time. An outside facilitator and junior officers can organize the information required for review prior to and during the annual planning sessions.

Survey

A strategic planning survey that addresses the most critical issues can help expedite the planning process. A survey stimulates strategic thinking and expedites the planning process by identifying controversial issues that are difficult to bring out in a group meeting.

The survey not only stimulates, it helps organize participants' thinking toward strategic issues and priorities before the planning retreat so that they can be more intelligently discussed during the planning sessions.

The survey responses must be kept confidential. They should be sent to one individual—an outside facilitator, if available—to abstract for use by the group for reference during the planning sessions.

The survey should not deal with vision, mission, master strategy, or the driving force. These issues are the responsibility of the CEO Focus Team.

The survey must be customized. For example, an organization that has been actively involved in the strategic planning process for a number of years will have a much more sophisticated and long-range series of questions on its critical issue survey. An organization that is just beginning the strategic planning process will likely concentrate on more short-term issues and on systems to create a more effective management and planning capability.

The Strategic Planning Retreat

Strategic planning sessions should be three hours long, with no more than two sessions scheduled each day. It is also important to schedule a minimum two-hour break between each session.

By limiting the planning time, participants remain alert and enthusiastic, which is conducive to creativity and responsiveness. More can be accomplished in a properly orchestrated split 6-hour session than in a 10- or 12-hour session.

The Planning Room

The planning room should be located where there will be no distractions. Participants should not have access to telephones or messages. Otherwise, planning sessions are less effective, continuity is lost, and timing and creativity are jeopardized. The location should be such that there are no peripheral noises, and the room should not be divided by fabric partitions.

Several years ago, a client scheduled a planning retreat in their board room. Even though the group was interrupted only one time by a well-intentioned secretary, the CEO became frustrated with the negative impact of that interruption. He instructed his secretary to schedule the second day of the session in a private club less than a block from the organization's headquarters. However, no one checked to be sure that the room was properly located.

My greatest fear was realized the minute I walked into the meeting room the next morning. A fabric partition separated our meeting room from an adjacent meeting room. The first two hours of the meeting proceeded as well as might be expected. At about 11:00 A.M., we became aware that the adjacent meeting room was being prepared for another group. Participants started to gather, and at precisely 11:30 our planning session was interrupted by an eight-piece brass band kicking off a rally for a United Fund Drive. I don't remember if we made a contribution to the Fund Drive, but there were lessons to be learned: (1) no fabric partitions, and (2) no brass bands in the strategic planning area.

Room Layout/Equipment Needs

The planning room should be spacious, with tables in a V- or U-shaped configuration. Participants should be seated so that they can look at each other when they speak and preferably do not have to turn away from the facilitator. Chairs should be comfortable so that participants are not preoccupied with certain parts of their anatomy and can instead concentrate on the issues at hand.

Equipment needs include an overhead projector, a clear wall and/or a large screen, two solid-back flip charts (no easels), large paper pads, marking pens, and a roll of masking tape.

Coffee and soft drinks should be available in the planning room; solid food is not recommended.

The Process

The chairperson or facilitator of the strategic planning retreat should set several ground rules. Initially, the vision statement, mission, and driving force must be presented, discussed, or, if in place, reviewed. Parameters should then be set for discussion and participation. The primary purpose of the strategic planning session should be reinforced with a statement that the organization is looking at the big picture. A basic ground rule: accuracy is defined by focus. Accuracy must come first, and momentum should follow accuracy.

Focus is the ability to achieve success at a targeted predetermined set of priority objectives that directly impact effectiveness in reviewing, refining, adjusting, and adapting to strategic accuracy. Once accuracy—in other words, agreed-upon focus—is determined, momentum can be instilled.

Momentum is the ability to control the level of success within a targeted time frame. Momentum deals with consistency in the process. Consistent intensity drives a group's ability to be successful. The process must be as concise, simple, and uncomplicated as possible. The objective of the planning procedure is to implement successfully, not to develop a plan. The objective is to create a blueprint as a resource to ensure success. Success is the product of implementation.

Strategic planning involves the recognition that we must do things differently in the future as we evolve in an ever-changing and competitive environment. To be committed to success, an investment in time and dedicated effort must be made to ensure that accuracy is first achieved and then reinforced through successful implementation. Consistency is essential; short-cuts result in mediocrity.

Strategic planning is a product of strategic thinking. It is a concentrated vision of the future. It defines where we are going and how we are going to get there. It should be creative, insightful, clever, and bold, and it should expand dramatically beyond what is currently being done. It should include previously unexamined options, possibilities, and alternatives. Vision is a prerequisite for a successful strategic program.

It is also important to inform all participants who have been invited to the group session that they are expected to participate. Those who do not participate are indicating by their inaction that it was a mistake for them to be placed on the participants' list.

It must also be reinforced that there is no such thing as a dumb idea. Embryonic ideas taken through the creative thinking process often develop into the most successful activities.

Finally, it must be communicated that there is no rank and that everything disagreed on should stay in the room. Only the consensus is carried forward. Suggesting that there are no titles in the participatory management process is not naive. Rather, it is a foundation from which successful creative thinking can begin. Each and every relevant idea must be thoroughly evaluated and discussed. The "no rank" guideline does, however, demand that the number of participants in the planning retreat be limited.

There are several important techniques for creative thinking and contemporary strategic planning. The most important is to think in bullet phrases and not get hung up on grammatical construction. Placing the emphasis on ideas rather than structure will stimulate and expedite creative thinking.

The Agenda

The planning retreat agenda should include discussions of

- *Market Opportunities and Limitations.* Discussion should include an analysis of market opportunities and market limitations. It is important not to confuse the concept of "market opportunities and limitations" with the organization's strengths and weaknesses or product development priorities. Market opportunities and market limitations deal primarily with the geographic locations, delivery units, and the market segments that can best be served.
- *Strengths and Weaknesses.* A review of the organization's strengths and weaknesses should be next on the agenda. It is helpful to categorize strengths and weaknesses in order to stimulate a response and to organize the participants' thought processes. The following categories of strengths and weaknesses often are used:
    a. Planning: strategic, business, financial.
    b. Management information systems and data processing.
    c. Communications: internal and external.
    d. Personnel and training.
    e. Business development: sales, cross sales, and referrals.
    f. Advertising, public relations, and promotion.
    g. Sales tools.
    h. Operations.
    i. Facilities.
    j. Equipment.

k. Products and pricing.
l. Customer base and/or share of market.
m. Financial performance.

- *Competitor's Advantages and Vulnerabilities.* This should entail a fairly comprehensive analysis of the primary competitor's advantages and competitive vulnerabilities. One of two approaches are effective. The planning team can discuss general categories of competitors such as regional or money center banks, nonbanks, competitive local independents, thrifts, credit unions, and captive finance companies. Depending on the market complexity, the team also can evaluate each specific competitor by name and location. The critical consideration is that only the most important and unique competitive advantages and competitive vulnerabilities are discussed. This is a very important stage of the planning process because the very purpose of strategic planning is to identify competitive advantages.
- *Competitive Advantage.* The discussion must now be directed toward the organization's competitive advantage. If an advantage does not exist, it is important to dedicate time to define what the organization does best and whether that edge can be translated into a competitive advantage. If not, a significant competitive advantage must be defined and action plans put in place to create a competitive position in the marketplace.
- *Goals.* The line items of the organization's strategic goal should now be reviewed or established. To stimulate discussion, the facilitator might ask, "How will we measure success in three years?" or "What are the most critical goals that we must achieve in order for this organization to maximize its potential?" The discussion should be directed to which line items are most important, not to quantitative values, although quantitative values or ranges put the discussion in perspective.
- *Research Needs.* During any one of several critical discussion points, it may be concluded that the planning team does not have enough information to make a decision or to conclude discussion. The discussion should not be terminated at this

time. Rather, the facilitator should recognize that additional information must be gathered and distributed. An action plan should be written that describes the activity to be initiated, the alternative methods that must be utilized, the time frame for completion, and the distribution of the necessary data. Otherwise, the facilitator should go to a flip chart and note, under the heading "Unknowns to be Researched," the topic and information that is to be required before a response can be made for that particular consideration. Subsequently, a series of action plans is created under the subtitle of "Necessary Research."

Strategic Statement

The first day of discussion should close with a strategic statement to summarize the analysis and critical conclusions in order to create a foundation for the following planning session. The agenda for the second day begins with action planning, followed by the assignment of specific responsibilities for each action plan and each action step and a preliminary implementation schedule.

Action Planning

Action planning is, in fact, an effort whereby the organization develops priorities and responds with specific activities to resolve the organization's weaknesses and market limitations while building on organizational strengths as they apply to market opportunities. Action planning must

- Stress the positive relative to opportunities and strengths.
- Shore up only those weaknesses that have direct impact on the ability to maximize potential.

Action planning must focus the attack on primary competitors' vulnerabilities as defined by the discussion of the organization's competitive advantage.

Strategic action planning tells management, officers, and staff which ropes to climb and which ropes to skip.

The action planning procedure is most effective when the group can be broken up into work groups. The participants should have special expertise or interest in the area to be action planned.

Creative Thinking Exercises

In creating action plans, participants will, from time to time, benefit from a variety of creative thinking exercises to resolve problems and to identify alternatives in order to take advantage of various opportunities. An experienced outside facilitator will orchestrate and stimulate the creative thinking process.

An Outside Planning Facilitator

Eight advantages should be considered when deciding whether to secure the services of an outside facilitator for strategic planning sessions. An outside facilitator:

- *Keeps the discussion on track.* Invariably, when senior management teams or planning committees meet, familiarity breeds unnecessary and unrelated discussion. The strategic planning process is a creative thinking experience. Therefore, it is very important to keep the discussion on track by following an explicit agenda and discussing only those issues that are most critically relevant to strategic focus. An outside professional facilitator ensures focus.
- *Stimulates participation.* An experienced outside facilitator has the skills to stimulate all participants to contribute regardless of title, tenure, or ownership. A professional facilitator not only inspires participation but manages all participation to assure that the discussion is relevant, timely, and not redundant.
- *Balances discussion.* An experienced facilitator reads verbal communications as well as body language and facial expressions. Typically, a speaker does not read nonverbal communications from a group of listeners. A senior officer, for example, may look directly at the individual he is speaking to, whereas a more junior officer may, when making a point that may be controversial or unpopular, speak directly to the facil-

itator, rather than the group. As a participant speaks, the experienced facilitator will read the nonverbal language of other participants and be prepared to call on individuals who have quietly communicated disagreement, point of order, or need for clarification. Also, an experienced facilitator balances discussion to ensure that strong personalities do not dominate the discussion.

- *Maintains priorities.* Discussions prior to the strategic planning session, as well as communications during the planning process, reinforce the facilitator's awareness of ownership's or senior management's priorities. This becomes critically important to ensure that participatory management does not result in a rearrangement of priorities. An experienced facilitator can ensure that priorities are maintained without losing perspective, objectivity, and the need for additional input.
- *Expedites consensus.* The very purpose of the strategic planning process is to develop an understanding of priorities in reaching a consensus on all strategic issues. Therefore, expediting that process becomes critically important. The involvement of an experienced outside strategic planning facilitator not only reduces the length of each strategic planning session by 50 to 60 percent, it also significantly reduces the number of strategic planning sessions required to complete the strategic planning retreat. Second, and even more important, efficient and effective use of everyone's time results in a more enthusiastic and, therefore, a more creative and focused session. The ultimate product is far superior to one orchestrated by an "insider."
- *Secures commitment.* The very nature of a senior management team's or a planning committee's interaction often results in hidden agendas and obscured commitment. An experienced outside facilitator can secure commitment more efficiently, more effectively, and more objectively by drawing out discussion and securing each participant's commitment verbally in front of the other participants.
- *Creates implementation tools.* Having worked with hundreds of other clients, an outside facilitator has learned and tested the most effective tools available, including automated imple-

mentation schedules, follow-up matrices, and change management methodologies.

- *Concise documents.* One of the greatest pitfalls in successful implementation, follow-up, and reinforcement is the tendency to over-document the unnecessary. The written plan becomes so all inclusive that participants have difficulty reviewing the key issues, strategies, their responsibility, and implementation time frames. An organization's strategic plan should never be more than 20 pages in length, including the implementation schedule. Subsidiaries and divisions within each organization can develop supportive documents of similar or lesser size. The key is to know how to exclude the unnecessary and to concentrate on the most pertinent details so that a concise, but comprehensive, plan is documented and easily accessible. A concise document can be reviewed monthly or quarterly to ensure successful implementation of strategic action plans.

Evaluating an outside facilitator consists of several considerations. The most important consideration, however, is the facilitator's approach: contemporary or traditional. Contemporary strategic planning is driven intuitively. The intuitive nature of the process recognizes that there is significant value in drawing on the experience of the existing management team. It is a very creative, fast-moving experience and cannot be jeopardized by references to predetermined statistical conclusions. Recognizing the value of the intuitive, creative mindset requires a contemporary strategic planning approach. Traditional, statistical-driven strategic planning techniques are no longer valid.

Therefore, caution should also be exercised for employing a statistically driven planning approach. The contemporary strategic planning process drives the numbers. The balance sheet and income trends must not drive strategic analysis. Strategic planning is not quantitative analysis. Strategic planning must precede statistical analysis.

Also, the contemporary strategic planning process should not be driven by market research. For example, traditional planners often require comprehensive data collection and market research relative to trends, image, and customer satisfaction prior to the first strategic planning session. This is totally inappropriate because the data will create parameters that are inconsistent with management's strategic priorities. The way the market research instrument is constructed will actually define and limit strategic alternatives. Rather, the strategic planning process must define what is important to research. Planning must precede research.

Senior management must identify and prioritize the type of market research required. That is, the strategic planning process identifies unknowns which must be researched before some strategic decisions can be finalized.

We facilitated a strategic planning retreat for a multibillion dollar holding company with approximately 100 branches located in a densely populated metropolitan area as well as throughout surrounding suburban and rural communities. The management team perceived its organization as a retail banking organization, a perspective that was not refuted by the bank's customer information files, balance sheet, income statement, and other accounting reports.

A prestrategic planning market research instrument had been constructed to determine how the bank could become more successful serving the retail market. Luckily, it was never utilized.

Prior to the planning retreat, secondary demographic market research data and other internal information about the various branches were prepared for review prior to the two-day planning retreat. During the first session, reference was made to these data on various occasions. A consensus developed. Fifteen minutes before the completion of the first day's session, the question was asked relative to market segment focus. It was concluded that the organization could best serve the commercial banking market and should remove itself from further activities in the retail market. That decision resulted in closing more than 50 percent of the bank's branches.

Had market research been implemented prior to the strategic planning process, the research would have been directed toward improving the organization's position in the retail marketplace. The lack of intuitive input and focus would have resulted in the market research driving the planning process. The commercial market opportunities would not have been considered, and the organization would have continued to pursue an inappropriate bank-wide strategy. The management team would have continued to do things right, but it would have been doing the wrong things. Market research must not drive the planning process.

CONCLUSION

Contemporary strategic planning is relatively new in the financial industry. It takes several years for the planning process to become fully operational.

The only purpose for a strategic plan is to create a focus on how the organization will differentiate itself from its competition. If there is little or no competition, there is no need for strategic planning. If there is competition and the number of competitors is increasing, the organization cannot survive without strategic planning.

The strategic focus and issues must be communicated and clearly understood by all of those involved in implementing the plan. The entire staff must understand the organization's priorities. The staff must become enthusiastic about the vision and commit to the mission, the organization's position in the marketplace, the prioritized market segments, and its objectives. Everyone must have a thorough understanding and acceptance of his role in bankwide and individual goal achievement. The effort is communication; the result must be understanding and an enthusiastic endorsement by all who are involved.

PART 2

INTERNAL FOCUS

The initial focus must be on internal strategies. Banks and thrifts are still operating with organizational responsibilities, cultures, and skills that are relevant only in a regulated business environment. That infrastructure is no longer valid.

The following chapters deal with why internal strategies are of such great importance. We will resolve many of the inhibitors to creating a successful sales organization, clarify the ability of all existing officers and staff in their unlimited ability to contribute to professional selling, and detail the role of the sales leader.

Corporate culture implications include a methodology for analyzing your organization's preparedness in creating a successful sales and service quality culture. These chapters also deal with how to evaluate performance measurement systems and the all important, but nonexclusive, reward for performance and incentive compensation programs.

CHAPTER 5

THE NEED FOR INTERNAL STRATEGIES

> Where absolute superiority is not attainable, you must create a relative superiority knowing where you are and by making skillful use of what you have.
>
> —*Karl von Clausewitz*

Many bank management teams are making a real effort to become more competitive. Internal strategies are the real challenge, however. There is rarely a consensus among management team members about "where they are" and therefore "what must be done next" and "who is responsible for what." These significant differences of opinion are a result of different perceptions about the internal implications of sales culture, service quality, and marketing in general.

Second, deregulation has had a substantially greater impact on banking than it has had on other industries. Airlines still compete only with other airlines. However, deregulation has expanded from banking to create a new industry called financial services, including many new nonbank competitors.

The nonbank competitors have cultural histories far more market-driven than those of banks, and many of them enjoy the benefits of being backed by national marketers. Therefore, *bank management must recognize that its business is driven by marketing.* Any management team that continues to perceive marketing as merely a delegatable staff function is courting disaster. A new commitment to marketing must begin with internal strategies.

Why is it necessary to begin with internal strategies?

Following the final session of an American Bankers Association conference for CEOs, I met with others who had participated in the program. We discussed the just-completed program and the receptiveness of the audience. We went on to share our experiences in assisting management teams to become more competitive in today's marketplace.

From our discussion, several common observations arose. First, none of us were satisfied with the degree of change going on in the industry. Second, we agreed that the industry's greatest challenges were internal challenges. Third, we had all observed that the vast majority of CEOs were preoccupied with external challenges rather than first dealing with the many critical internal challenges that are prerequisite for success.

If our conclusions were accurate, then the consultants, who are advising financial institution management teams, and the CEOs, who are in charge of implementing priority strategies, are advocating two completely different, and possibly counterproductive, activities.[1]

The conclusions from the informal discussion were unanimous; however, these conclusions were based on a very small sample. Subsequently, the author surveyed a group of nationally prominent marketing consultants who specialize in serving the financial services industry. Concurrently, over 200 CEOs and their senior management teams were surveyed. The respondents represented banks throughout the United States. The purpose of the survey was to determine perceptions relative to the industry's priorities to become more competitive and the degree of change necessary to be successful.

The results confirmed the earlier conclusions. The consultants' priorities related a consistent and dominant message: the prerequisites that have not yet been resolved for competing successfully in a deregulated environment are internal challenges. Banks must first focus, organize, and, then, truly commit. The consultants all believe that *the major challenges are people, not products and systems and the people challenges that need to be resolved are management, not staff.*

Looking at the CEOs' priorities revealed quite a different opinion. They felt that the people challenges are staff, not management,

---

[1]Karl von Clausewitz, *On War.* Translated by Michael Howard and Peter Paret. Princeton, NJ: Princeton University Press, 1976, p. 186.

and that products and systems are the most critical issues. The CEOs' own senior banking officers, however, concurred with the consultants. They unanimously reported a concern about their banks' commitment to change vis-à-vis marketing, training, and creating a sales culture.

The missing link is commitment from CEOs. Of 200 CEOs, only one registered commitment as an unresolved prerequisite to competing in a deregulated environment.

As traditional financial institutions prepare to do battle in a more competitive environment, it is now apparent that there are significant differences of opinion on where to begin, what to do, and how to do it. The ultimate decision makers—the CEOs—are looking for answers to create external strategies, while those responsible for implementation are pleading for internal strategies. The critical challenge, therefore, is to seek an understanding of the significant differences of opinion within each individual management team, the comprehensive implications, the need for reorganization, and a commitment to manage change effectively.

The purpose of this chapter and the following chapter is to clarify the very apparent confusion about critical issues and priorities. To do this, we must construct a chronological series of strategies and options to resolve the ever-increasing challenges created by a deregulated marketplace. We must begin with internal strategies.

In the majority of institutions, the current generation of CEOs grew up in a regulated and protected business environment. This background was perfect for the times, but it did not prepare them to compete in today's deregulated and unprotected environment.

The new environment creates an urgency that cannot be ignored. If traditional banks had to compete only with other banks (and primarily local banks), the banking industry could wait for a new generation of management who would have the necessary orientation and skills. However, this luxury of time does not exist; the money center banks and nonbanks are too skilled and too hungry for market share. Furthermore, in most instances the new competitors have cultural histories far more market-driven than the smaller financial institutions, and many of them enjoy the benefits of being backed by national distribution systems and significant economies of scale. The competitive environment will be very unforgiving.

A traditional approach to strategic thinking—that is, to focus on external opportunities—will be counterproductive. Financial executives need and deserve a clearer understanding of the implications for requisite internal strategies, as well as a more refined focus on external strategies, priorities, and options. This begins with a better understanding of why internal strategies are so necessary and why they are prerequisite to external strategies.

This author interviewed nationally prominent marketing specialists who assist financial institutions to become more competitive. The respondents represented a variety of disciplines, including strategic planning, market planning, market research, sales management, sales training, sales performance measurement, mutual funds, telemarketing, communications, customer service, and productivity-profit improvement. They have worked with thousands of financial institutions and encompass a variety of skills and services. Despite this diversity, their responses consistently pointed to five specific priorities for banks to become more competitive:

- Strategic planning and implementation.
- Senior management understanding the commitment to create a market-driven environment.
- Senior management's positive response to change.
- Selection of a marketing director with expertise and clout.
- Bankwide compensation based on performance.

Each nationally prominent marketing specialist elaborated on his opinion relative to the single most critical challenge. A representative sample of their replies follows, with pertinent observations highlighted.

Committing to a Market-Driven Environment

Glen Johnson
President, Federated Investors, Inc., Pittsburgh, Pennsylvania

Senior management must design, implement, and *be committed to a specific course of action* when pursuing new marketing opportunities, but there is a twist. Instead of setting a goal at the top and selling it "down" to the customer level, it makes more sense today to know what the customer wants and sell that "up" to the senior level.

The new role of bank marketing is to *know customer needs* and communicate them upward to initiate new marketing goals. This approach needs a strong commitment from senior management to follow through on customer preferences. Management must also positively respond to changes brought about by the market-driven approach and reinforce that positive response through a strong commitment to training, as well as an ongoing communication of goals and plans to the customer support staff level.

A closing thought: senior management must adopt the attitude that *there are no marketing problems, only marketing opportunities.*

Mastering Change

Kent Stickler
Stickler Learning, Clearwater Beach, Florida

The real issue is whether bank leadership can market, sell, and manage in the new competitive age of banking. *The jury is still out!*

The challenge is senior management's *understanding and commitment* to the contemporary marketing discipline. This issue becomes more timely and relevant because CEOs have been traditionally groomed from the lending and operational divisions. There, too often, managers confront a product-driven environment, without a specific perspective on market needs and expectations.

As in other deregulated industries, bank CEOs must begin to focus on strategic issues to position the bank for improved growth and profitability. They must focus on positioning and delegate administrative support needs. This allows the CEO to define the accountability of his operating units in terms of customer service, delivery and sales. In other words, by delegating all responsibilities *other than* sales and service quality, the CEO can concentrate on building the company by managing every opportunity to create and retain customers.

Restructuring by Markets, Not Function

Laird Landon
Laird Landon Consulting, Humble, Texas

Banks have always specialized labor by function to reduce errors and costs. With deregulation, we must consider demand as well as supply. A market structure brings all relevant banking functions together in a profit center directed to a relatively homogeneous group of customers (for example, middle-market manufacturers, large retailers, cattle ranchers, and professionally employed consumers). *At present, a customer is shunted to process-driven specialists,* rather than served by customer-driven consultants. Renaming the lending department "commercial banking" and the branch administration "consumer banking" is a positive symbolic step, but has anything really changed?

Differentiating from Your Competitor

Cass Bettinger
Bettinger Isom and Associates, Salt Lake City, Utah

Most bankers do not understand that success comes only by taking business away from the competition, because there is not enough new business to go around. We must acquire the vast majority of new business from competitors. This requires that the banker understand customers' needs better than competitors do and create products that clearly meet those needs better. *Management personnel must positively differentiate their bank.* Bankers agree with this conceptually, but do they really know what it means or how to do it? Furthermore, it cannot be done without a significant investment. Bankers must learn that they have to spend money to make money.

Consensus

The overriding message is that the challenges are internal challenges. They are people, not products and systems; and the people challenges are management, not staff. The prerequisite for competing successfully in a deregulated environment is to focus, organize, and then truly commit.

We must build an internal foundation of understanding and purpose. The consensus is that we have yet to assign ourselves to the internal challenges that must be resolved in order to successfully deal with the new and expanding external forces.

INITIAL SURVEY: MANAGEMENT

Banking CEOs and their senior management teams, including marketing officers, were surveyed about the same issue. As might be expected, their responses were less consistent than the responses from the national marketing specialists. The bankers were from every region in the country. They represented banking institutions experiencing a wide range of external economic and market influences, as well as varying internal state-of-the-art, asset size, and organizational relationships.

Between the bankers and nationally prominent marketing specialists there was agreement on only one of the most critical challenges:

- Strategic planning and implementation.

There was significant disagreement on all other issues. The implications relative to the areas of agreement become more meaningful when compared with the priorities for which there was no agreement. The CEOs considered the other most critical challenges as:

- Commitment to quality service.
- Customer information systems with total relationship analysis.
- Customer needs analysis.

Conversely, as previously mentioned, the national marketing specialists identified the following as the other four most important challenges:

- Management understanding of the commitment to create a market-driven environment.
- Bankwide restructure to provide market-driven organizational responsibilities.

- Senior management's positive response to change.
- CEOs' selection of a marketing director with expertise and clout.

National marketing specialists were almost unanimous in their opinion that bankers must first build an internal foundation of understanding and purpose. Only then can the necessary tools (such as customer information systems and customer needs analysis) be utilized for banks to become more competitive. In addition, only then will quality service become a reality. The overwhelming consensus among the specialists is that there are significant *internal* challenges that must be resolved *before* bankers can become successful in dealing with the new and ever-expanding *external* competitive forces.

None of the CEOs identified "senior management's positive response to change" and "selection of a marketing director with expertise and clout" as significant issues. According to the national marketing specialists, both issues were considered a top priority and prerequisite to achieving operational goals and objectives.

Another difference of opinion dealt with the "commitment" issue. Senior bank officers and marketing directors were in agreement, identifying commitment as a top priority. Further, senior officers said that commitment is obviously needed from their CEOs. Bank CEOs, on the other hand, did not consider "commitment" a critical issue.

The importance of addressing the "commitment" issue was reinforced by the senior and marketing officers who expanded on their survey response. A representative sample of replies to "What is your single most important challenge?" follows:

> Commitment. Consistent and comprehensive direction from senior management is the most critical. We, as a group, must have a better understanding that almost all corporate decisions impact the external and internal marketing environment.
>
> Commitment by executive management to the creation of a "sales culture."
>
> Commitment from the CEO and senior management to involve all 440 people in our bank in *selling their bank.*
>
> Support from top management and acceptance of a pure marketing concept.

Senior management's understanding of the commitment to create a market-driven environment.

Senior management's misconceptions about what "marketing" is and can do, and resulting lack of resource commitment.

Because of merger activities and solving affiliate problems, management has not placed an emphasis on marketing/sales. Bank management at most levels has been occupied putting out fires, consolidating offices, etc. Marketing/sales needs to be pushed to the top of the priority list.

These comments should not be construed as an indictment of CEOs. Rather, they point to the many significant differences of priorities between CEOs and their senior management teams. *The most significant difference is perception of commitment.* Although CEOs obviously think they have made a commitment, their officers responsible for implementation definitely have not felt that they have that commitment. In other words, senior managers do not perceive that commitment exists to the degree necessary to make things happen and to change their current environment enough to become competitive.

Commitment is the issue. Furthermore, until it is resolved, *commitment is the only issue.*

The importance of commitment is illustrated by the experience of a midwestern bank with $600 million in assets. The chairman and the president directed the marketing coordinator to create a comprehensive sales organization throughout the bank. Most of the critical elements were introduced. A strategic plan was created and updated every year. A marketing plan and individual market segment plans were defined. Sales training was introduced. Very comprehensive sales organization and sales administration to include measuring sales, cross-sales and referrals were implemented. Goals were set for departments, teams, and individuals. A significant budget was allocated to creating a sales culture. But nothing happened.

The president was challenged to evaluate his commitment. He became angry and defensive. He itemized the effort he made to communicate his support: the demands he placed on the marketing director and the budget and time allocated to schedule training, purchase measurement systems, and make plans. In fact, he said, "I've talked sales and sales culture until I am blue in the face. I'm satisfied we've got it." However, the marketing director thought differently, and the other senior officers knew better because:

- The marketing director did not participate in the development of the strategic plan; the chairman felt that strategic planning and market planning were two separate activities.
- Goals were set but no one was ever held accountable.
- Some officers were not required to complete call reports.
- Measurement systems were put in place, but no one ever read the reports.
- New accounts personnel received extensive sales training but were never invited to attend a sales meeting, never received feedback on their performance, and goals were never set.
- Weekly sales meeting were often postponed and finally scheduled only once a month.
- The chairman and president attended only two sales meetings in two years.
- Rewards for sales performance were created only for calling officers. When the officers did not achieve their goals, the goals were lowered.
- No one was held responsible for departmental or market segment goal achievement.
- Sales performance was not included in annual reviews.

The list goes on and on! Nevertheless, the president honestly felt he had made a commitment. He had invested in the systems that were necessary, and he gave verbal support.

RECONFIRMATION

Since 1984, this author has surveyed senior managers to evaluate their perceptions of how successful their institutions have been in creating a successful sales organization. Specifically, the survey asked 60 questions of senior management, having them rate their institution's efforts to become competitive in a deregulated environment. In other words, they evaluated their institution's status with regard to being able to create a market-driven sales culture.

The survey, which will be expanded upon in the next chapter, deals with:

- Strategic planning.
- Market segment planning.
- Client and prospective client prioritization.
- Staffing.
- Management's commitment to a sales culture.
- Performance measurement systems.
- Reward programs for goal achievement.
- Customer information systems.
- Training priorities.
- Product development systems.
- Profit improvement programs.
- Asset and liability management systems.

Each participant was asked to rate their organization's position (assigning scores of between 1 and 10), with 10 representing a totally prepared position or state-of-the-art relative to that specific question. Table 5–1 presents examples of various questions and typical responses from a nine-member senior management team:

In general, the responses to the questions are typical of the responses that were received from most senior management teams. Opinions vary dramatically, and dramatically different opinions about critical issues and priorities will have a significantly negative influence on the group's ability to manage.

Rarely did a respondent assign consistently high or low ratings to all of the questions. Responses appeared to be honest observations or opinions relative to an organization's commitment and ability to become competitive.

CONCLUSION

It can be concluded that critical internal strategies must be in place before an organization can maximize its potential. Strategies must begin with prioritization and development of an understanding of:

1. The need for a consensus of the organization's status.
2. Where the organization should be in the development of those critical disciplines.
3. A clear definition of who is responsible for what tasks.
4. An understanding of what are the most important priorities

TABLE 5-1

	Answers	Avg.	High	Low
1. Has your organization conducted internal and/or external market research to identify the needs and wants of your				
a. Priority customers	7,4,5,1,5,2,4,3,2	3.7	7	1
b. Priority prospects	2,3,5,4,5,9,5,3,1	4.1	9	1
c. Customer satisfaction with existing services	10,7,5,1,8,5,2,3,8	5.4	10	1
2. Does your senior management have a specific plan in operation with quantitative goals for the following:				
a. Priority customers	6,4,7,3,9,2,6,8,2	5.2	9	2
b. Directors' participation in business development	1,2,2,1,3,1,0,2,2	1.6	3	0
c. Bankwide cross-sell program to integrate retail, commercial, and trust services	3,2,6,2,7,2,7,2,2	3.7	7	2
3. Does your organization have				
a. Measurement systems in place to track bankwide sales performance, bankwide cross-sell as well as referrals throughout the entire organization	7,6,3,2,7,6,7,7,0	5.0	7	2
b. Incentive programs for business development and goal achievement	2,4,7,4,8,7,2,1,3	4.2	8	1
4. Market segment services				
a. Has your organization identified the				
i. Market segments that provide the greatest potential relative to the mission statement, position of the marketplace, goals and objectives for the next three years	7,4,2,1,3,8,6,4,1	4.0	8	1
ii. Priority list of existing and prospective customers	2,3,5,4,5,9,5,3,1	4.1	9	1

and activities to be emphasized in order for the organization to maximize its potential.

These activities, which are prerequisites for success, are all internal challenges. They must be resolved *before* external challenges can be dealt with successfully. The entire management team must agree that to compete successfully in a deregulated environment they must first focus, organize, and then truly commit to a series of clearly understood priorities and responsibilities. Second, they must understand that the overriding challenges are people, not products, parity, or systems. Finally, they must all recognize that the people challenges that must be resolved first are challenges dealing with management.

CHAPTER 6

CREATING THE CULTURE TO COMPETE

> The preparation for total war must begin before the outbreak of overt hostilities.
>
> —*Erich Ludendorff*

In a speech before attendees of the 1988 American Bankers Association Convention, R.L. Crandall said, "We had to learn about serious cost cutting. We had to learn to court the customers, not the regulator. We had to learn to define our markets, to price by thinking. The free market is not tolerant of inefficiency or arbitrary pricing."[1] Mr. Crandall was speaking to bankers, but he was speaking from the perspective of the chairman and president of American Airlines. Nonetheless, these caveats apply to banking. Putting these caveats into practice begins with internal management strategies.

Internal management strategies must be created for any organization that is in transition. Banking's transition from a product/operations-driven industry to a market-driven industry will require internal management strategies that must begin with a rewrite and a commitment to change the corporate culture. The culture demands new management skills and new leadership skills in order to build teams and maximize the great potential of each team member. That is the essence of creating a more competitive corporate culture.

[1]Bill Poquette, "Pointers Offered for Managing in a Deregulated Environment," *Bank News,* November 15, 1988, p. 9.

WHAT IS A CORPORATE CULTURE?

Corporate culture is the learned pattern of thought and behavior of an organization. It is the way an organization has agreed to do things. In successful organizations, there is a corporate culture—an observable pattern of behavior—from the board room to the supply room. The ability to compete successfully in a deregulated environment will require all institutions to create a service quality/sales culture.

To create a successful sales culture, it is necessary to build a belief in service quality that will serve as the lifeblood of the organization. This belief will result in a set of values, standards, and customs subscribed to by all personnel. Service quality must have a meaning for each and every individual in the organization.

When a service quality/sales culture permeates an organization, everyone works hard to reinforce the culture. All employees think in terms of customer service as their top priority. Selling is not the focal point. Selling is not an isolated activity. *Need* is the focal point in a professional sales culture. Customer service begins with identifying and resolving customer needs. Professional selling becomes a process from which customers' needs can be best served. Professional selling, then, becomes synonymous with service and, indeed, becomes the very purpose of a service organization.[2]

When speaking of a sales culture, it is service quality that is sought. Service quality requires the use of professional selling techniques, and from the use of professional selling techniques comes increased sales. Values, standards, and expectations are the core of a sales culture through which quality service is delivered. Values are ingrained by setting goals and establishing a system for measuring and rewarding goal achievement.

Coining slogans and making statements about instilling a sales culture does not create a sales culture. It cannot just sound good; there must be belief. Management must constantly demonstrate its commitment to a sales culture, both by articulating its commitment and by example. By repeatedly demonstrating its commitment to

[2]Michael T. Higgins, "From the Field: Making a Sales Culture Happen," *ABA Banking Journal,* July 1988, p. 82.

quality service through professional selling, selling becomes a part of the corporate ritual. A successful sales culture then spreads throughout the organization as a value appreciated by the people who believe in expanding the richness of their commitment to service quality.

BUILDING A CONSENSUS FOR A SALES CULTURE

Before change can succeed, there must be a consensus among senior management. Next, there must be a process that will help the organization understand that consensus and recognize that the existing culture is the major barrier to change.

The process for successfully implementing and reinforcing a sales culture is shown in Figure 6–1. There are nine critical steps in the process, beginning with developing a vision and culminating with reward for performance. Each of these steps requires a comprehensive set of activities and responsibilities that must be clearly understood by all members of the senior management team. All steps are equally important, and each step is dependent on all others. If one of the nine critical steps is minimized or not implemented, the entire pyramid crumbles.

Building a consensus for a sales culture encompasses the first three steps of the nine-step process. Steps 1 and 2—vision and strategic planning—were discussed in length in previous chapters. Step 3—market segment planning—will be the topic of a subsequent chapter. However, it would be useful to again touch upon these subjects in looking at how an organization can build a consensus for a sales culture.

The most successful implementors of a sales culture reach a common understanding about what they want to accomplish. They also know who is responsible for handling or directing each priority activity. Equally important, everyone accepts that role and agrees to levels of performance and implementation within an agreed-upon time frame. A sense of urgency rules the actions of the team members.

The least successful management teams do not take the time to discuss how to get the job done, or they assume that only sales and product knowledge training are necessary for their employees to in-

FIGURE 6-1
Steps to Reinforcing a Successful Sales Culture

stantly become better salespeople. They do not yet understand that selling is not the culture.

To build a sales culture, senior managers must first reach a consensus about what a sales culture is, what selling is, and what being market-driven is. In short, they must decide what the organization wants to accomplish and, in the process, build a mutual understanding and consensus. To be effective, the process must be structured and deliberate. There must be:

- A formal agenda.
- Time must be set aside to cover the characteristics of the new cultural environment;

    The management skills required.
    Organizational responsibilities.

The decisions that must be made to successfully implement the culture.
The implications for the organization.

There is no shortcut to taking this step. This consensus-building process need not take long. However, a 6-to-8 hour session is critical. Afterwards, the participants will wonder how they could have gotten started without agreeing on where they were going to take the bank in the first place.

Following the session, the CEO must reinforce that consensus. In one of the most effective reinforcements I have ever witnessed, a CEO wrapped up a consensus session by saying, "I want you all to know that our sales culture/service quality train is leaving the station. Some of you are already on board. Some of you are trying desperately to climb on board. I know and respect that it will be more difficult for some than for others. For those who find it most troublesome, my hand is out to help get you on board. But you've got to make it. We aren't going back to the station."

The consensus that is reached among senior management must first reconcile the current status, then resolve future requirements, timing, and responsibilities to implement and reinforce the prerequisite steps in creating a successful sales culture. Once a consensus has been reached, the next step is to reinforce survival skills and to create a market-driven organizational chart of responsibilities.

NEW SURVIVAL SKILLS

In the new, deregulated environment of today, management must reexamine its leadership philosophy. A new breed of skillful competitors now threatens the very survival of any bank or thrift institution unwilling or unable to change to meet the demands of a deregulated environment. The opportunities for success are unlimited, however, for those managers willing to adapt.

To prosper in a deregulated, competitive environment, bankers need to manage from an entirely new point of view. This new perspective can best be appreciated by comparing the management skills and activities that worked in the past with the management priorities that are needed in today's financial market.[3] The differences are significant and are presented as Appendix B, a comparison of the management skills required in a regulated, product-driven environment with those skills demanded in a deregulated, market-driven environment.

ORGANIZATIONAL LEADERSHIP

Financial organizations have traditionally been organized along product lines, as shown in Figure 6–2. This product-driven approach, in which product managers are responsible for loans, deposit

FIGURE 6-2
Traditional Organizational Responsibilities of Product-Driven Companies

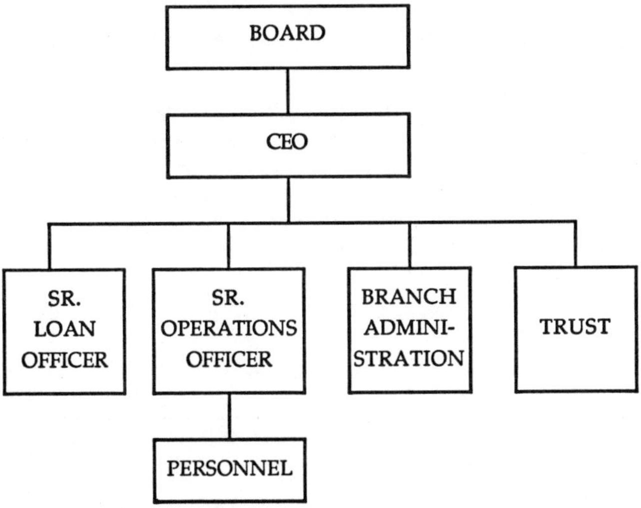

[3]Michael T. Higgins, "New Survival Skills," *Bank Marketing*, February 1986, pp. 30–33.

services, trust services, and so forth, is outmoded.[4] Instead, banks need to be organized according to the markets they serve and the customer's perspective, in other words, by market segment and subsegments.

Banks that retain their product-driven structures are living in a house of cards. They are not prepared to operate in a competitive environment because they cannot make market-driven decisions from a perspective of product-driven organizational responsibilities.

Market-driven organizations in transition (Figure 6–3) are structured to serve specific market segments. Senior managers should be responsible for commercial services or consumer services, with middle management focused on such subsegments as small businesses, executive/professionals, and retirees.

To survive in a competitive environment, banks must be responsive to the client—first by identifying priority client needs, then by focusing on providing those clients with the best possible combination of products at the best possible prices. Form follows function.

The author has worked with financial institutions serving large and small, metropolitan, suburban, and rural markets. Management teams that have made the transition from product-driven to market-driven organizational responsibilities cannot believe how easy it is to

FIGURE 6–3
Market-Driven Organizational Responsibilities in Transition

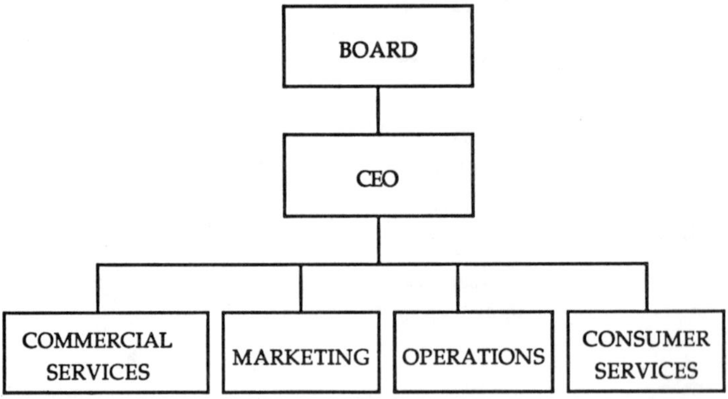

[4]Michael T. Higgins, *Competitech,* American Bankers Association, Washington, D.C., October 1984.

think "market" when their organization is defined along market-driven lines of responsibility.

An institution's response to a competitive environment often shows in the human resource management function. Traditionally, the personnel department either reported to or was the responsibility of the senior operations officer or cashier. Why? Because, in the old days, personnel management was pure "numbers" management: salaries, fringe benefits, and problem-solving-by-hiring-more.

In a competitive environment, personnel management becomes human resource management. The terms "personnel management" and "human resource management" should be taken very literally. Most operations managers and head cashiers are ill-prepared to deal with employee attitudes, customer service considerations, sales training skills, career development, and incentive compensation issues. Human resource management requires far more than the bookkeeping skills that the traditional personnel function once demanded. In today's market, operations managers and head cashiers will be more productive by concentrating on what they do best, that is, improving management information reporting.

Like change, structure is a tool to be used toward an end. A successful end requires an approach to the future that is unlike the practices of the past. Banks that are structured to provide services of superior quality at the least cost will be the ones that survive against competition. Banks that are organized according to the way things used to be done will be left behind.

In small to medium-sized banks, the human resources manager should report through marketing. In larger banks, the human resources manager usually reports to the CEO.

The single most important reason to dismantle the product management organizational model in a market-driven environment is that product management perpetuates product-driven priorities. Product managers tend to protect their turf regardless of market demand. This is typical of any industry in transition. It results in an organization continuing to do many things right, but rarely ever concentrating on doing the right things. Senior loan and trust officers manage loans and trust business rather than relationships. Antiquated product lines are protected to preserve title and position rather than to respond to client needs.

However, it will take more than a change from product-line

boxes of responsibility to evolve into an effective market-driven organization. It will take sales-leadership strategies to ensure that the untapped potential of human resource talent is maximized.

SALES LEADERSHIP STRATEGIES

In Chapter 1, Glen Johnson was quoted as saying that a CEO, to be effective in a competitive marketplace, first has to be a sales leader. If the CEO has neither the desire nor the aptitude to assume those responsibilities, then they should be delegated to a second in command. And, because a sales culture must focus on service quality, what is really necessary is service quality leadership. In sum: the sales management skills the CEO must possess are no different from the skills necessary to ensure "service quality leadership."

Service quality leadership begins with a commitment to implement the prerequisite skills, tools, and systems and to provide the necessary reinforcement to achieve the desired results. Sales management via successful sales/service quality leadership can be limited to

- Recognizing potential sales talent.
- Coordinating talent with expectations for success.
- Coordinating talent with targeted market segments.
- Creating an environment to maximize potential.

Recognizing potential sales talent and coordinating that talent with expectations for success begins with identifying how each individual can participate in the service quality/sales process.

WHO CAN PARTICIPATE AND HOW THEY CAN PARTICIPATE

Some organizations require all officers to make a specified number of sales calls per week. Such an arbitrary quota becomes a mandate for failure. In contrast, professional sales leadership recognizes that everyone can make a contribution to the bank's business development effort, but each participant will contribute differently. This is the essence of creating a successful sales culture.

The way to get people excited about professional selling is to reinforce the fact that they can all make a significant contribution. Too often in the past, people have been forced to participate at levels of selling at which they were not comfortable. However, if officers and staff are allowed to participate at a level at which they are most comfortable, they will be enthusiastic and they will succeed. In addition, each success experience will stimulate them to stretch to succeed at the next level of professional selling.

How individual skills are employed is critical. For example, relative to outside business calls, customers generally fall into one of three categories, whereas bank officers and staff can be classified according to one of four skill positions. Interestingly, banks typically have the proportionate number of people with the right kind of skills to call on a similarly proportionate number of client styles (Figure 6–4). It takes sales leadership awareness to identify skills and to match those skills with client needs. That awareness can be learned. Training reinforces that balance.

Management has the responsibility to recognize strengths and to assign the appropriate business development responsibilities to maximize those strengths. This is the most critical sales management–sales leadership function, because it will ensure that everyone can participate at a level of professional selling at which they have the ability

FIGURE 6–4
Business Call Participation

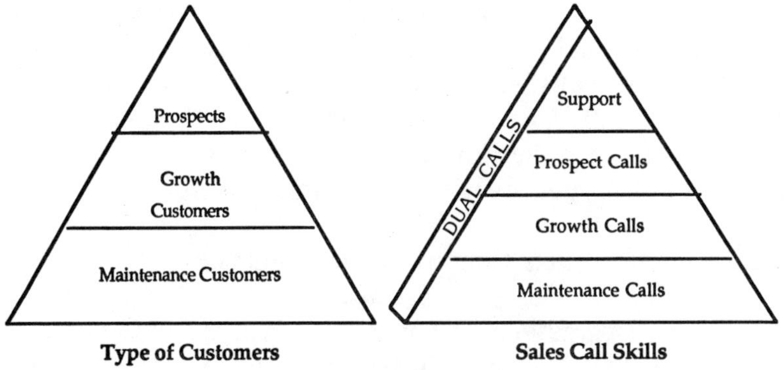

and therefore the confidence to be successful. With each success, the employee's confidence will motivate him or her to reach for a higher level of participation. Everyone can contribute, but everyone will not, cannot, and should not be required to contribute in the same way. This entire concept is expanded on in Chapter 11.

Bankers must overcome the negative perception that their staff does not know how to sell and, therefore, cannot sell successfully. The way to resolve this inaccurate perception is to assume—and rightfully so—that everyone in the organization—every customer contact person and backroom person—has tremendous potential to contribute to the sales effort but that each will contribute differently.

Employees should not be forced to sell under conditions they are incapable of handling successfully. Sales leadership activities should be directed in such a way as to assure everyone that they can be successful selling at a level that they have identified they can maintain. Initially, sales success builds slowly, but in time sales increase, confidence builds, enthusiasm is generated, and a momentum for professional selling is created that leads to even greater success (Figure 6–5). This momentum is required to create and reinforce a successful sales culture based on service quality through professional selling.

The industry has wasted a tremendous amount of time trying to get people involved in selling at skill levels beyond their abilities. As a result, very few bankers have experienced success, leading skeptics to conclude that very few traditional bankers can sell. The key is to get everyone to contribute at the level that ensures that they will be successful, even if it is less than what a bank is trying to accomplish at that particular point in time.

How can it be determined at what level employees can contribute? Psychological testing is not the answer. Past experience in making business calls is not the answer either, because, in general, most business calls have not been successful. Why? Employees do not want to do what they know they are going to be unsuccessful at. Thus, they fulfill their own prophesy. In other words:

Self Concept = Performance

because

To the Degree People Think They Will Be Successful,
They Will Be Successful

FIGURE 6–5
Sales Momentum

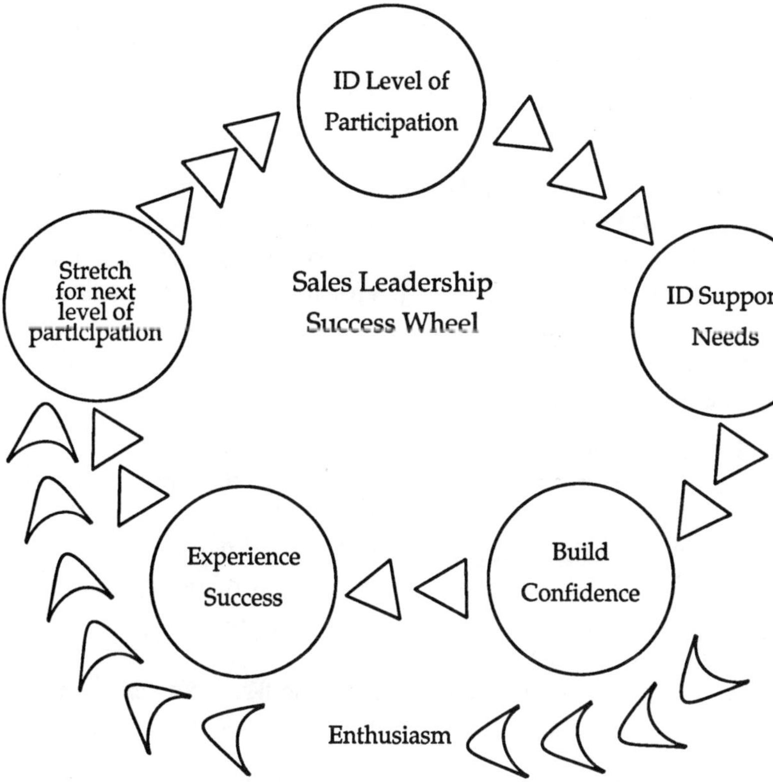

People really want to participate; they really want to contribute. However, they want to contribute at a level they can be successful at. Once they are successful and are committed to selling, they will do an exceptional job. As they continue to succeed, they will ask for additional responsibility, thus building momentum toward a total bankwide sales force. This is how a positive sales culture is created and molded. By allowing this critical internal strategy, banks will not only have greater success, they will have greater numbers of people from throughout the organization participate. This increased participation will dramatically increase results.

This strategy is critical because there are so many customers who need and deserve to be called on. We do have enough people, and we have the potential resources to call on all of our priority customers if we employ those resources appropriately.

SALES MANAGEMENT = SALES LEADERSHIP

The role of a sales manager is one of sales leadership. Sales leadership is required to nurture self-esteem in those who must do the job. The more self-esteem is nurtured, the more people feel great about being involved with what the organization is trying to accomplish and the better they are going to perform. Self-esteem begins with assuring people they can be successful.

To grow in self-esteem is to grow in positive experience. The higher the self-esteem, the more likely people will be able to

- Cope with adversity.
- Be innovative, rather than ritualistic, in their business activities.
- Avoid becoming tradition-bound in their work; this improves a bank's chances for success in a world of rapid change.
- React ambitiously to all creative opportunities.
- Build stronger personal relationships.
- Treat others with respect because self-respect reinforces respect for others.

High achievers and productive customer service people can be described as extremely motivated and dedicated to excellence in their performance of responsibilities. With proper sales leadership, they will work with very little supervision. Most managers agree that if they had more of these kinds of employees, their jobs would be a lot easier and the results would be a lot better.

In the military we had a saying: there are no bad soldiers under a good general. It all comes from the leadership.

SALES MOTIVATION: THE HIERARCHY OF NEEDS

How are people motivated to provide exceptional service quality, that is, to sell professionally? People do things for one of two reasons. They do a good job because they want to, or they do a good job because they have to. When employees want to do a good job, they are much more likely to perform.

This basic concept is an expansion of Maslow's hierarchy of need. The importance of reviewing Maslow's pyramid is reinforced by our industry's previous management strategies, which have proved unsuccessful in creating a successful sales culture. The very foundation of everyone's needs is the basic physiological need to survive. Once a person's fear of failure is resolved, all motivation to prohibit failure ends. When traditional bankers are asked to sell, their fear of failure will result in their doing everything they can possibly think of not to participate. It is a survival fear, and we must respect it and manage it into something great.

The next level of needs is the need for security. The fear of being fired and the fear of being dealt with in an arbitrary fashion are threats to security. The threat of firing employees will motivate them to act, but it will only motivate them to do just enough not to get fired. This is the basic reason why most officer call programs have been less than successful.

The third level is the need for belonging, that is, the need to be affiliated and accepted by other people. When a person is not accepted by other people, it triggers the fear of rejection. The fear of rejection, again, is a motivator. Employees can be scolded, shouted at, chastised, or approval withheld, but the only result will be that they will do exactly what they need to do in order to avoid the negative experience, and no more. The critical parallel to be drawn is that people who are not confident in making certain kinds of business calls will not participate if they have even the slightest fear of rejection. Rather, they will find excuses not to participate, or they will participate only by stopping by to say hello, the traditional ineffective "howdy-doody" call.

Even higher in the pyramid of needs is the desire for esteem or recognition. People have to feel great about themselves and be praised and recognized by others for their performance. As a matter of fact, one of the two biggest irritants and demoralizers in all of business is that management often does not recognize an employee for a job well done. There is nothing more demoralizing to a person than to do a job as well as he or she possibly can and have it completely ignored by management. In effect, management is saying that no matter how well you do the job it really does not matter.

If performance is not recognized, how motivated will a person be to go that extra mile and do a little bit more next time? Most managers do not realize that their people are dying for recognition. We all are! Most employees are dying to give their whole heart to their work; they want to make a contribution. Companies that recognize their employees, praise them, and give them continuous approval are always companies that are highly motivated to succeed.

Finally, the very highest need is the need to achieve and fulfill potential. If management can create a corporate environment in which employees have the opportunity to fulfill their potential, to become everything they are capable of becoming, and to achieve all the success they can achieve, they will make a commitment and will throw their whole heart and soul into their job.

The survival need, the security need, and the belonging need are all *deficiency* needs. Deficiency needs are such that once they are satisfied, motivation to perform is no longer present. The higher level needs—the need for self-esteem and the need to achieve—are *growth* needs. If management can get their employees plugged into their growth needs, it will find that they become excited about fulfilling themselves and achieving everything they are capable of achieving.

Growth needs act as a perpetual motivator. A week or a month or a year later, employees will still be motivated to do the very best they can. In contrast, if management motivates with deficiency needs—fear of failure, fear of rejection, withdrawal of approval, or dismissal threats—the motivation will work only as long as management keeps up the threats.

Negative reinforcement is a full-time job, and no one can afford the effort or the results. The minute a manager's back is turned, the people stop performing. Therefore, the key to sales leadership is to move as many people up the pyramid of needs as rapidly as possible by removing barriers to motivation while increasing reward. This is leadership ability; the skill to elicit extraordinary performance from ordinary people. Leadership is building a winning team.

BUILDING A WINNING TEAM

Building a winning team consists of five steps.

Step 1 is purpose. What is the purpose of the company? What is its mission? What are its basic values? People need purpose. The company has to stand for something greater than simply making money!

Experience in the field confirms that one of the most wonderful purposes that motivates and inspires people is to know what they are doing is helping other people. The most inspiring external purpose is serving other people by doing something important. That is what keeps people motivated; that is what keeps people working long hours in hospitals; and that is what keeps people working long hours during disasters. Everyone wants to help, which is why the idea that professional selling is helping people achieve their financial objectives is an internal strategy that should be constantly reinforced among all employees.

Step 2 is excellence. Striving toward excellence is one of the most influential, perpetual motivators. Excellence equals motivation because excellence is a journey, not a destination. Excellence in an organization is never achieved; it is always aspired to. When everybody in a company is striving to do things in an excellent fashion and is succeeding, even if only on occasion, everyone in the company feels very good about continuing to contribute. Everyone wants to be on a winning team, and winning in business is doing things well. This is why an environment must be created and reinforced in which people are asked to participate only in activities that they know they can be successful at. First, ask employees to do only those things they know how to do well. Then, after they experience doing something well, they can be asked to extend themselves; they will have become enthusiastic about their ability to contribute by being successful.

Step 3 is building a consensus. Getting people to become involved in the decision-making process is critically important. There is a one-to-one relationship between the degree of consensus in a decision and the degree of commitment. That is not to say that there has to be universal agreement on every decision. Sometimes consensus can be created just by understanding why decisions were made. Whether doing long-range planning, preparing budgets, or forecasting sales, it is very important to get people together and ask them how they feel about it. When decisions are handed down from above, they have little impact on commitment. In contrast, when people are involved in the decision, they will work very hard to achieve the goals and to achieve them within the time frame and the budget agreed upon.

Step 4 is team-building. Traditional thinking calls for management to assume a role in which it is a stern taskmaster, to stay aloof and keep a distance from the staff. Although this thinking is still being taught today, it has no place in a competitive environment. Successful organizations no longer work out of the traditional pyramid. Today, in order to maximize everyone's contribution, companies actually function so that decision making is the focal point around which everything else revolves (Figure 6–6). The result is a centrally focused organization of coordinated functions, thus maximizing the potential of the company's limited financial, physical, technological, and personnel resources.

Step 5 is reward. Rewards to include recognition and value must be linked to team performance first and then to individual contribution. If an organization has a history of promoting or compensating employees on the basis of seniority rather than on the basis of performance, management *must* undo the inequities before it can prepare the organization to compete successfully. Successful organizations do not tolerate reward for experience. High achievers, highly

FIGURE 6–6
Market-Driven Organizational Responsibilities

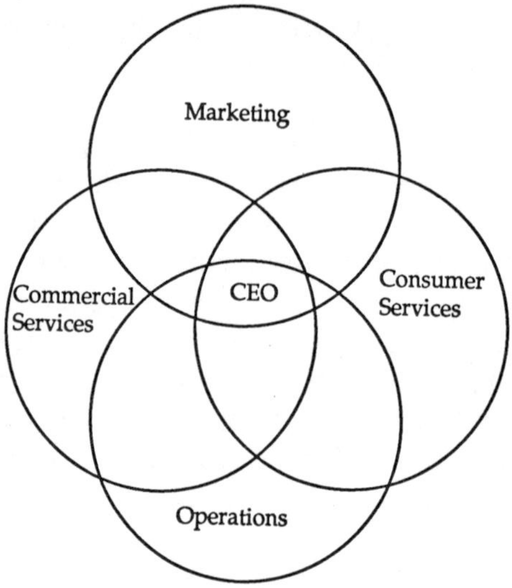

productive people, and the most effective customer contact or quality service people will demand an environment with performance specifications.

Who stays in an environment in which people are compensated for tenure and experience? Those people who cannot perform. Who stays in an environment in which people are compensated for performance? High performers!! The people who opt for security are not always the nonperformers. However, if a system is created in which people have a great deal of security, do not expect high performance.

The best way to begin to create a successful compensation system is to establish a corporate goal to work toward 10 to 25 percent of each person's total compensation based on performance. However, the 25 percent goal should not be established during year one. In other words, if a person makes $12,000 a year, he or she should in time be able to get at least another $3,000 as a result of performing better. If another employee's salary is $40,000, that person should be able to earn at *least* another $10,000 for improved performance. Eventually, there should be no cap on what an individual can receive for improved performance.

Management personnel must be able to measure performance so that they can recognize when performance is great and why it is great. Also, they must know when performance is poor and why it is poor. People have to know how they are doing. It requires constant communication, with lots of feedback—day-to-day, week-to-week, and month-to-month—on how the company is doing, how teams are doing, and how individuals are doing.

CREATING SUCCESSFUL SALESPEOPLE: AN EXAMPLE

Some readers may feel that all of their customer contact people have the aptitude, the skill, and, most important, the enthusiasm to be very successful selling financial services. Many others, however, may have concluded that "We don't have the people who can sell!" and therefore "we have to recruit people who have natural selling skills."

The latter conclusion is wrong! First, there is no such thing as a natural salesperson. All skills are learned. Second, the alternatives are not practical.

The only difference between those who can sell and those who cannot sell is:

> Those who can sell successfully, want to. And they want to because they know they can be successful. Those who think they will not sell successfully, will not be successful. And, because they do not think they will be successful, they will not participate.

Management should look at what its employees can do best and build on that. Successful people define success by the achievement level they set for themselves. Successful sales leaders understand this!

An internal strategy should convince people that they are successful—not that they will be successful, but that they *are* successful. The focus is on the present.

To prove this point, consider for a moment one person in your organization who could sell more successfully if he did not always find excuses not to try. Consider that you have just received a report from a very reputable market research firm. The firm has just given you five prospects who are among the most desirable prospects in your market. The list includes everything one could possibly need to know to be comfortable in making a sales call. Each wants to do business with your bank and will move all of their accounts to your bank only if that "one person" in your organization calls on them within the next 24 hours.

Do you think your lackluster salesperson would find excuses to make sales calls? He would be so excited about the prospect of success that nothing would stop him. He would probably work every one of those 24 hours, without any fear of being rejected or turned down or of being unsuccessful. With that confidence, he would be incredibly successful, because he would commit his effort to those activities without limitations. He would set all other priorities aside because he had been assured of success.

That feeling of commitment to a successful endeavor is the very feeling that successful salespeople have all the time. This feeling must be reinforced in all employees who do not feel that they can be successful at selling.

Successful salespeople have built their success into a mindset. They have absolutely no fear of rejection because rejection is irrelevant. A "no" is nothing more than finding out what will not work. That is success! They will be successful with each contact. Some contacts will just be more successful than others. Their self-concept is so strong that the question of rejection or failure is never in their mind because it is not a part of their success formula.

SELF-CONCEPT = PERFORMANCE

There is not much difference between the top 20 percent and the lower 20 percent of salespeople. The top 20 percent just do the little things a little bit differently; they have what is called the "winning edge." In thoroughbred racing, the winning racehorse is consistently less than three-tenths of a percent faster than the horse that finished in fourth place and out of the money.

Similarly, the difference between a great salesperson and an average salesperson is about 0.3 percent, and that 0.3 percent is so critical because 99.9 percent of the difference has nothing to do with skill, it has nothing to do with aptitude, it has nothing to do with age or experience. Ninety-nine point nine percent of the difference between winners and losers is individual self-concept about what can or cannot be accomplished.

The difference is understanding that there is a direct relationship between self-concept and performance. Self-concept regulates everything people do, and, interestingly, people can *never* perform beyond the level that they are convinced that they can perform. What that really says is that a bank's officers and staff will never perform beyond their level of self-concept.

There have been extensive studies proving that people perform within the parameters that they set for themselves. If management wants more, it must plan and set goals with employees that they can achieve—first, in their minds; next, in reality. Note that this is not the same as the power of positive thinking. This is belief!

The banking industry can create a self-concept—a self-esteem—that results in successful selling based on service quality. The players need not be participants recruited from other industries. Our people have the capacity to get the job done.

Performance is always governed by self-concept. Self-concept is very, very subjective and has nothing to do with reality. Self-concept has to do only with perception. If people think they will be ineffective making business calls, they will be ineffective making business calls. Many people do not like to think of themselves in terms of "selling." It is not because they cannot be successful; it is because they do not think they can be successful. They have no belief!

Successful sales leaders give employees the confidence to believe in what they can do. They do not force employees beyond their level of self-confidence. Most important of all, people need winning experiences. The only thing management should insist upon is that their employees continue to improve their self-concept of what they want to do and then work to reach the next step beyond their level of performance. Employees will do that because they know they can never be unsuccessful doing what they know they can do.

CONCLUSION

Sales leadership strategies may be something entirely foreign to some bank managers. However, placed in the proper perspective and provided the necessary tools, bank managers can take comfort in knowing that professional selling and service quality are synonymous in a financial services environment. Quality service is the epitome of professional selling. Therefore, professional selling must be introduced if the contemporary bank manager is to become a leader in service quality—something that seems much less complex than managing sales. Once commitment has been made to master professional sales leadership, there are other necessary internal strategies to consider. These are the subject of the next chapter.

CHAPTER 7

INFRASTRUCTURE FOR SALES AND SERVICE CULTURE

> The results of a successful sales culture will be that everyone believes in quality customer service first. And, they will understand that professional selling becomes the focal point from which customer needs can be best served. Professional selling and service quality then become synonymous because quality service results in sales. Therefore, professional selling becomes the very purpose of the organization.
>
> —*Mike Higgins*

Once the appropriate leadership strategies are in place, management must carry its commitment throughout the organization to reinforce the newly defined corporate culture. Reinforcement comes from three critical activities: on-going training, expanded responsibilities for marketing, and a structured organization-administration for bankwide sales activities. Mastery of these three strategic issues are prerequisite in building a strong and positive new culture. An organization performs more effectively if it has a strong and positive corporate culture. In fact, the stronger and more positive the corporate culture, the better the organization maximizes its performance potential.

When an organization has a weak or negative corporate culture, its performance suffers. Many banks now have a culture that stresses tradition and conformity. This type of culture is a reflection of the past in which the market was regulated and marginally competitive and the economic environment was relatively stable.[1] Innovation was

---

[1]Cass Bettinger, "Corporate Culture and High Performance," Bettinger Isom & Associates, Salt Lake City, UT, December 1988.

not encouraged, risk-taking was controlled, and aggressive competition was discouraged. Today's environment is much different. If banks are to succeed, management must have a new commitment. This begins with an orientation that requires training.

TRAINING STRATEGIES

There are many excellent sales and product training programs available in the marketplace. Also, many equally beneficial training programs have been developed within various financial institutions. The critical issue is that sales training and product training do not stand alone. All nine steps in the sales cultural reinforcement pyramid must interlock because all are necessary to create and sustain a successful sales culture.

Equally important is that any one training program, whether developed internally or acquired from an outside supplier, is inadequate. There are two reasons for this. First, training, like all the other steps in the pyramid, is an on-going reinforcing process. Second, different training programs take different perspectives relative to how topics are approached and designed. Therefore, financial institutions should schedule on-going sales training and reinforcement programs by using any number of resources and suppliers not only to reinforce, but to keep the training environment fresh and stimulating.

This point is substantiated by the fact that nonbank brokerage firms—the banking industry's new competitors—commit up to 10 percent of gross revenues for training their professional salespeople, sales managers, and office managers.

Many parallels can be drawn between the manufacturing industry's transition to a market-driven environment in the 1950s and 1960s and the banking industry's transition to a market-driven environment today. This author's first position was selling aluminum ingot and industrial products for the Aluminum Company of America. Before I was allowed to make my first sales call, I had to undergo 18 months of product knowledge and sales skills training, followed by 6 months in serving as administrative support for three other professional sales representatives, which is a typical agenda for preparing professionals to sell successfully.

Four strategic areas of sales training are not being adequately presented in most training programs. The first and most important void is a positive understanding of *professional selling*. The second area deals with *listening* in professional selling. The third area concerns the *planning* of sales calls, while the fourth area is the understanding of *selling perceived value* rather than selling rate.

There are many excellent training programs available, however, there are four strategic areas of sales training that are not being adequately presented. The first and most important void is a positive understanding of *professional selling*. The second area concerns the *planning* of sales calls. The third area deals with *listening* in professional selling, while the fourth area is the understanding of *selling perceived value* rather than selling rate. Each deserves special note in this test.

Professional Selling Defined

Strategically, it is important for management and all customer contact personnel, as well as support personnel, to have a clear understanding of what professional selling is really all about. First, they must have a positive attitude regarding their selling responsibilities. Professional selling can be likened to a physician in a hospital emergency room. The difference is that the physician's responsibility is to help people survive and to maximize his or her patient's physical well-being. Professional selling in a financial institution has a similar mission—helping people survive financially and maximizing their financial well-being. In both cases, professionalism requires that the provider do only those things that assist the client in maximizing his or her potential. Both deal with survival: one physical survival, the other financial survival.

Second, all customer contact and support personnel must have a good understanding of the definition of professional selling. Professional selling is not pushing product. Professional selling is *the enthusiastic transfer of belief in your service and the organization you represent.*

This is an entirely new concept of selling. It is a concept that is significantly different and much more positive than believing that selling is pushing products.

Traditional "push product selling" has an inverted series of priorities relative to professional consulting or professional selling (Figure 7–1). With professional selling, the salesperson spends the vast majority of time and effort in understanding the client and identifying specific needs. This positive focus is clear because preparation and planning for each sales opportunity is a prerequisite. There is very little need to push the product and hardly any effort in closing because the professional salesperson and the client are walking hand-in-hand in solving challenges together.

Planning the Business Call

In financial institutions throughout the United States, bankers, for the most part, do not appreciate the need to plan a sales call. A lack of planning results in a salesperson being inadequately prepared for selling financial services professionally. Being inadequately prepared, in turn, results in a salesperson not achieving an acceptable level of success. A lack of success causes the salesperson to think poorly of the experience. He or she has not used time productively, and there is a feeling of having imposed on the client. The inefficient use of time reinforces the salesperson's perception that there are more productive things to do than make business calls. As long as they do not plan sales calls, their negative perception is accurate. Then, they find excuses not to participate.

FIGURE 7–1
Selling Priorities

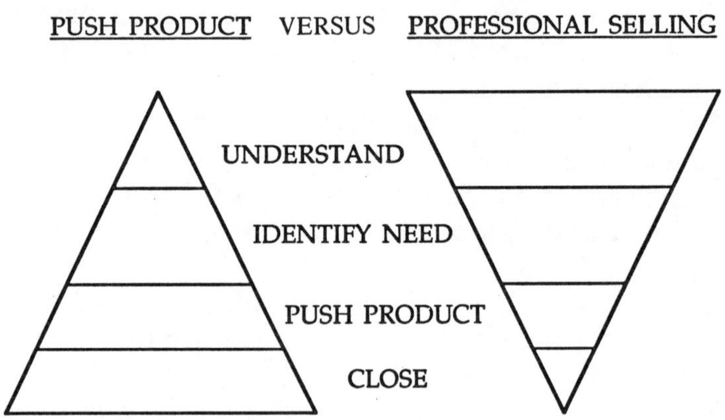

To demonstrate professionalism in selling, bankers must first appreciate the value of planning a sales call. Professionalism is creating an environment of trust. Caring enough to prepare for the sales call is the first step toward establishing that environment. The benefits of preparation provide immediate results: they instill a feeling of confidence that comes from resolving the inherent fear of the unknown. A banking officer who can resolve the fear of the unknown and proceed with clarity of purpose will be rewarded by being able to create an environment of trust throughout the sales call.

Properly planned business calls builds a confidence for success, and a confidence for success results in success. As has been noted many times in this book, people take the initiative only when they can be assured of success.

Many bankers do not perceive the need for an aggressive sales organization and aggressive sales activity. They view aggressive selling as being at odds with the professionalism that is necessary in a banking environment. In fact, the degree of sales aggressiveness has little to do with professionalism. However, to the extent that sales aggressiveness embodies preparedness, then sales aggressiveness is the epitome of professionalism. Professionalism requires preparedness. Preparedness requires planning. And planning requires major effort *prior to* each and every business call.

Being thoroughly prepared requires more than the technical knowledge of the features and benefits of various financial products. Preparedness is an internal strategy to ensure professionalism. Professionalism in selling bank services requires a complete understanding of the client's personal idiosyncrasies, past and current financial relationships, and the business trends. Preparation also takes work. The officer must learn as much as possible about the individual, the company, and the implications of the client's needs. Finally, written objectives must be developed in order to execute a successful professional call.

Listening

I wish I could give credit to the individual who said, "God gave us two ears, two eyes, and one mouth to communicate. I think he was trying to tell us something about the importance of listening."

There is no more important internal strategy in a professional sales environment than to master listening. The good news is that listening can be taught and it can be learned extremely well. In fact, if golf could be taught as effectively as listening can be taught, all students would be shooting par by the end of the second day of class.

Listening builds self-esteem in the person who is being listened to as well as in the person who is listening. There is a need to reinforce this very important concept: when a person is talking instead of listening, he or she learns only what is already known. It is only by listening that salespeople can truly understand the needs of their clients.

Perceived Value

The banking industry has another significant training hurdle. Traditionally, customer contact people have concluded that people do business with banks based on interest rates. Nothing could be further from the truth. Research (Figure 7–2) has confirmed that interest rate is typically one of the least important factors in determining where a corporation or small business conducts its banking.

If price were the only basis on which banks were chosen, there would be no reason to initiate a business call; the customer could easily find the lowest price among financial institutions. Consequently, any organization (or individual) that establishes price (rate) as its overall marketing strategy will not survive.

Although everyone has price resistance, there is a big difference between ability to pay and willingness to pay. People are willing to pay a premium when they are convinced that the price or rate is less than the value received.

Having determined that the client or prospect can benefit from a sale, the professional salesperson's strategy is, then, to convince him or her that the value of the product is far greater than its price. As long as the salesperson is talking about the value of the product that is being offered, the focus is off the price. As long as the focus is on price, there is going to be an argument that goes on forever.

If a prospect asks, for example, "What is your lowest loan rate?" before the banker has had a chance to explain the bank's service, the banker should reply, "If our total service package isn't exactly right for you, then there is no charge because you will have chosen not to do business with us. So let's talk about what we can

FIGURE 7-2
The Most Important Factors to Decision-Makers of Corporations and Small Businesses in Choosing a Bank

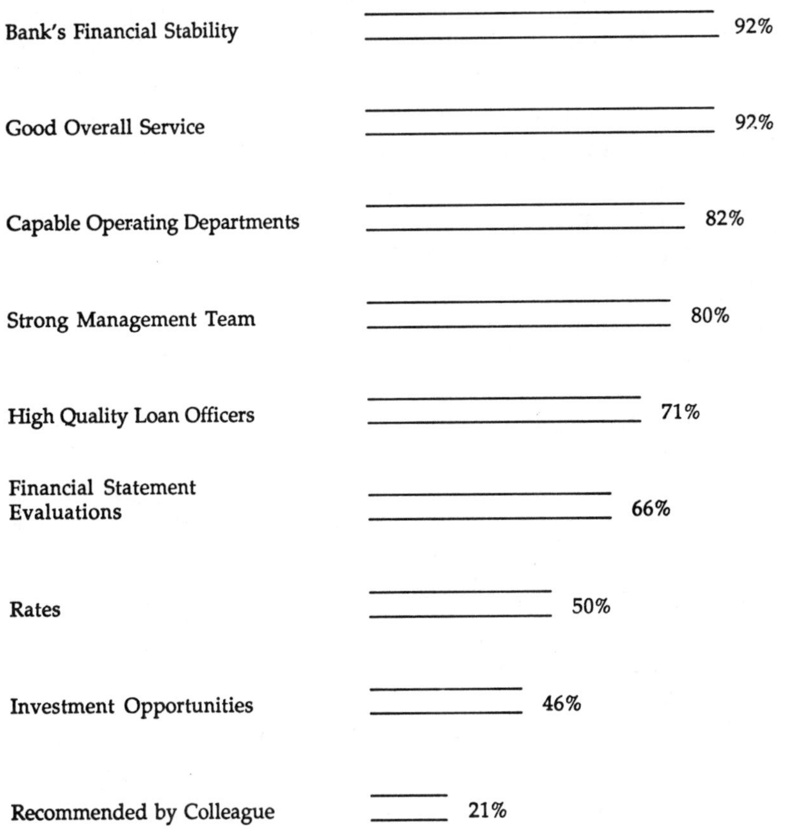

do for you and then you be the judge of whether or not our service has a value equal to or greater than our rate."

There are many ways of handling price or rate objections, and they must be reinforced throughout the organization. In handling objections, the goal should be to create perceived value. Creating perceived value can be very challenging, but it provides an opportunity to improve sales. The seller must understand that what is valuable to him or her may not be valuable to the client. What is considered real value to the salesperson may differ from the client's notion of real value. Value is a subjective term. Real value is determined by needs, wants, and desires. The first rule in selling value is to start thinking in the customer's terms.

Value-added selling is when the professional salesperson embraces a customer-oriented philosophy, recognizes a mutual benefit objective, and actively seeks ways to add value in every step of the selling process. When bank personnel become value-added sales professionals, they will be able to sell more profitably because price becomes less of an issue. Value-added sales professionals demonstrate their real concern for the customer, and it is this visible concern that builds relationships. Increasing value for the customer and building stronger relationships enhance the organization's position with the client. The organization is more firmly entrenched because it is worth more to the client.

Value-added sales professionals are characterized by three qualities. First, they embrace a customer-oriented philosophy. They think in terms of solving problems for the customer. In fact, they share an equally high desire to solve problems as well as sell products. It is because of this genuine concern for solving problems that the value-added sales professional is so successful. Being customer-oriented means that the salesperson is thinking in terms of how the product or service offers a solution for the customer. Customer-oriented sales professionals establish a special kind of relationship with their customers that neither price nor competition can disrupt.

Second, value-added sales professionals also believe in a mutual profit objective. They recognize that it is unwise to charge too much or too little for their services. Selling value is not permission to gouge the customer. The value-added professional realizes that charging too much diminishes the customer's strength in the marketplace by destroying their profit margins. If the customer's market position is weakened, future sales will fall.

By the same token, charging too little diminishes the banker's market position. If the bank is not making a profit on what it sells, it will be unable to remain competitive with regard to service, quality, research, new product development, and all the other things that answer to customer needs and, therefore, make a great organization. Value-added professionals feel that they are doing their customers a grave disservice by selling "rate" because they will not be able to provide the quality level of service that is necessary for that client to maximize his or her profit potential. Value-added professionals realize this because they understand that lower margins adversely affect the "extras" of professionalism that they have been able to offer in the past.

A mutual profit objective means that the price of a product is mutually beneficial. A client does not mind spending more for a product when a bank delivers more value than competing products. The value-added professional salesperson makes some big claims about offering more, but delivers even more than is promised.

Third, value-added sales professionals actively seek ways to add more value to the sale. They define value in terms that are relevant to the customer by analyzing the marketplace, competition, and the customer, to look for windows of opportunity.

Value-added selling is a long-term commitment. It also allows the salesperson to feel more professional about selling. Value-added selling demands consistency; creating a portrait of value requires time and patience. Each action is like a piece of a jigsaw puzzle. Individually, the pieces mean very little, but collectively the actions of the value-added professional create a panorama of value to the customer.

A competitive price situation can be met in one of two ways: either more value can be offered while maintaining the integrity of profit margins or prices can be cut, which will result in erosion of profit margins. These two options are the foundation for every pricing strategy. In the traditional banking environment, loan committees and/or lending officers established a rate and, more often than not, presented it to the client on a take-it or leave-it basis. Perceived value strategies with value-added commitments were rarely ever considered.

The next time a lending officer or customer service representative wants to impose a rate or, more importantly, wants to cut a rate, ask the question, "Are you cutting our price or cutting our throat?" Actively seeking ways to add value is a strategic consideration, and it must be introduced at every level of training throughout the organization. Adding value to each service must be on the agenda at every weekly sales meeting.

In summary, sales training should not define specific selling steps nor rehearse manipulative questions with boiler plate answers.

Rather, professional selling is a process that begins with planning to gain confidence so that the sales professional and the client can walk hand-in-hand to address the client's or prospect's financial challenges. Just as important is the expanded role of marketing, another critical strategic concept that must be introduced and reinforced throughout the organization so that the bank can compete profitably and achieve beyond survival.

MARKETING'S ROLE

A recent survey of bank marketing consultants and bank CEOs revealed a significant difference of opinion concerning priorities between those who give advice to banks on how to become market-driven and those who are responsible for implementation.[2] A near unanimous opinion of the outside consultants recognized *selection of a marketing director with expertise and clout* as one of five most critical challenges facing the industry. None of the CEOs surveyed considered it an issue.

This finding reveals one of the most important reasons for the industry's less-than-satisfactory progress in creating successful sales cultures. It also explains why many CEOs have become so disenchanted with the results of their marketing activities. Yet, such results should not come as a surprise since, in most cases, the CEO

- Has not selected a marketing director with the necessary expertise, and/or
- Has failed to delegate the necessary responsibility and authority to allow successful implementation of a sales culture.

In either event, rarely is the marketing director considered a peer by the senior management team. The inevitable result is that marketing is too often relegated to a middle management responsibility, which practically guarantees failure.

---

[2]Michael T. Higgins, "Community Bank Strategies: Commitment & Consensus. Keys to a Successful Market Strategy," *Bank Marketing Magazine,* October 1988, pp. 6–10, 99.

Clearly, a serious and generally widespread credibility problem exists. The primary reason is that all too few bank marketers have a CEO's perspective, that is, an understanding of how banks make money and a full appreciation of the implications of increasing shareholder value. As a result, marketing has little or no credibility with the CEO, the board, or the staff. The marketing director's role is simply not taken seriously.

Selection and/or Training

Significant leadership and management complexities exist in a deregulated, highly competitive environment, especially when many competitors still enjoy substantial regulatory advantages. In order for the marketing director to earn the responsibility as well as the authority that brings credibility, he or she must understand the bank's overall management priorities from the CEO's perspective. If not, the marketing director must at least have the capacity and the commitment to develop that perspective. The CEO, after all, is accountable to the shareholders. The CEO's primary role is to maximize shareholder value over the long-term. In accomplishing this task, bankers can pursue one of four master strategies:

- Emphasize growth.
- Emphasize profit.
- Balance profit and growth.
- Sell or merge the organization.

Each of these master strategies requires significantly different priorities and, therefore, different strategic and tactical action plans and implementation commitments.

The master strategy must precede the marketing strategy. Once consensus has been reached on the master strategy, the appropriate marketing strategies become much more clear. Therefore, in developing a CEO's perspective, one of the first things that the professional bank marketer must do is develop an in-depth understanding of what the bank's master strategy is, the critical implications of that master strategy, and how the marketing strategy will influence the marketing priorities.

Responsibility and Authority

Successful, market-driven organizations recognize that there are three prerequisites relative to the marketing director's position and responsibility in any successful organization.[3] These prerequisites include:

- *Title and position.* If the marketing function is to be taken seriously, both the title and the position of the marketing director as a peer member of the senior management team are paramount. "No title, no position" equals "no clout, no authority." The wrong person has been selected if the marketing director cannot qualify for a title and position placing him or her on *at least* a par with other senior officers. In the traditional, regulated, product-driven organization, the senior loan officer was typically second in command, and that was entirely appropriate. However, in a highly competitive, market-driven environment, the CEO must challenge the primary responsibilities of everyone: "Is loan volume and loan quality management our primary responsibility?" Traditional bankers will reply "yes." The answer is "NO!" The primary business of a bank in a deregulated competitive environment is to get and keep customers, and you do not achieve that by managing loan quality. Loan quality management is as important as ever, but it now comes from a different point of reference. In *Megatrends,* John Narsbitt warns, "Unless banks reconceptualize what business they are in, they will be out of business."[4] Theodore Levitt, in "Marketing Myopia," presents several compelling examples of how defining a bank's business incorrectly will lead to failure.[5] Management must focus on needs, not product.
- *Senior management responsibilities.* Other members of the

---

[3]Cass Bettinger and Michael T. Higgins, "Marketing: It's Not a Middle Management Responsibility," *ABA Banking Journal,* Vol. 80, No. 5, May 1988, p. 171.

[4]John Naisbitt, *Megatrends* (New York: Warner Books, 1982), p. 92.

[5]Theodore Levitt, "Marketing Myopia," *Harvard Business Review: On Management* (New York: Harper and Row, 1975), p. 176.

senior management team must also commit to their marketing responsibilities. They must understand the invaluable role that marketing strategy plays in helping them achieve their goals. The other senior managers' marketing performance must be thoroughly evaluated by the CEO and compensation adjustments should be made accordingly. One recommended strategy is to have the bank's management team earn a significant portion of its compensation based on specific bankwide performance and marketing goal achievement. Measurement systems and performance models, which will be discussed in subsequent chapters, are readily available to reinforce that commitment.

- *Marketing Officer's responsibilities.* A competitive environment requires comprehensive marketing skills that are just as complex as lending and data processing skills. The marketing director should have hands-on experience; the capacity to learn; and/or working knowledge of market research, strategic planning, market segmentation planning, sales organization, sales management, sales training, sales goals and performance measurement, reward for goal achievement-incentives, internal and external communications, as well as motivational and other people skills.

An individual with the appropriate skills and CEO perspective will assume the responsibilities of the Chief Marketing Executive (CME) and play a pivotal role in the bank's transition to become a market-driven organization. As in other market-driven industries, the CME must have comprehensive skills. According to a 1988 study, the CME of a large U.S. company earns, on average, $170,000 a year and assumes the important task of increasing profits and determining strategy and tactics.[6] The study also confirmed that marketing will play an increasingly more important role in all American corporations as the United States strives to become more competitive in the global marketplace. Further, the study said that marketing

[6]H. L. Heidreck and B. J. Struggles, "Marketing Monitor," *Banking Week,* December 27, 1988, p. 6.

skills will be more critical in the financial services industry than in any other industry.

In order to gain credibility, the bank marketer must develop a CEO's perspective. He or she must have a clear grasp of the bank's master strategy and the role that marketing must play in implementing that strategy. In addition, he or she must have a clear understanding of how the bank makes money and must be able to relate marketing strategy to improve bank profitability.

Once the bank marketer can demonstrate a CEO's perspective and can create strategies that clearly enable the bank to achieve its objective of increasing shareholder value, credibility will have been established.

If credibility cannot be clearly established, then the selection process must be re-evaluated. It is essential that the marketing director reflect an in-depth understanding of the CEO's perspective, or at least have the capacity and commitment to do so. Without the credibility resulting from having a CEO's perspective, the marketing position will never be taken seriously.

Marketers cannot have it both ways. Their pleas for responsibility and authority and for title and position must be qualified by capability and capacity. The bank's staff, customers, and shareholders deserve no less.

Marketing in many banks is still very much a second-class profession relegated to nice people. Marketing is rarely at the forefront of strategic planning, is infrequently represented on asset/liability committees, and is the first department to suffer budget cuts when the bank has earning problems. While it may have been a popular way to manage in the 1970s and 1980s, it will not be an acceptable survival strategy for the truly competitive 1990s.

Budget Cuts

The mid-1980s was a time of fiscal austerity for many banks, which were having loan quality problems. Bankers responded with across-the-board budget cuts. Although an indiscriminate cost-cutting strategy may have been appropriate in the 1980s, it will prove disastrous in the 1990s. Across-the-board budget cuts are appropriate only in a monopolistic, regulated environment because everyone in that environment is experiencing the same negative impact on their business.

In a deregulated, competitive environment, things are different. The majority of competitors are nonbanks. The nonbanks are not directly affected by agriculture and energy slumps. They will continue to place their bets on marketing to ensure a viable future. Multi-industry players do not follow the traditional regulated banker's rule book. Banks that restrain their marketing efforts by across-the-board cuts in a deregulated marketplace are playing into their competitors' hands.

Budgeting must be prioritized. It must *not* be maligned by across-the-board decisions. Marketing is a bank's hope for the future. To cut marketing budgets is to destroy the potential of long-term opportunities in response to short-term needs. Think about the last nationwide economic recession or industry-wide reversals. Did McDonald's cut back on training? Did IBM cut back on product development? Did Ford Motor Company cut back on product enhancement and strategic planning? No. They kept the future alive. They fed and nourished it. Strategically, banks must do the same.

Marketing will enable banks to survive, both literally and psychologically. Marketing is the one discipline in the entire banking environment in which people can set their day-to-day challenges aside for a moment and look positively toward the future. It is a future in which employees throughout the organization instinctively make decisions and relate to clients in ways that bring the maximum benefit to the overall enterprise.

Expense consciousness is too often out of balance. The person who treats marketing as just another budget item is going to suffer the same fate as the person who got a good deal on a bunch of off-brand phones. The price was right, but the off-brand phones did not have a number five on them.

Perhaps the bankers who are downplaying marketing are overlooking its basic purpose—which is to define opportunity and create hope. They are too overwhelmed by short-term challenges. Worse yet, too many are simply short-sighted people who fail to understand the implications of a competitive, deregulated environment. They are the ones who respond to creative ideas with "let me tell you why that won't work." They are the ones who are preoccupied by technical unraveling rather than positive, creative, opportunity-building. Unconsciously, these managers are moving away from the threatening marketing arena because distance gives them a greater comfort level. If they did not do so, they would have to ask themselves whether they were really capable of making a contribution in a deregulated, competitive industry.

In addition to on-going training and an expanded role for marketing in the scheme of things, each institution must structure new organizational responsibilities and introduce administrative programs and disciplines to ensure success.

ORGANIZATION AND ADMINISTRATION OF THE SALES FUNCTION

All of the tactical organizational activities and all the administrative formats necessary to manage a successful sales and quality service organization will not be covered here. However, it is important to offer strategic parameters from which to design the necessary support systems to ensure that sales and service quality momentum is maintained and expanded.

Many bankers have unsuccessfully tried to build a sales organization by borrowing a concept here, a discipline there, a training package from somewhere else, and administrative support from any number of resources and suppliers. When the package is put together, it does not look very good, and it works about as good as it looks. The process of gathering ideas and systems from peers and trade associations is a good one—if the manager is operating in a stable, regulated environment. It is in that environment in which the habitual idea-gathering experience was first learned. However, such a process is no longer valid.

Sales organization and administration in a competitive environment must be customized to fit each bank's marketing priorities and management style. They must be comprehensive and tested to ensure that constant reinforcement is provided and that voids are filled to sustain and expand success. For example, in an external business call program alone, there are 39 elements and systems that must be customized, coordinated, and reinforced to ensure success. All too many sales programs die a cyclical death because all of the appropriate systems and elements are not in place.

Objectives and Goals

Bank objectives and goals are an extension of the marketing opportunities defined in the strategic and market planning process. They become the targets for resolving challenges and maximizing opportunities that have been prioritized by the process. The long-term results established by the bank's CEO as the sales and quality service leader and marketing manager become the corporate objectives in the marketing function. It usually takes more than one year to achieve each strategic objective, because most objectives require the completion of several intermediate goals. Therefore, objectives are usually long-term and can be qualitative, quantitative, or a combination of both.

Goals constitute a quantitative statement of purpose for the marketing strategy. Goals are usually established on the basis of an actual result to be achieved within a shorter period of time and can be set for the bank as a whole, for a department or division, or for a team, group, branch, or individual.

While setting objectives and goals are necessary to establish the specific intent for a marketing action, they must follow the selection of the recommended strategy and the designation of targeted markets. The terms "objectives" and "goals" are often used interchangeably, although, in fact, they should be used to denote two different entities.

> An objective is more of an aspiration to be working toward future accomplishment. It may even be timeless in certain instances in the sense that a qualitative objective is often continuous. On the other hand, a goal is quantitative and covers short-term, intermediate steps on which objectives are achieved.

There are two important points with regard to goals. First, they have to be quantified. Individuals, departments, divisions, and bankwide goals must define clearly what is to be accomplished. They also must be measurable. What gets measured gets done! Second, goals must be written down in very clear and precise language. Then, a written plan of action for accomplishing the goals should be created. A manager who does not write down his or her goals is a manager who is engaging in self-delusion.

Many managers say, "Well, I don't need to write down my goals because I know what they are.'' The reason they do not write down their goals is because it entails making a commitment. Most people subconsciously resist writing down their goals because if they never write them down, if they never quantify them, if they never make plans and set deadlines for their accomplishments, then when they do not achieve their goals they can rationalize that they have not failed. Writing down a goal on paper and making a plan for its accomplishment is a starting point of achievement, because it represents a clear commitment to the future. When people put something down on paper, they are making a commitment to take a great leap of faith into the unknown. Setting goals is an act of courage. Writing a goal down on paper places it indelibly in the subconscious, thus serving as a catalyst for creative thinking in how to accomplish it.

In contrast, when people do not have clear, specific goals to which they are committed, the result is usually aimlessness, confusion, unhappiness, underachievement, and possibly failure.

Goal Setting

Setting goals is essential for strategic success. Goal orientation is evident in *all* successful people. It is their number one priority. Preferably, goals should be set for five-year, three-year, one-year, quarterly, and monthly intervals. The most successful people even have daily quantitative goals. Successful organizations are just like people; they thrive on goal-setting.

Successful managers are able to recite, on a moment's notice, the most important goals that they want to accomplish in a one-, three-, and five-year period. It is critical to have explicit quantitative goals that must be accomplished.

To accomplish three- and five-year goals, it is not necessary to know how each of the steps toward those goals will be accomplished. However, it is important to establish the steps for accomplishing the one-year goals and to have an outline for meeting the three-year goals and a general agreement for accomplishing the five-year goals.

It is important for managers of divisions, departments, groups, and/or teams to encourage team members to write their own personal goals. Less than 5 percent of all people have clear, written, specific goals, and those are the people who seem to accomplish everything.

A Yale graduating class in the 1950s was surveyed to determine who in the class had written down their personal goals. Only 3 percent of the graduating class had done so. Twenty-five years later, the 3 percent who had previously written down their personal goals had achieved 84 percent of the total net worth of their graduating class.

This story is not meant to imply that the only measurement for success is making money or achieving a high net worth. However, it does relate the very favorable developments that can come from putting goals down in writing.

Written goals make things happen and making things happen is the very essence of successful professional selling.

CONCLUSION

W. Clements Stone, one of the world's most successful sales professionals, concludes that everyone is a salesperson. People are constantly convincing or trying to convince someone to do something. Even a child who is too young to talk is a great salesperson. All the child needs to do to get mother to respond is to cry out. A proposal of marriage is a sales job, and you damn well better be prepared if you want the proposal to be accepted. Since everyone is a salesperson, it pays to learn to be a *good* salesperson. Professionally, it pays to set goals and to help people make decisions you want them to do only if it is in their best interest. Professional salespeople recognize that selling is nothing more than motivating a person to make an appropriate decision and the only way to do that is by *the enthusiastic transfer of belief in the service and the company they represent.*

This is the essence of improving performance. Because we must be committed to improving performance substantially it will be timely to discuss how to first measure and, then, reward improved performance.

CHAPTER 8

PERFORMANCE MEASUREMENT AND REWARD STRATEGIES

Organizations are not more effective because they have better people. They have better people because they motivate to self development through their standards, through their habits, through their climate.[1]

—*Peter F. Drucker*

Prior to 1970, few, if any, banks had sales tracking. Although some banks could "ring up" sales volume totals, management could not determine who had sold what. Most importantly, bank management could not track purchases by customer or measure sales productivity by individual sales persons. The creation of sales tracking systems for banks evolved with the eminent transition to a deregulated environment and the need for banks to become more sales oriented. By creating sales tickets at the new accounts desk, external processing centers or internal microcomputers could function to track sales by individual, location, and customer. However, of these bank sales tracking systems created in the seventies have become obsolete. They simply do not provide today's sales managers with the critical information needed to actively manage sales and to develop new business. In the increasingly competitive environment, there is a critical need to coordinate bankwide sales performance. Therefore, the need to measure external bankwide business calls with bankwide cross-sales and bankwide referrals has resulted in a need to acquire much more sophisticated performance measurement systems (see Appendix C,

[1]Peter F. Drucker, *The Effective Executive* (New York: Harper and Row, 1966), p. 170.

"Evaluation of Alternative Sales Measurement Systems") to support the Sales Manager's needs.

Effective sales management is based on four fundamental feedback principles:

1. It is difficult to aim without a target.
2. It is impossible to improve if you cannot keep score.
3. People do what is inspected rather than what is expected.
4. Managers cannot manage results that are not measured.

The quality of the sales management information system determines the ability to manage results.

Retail Sales Measurement

In addition to tracking sales, today's sales management information systems should include the following critical components:

- *Bankwide cross-sell measurement.* Most cross-selling tracking systems were designed and implemented for new accounts personnel. However, cross-selling is a bankwide opportunity and, therefore, a bankwide responsibility. To maximize relationship banking, it is just as critical to measure whether loan officers cross-sell deposit accounts and refer trust services, as it is to measure customer service representatives' cross-sell activities and referrals of other services.
- *Referral quality as well as quantity.* Not every employee has the opportunity to close the sale. However, everyone in the bank has the opportunity to refer. Failing to actively measure and manage referrals is tantamount to throwing away opportunities to improve both customer service and the bank's bottom-line. Today's systems should track the status of each and every referral that is made from the boardroom to the supply room. In addition to referral quantity, the system should measure referral quality in terms of the number of referrals sold, as well as the accounts and dollars generated.
- *Bottom-line productivity ratios.* Many banks that track the traditional cross-sell ratio have not experienced a corresponding increase in deposit growth. This is because the typical cross-sell ratio is based on sales of all services (for example,

automated teller machines [ATMs] or safe deposits boxes). While this is an important index of relationship selling, specific measurement of deposit/deposit and a deposit/loan cross-sell ratio provides a better indicator of sales performance that shows up on the bank's bottom-line. Top sales performers do not just ask for minimum opening deposits. They generate additional core deposits and new money. Other key performance ratios must include average deposit per account, new money, and new dollars as a percentage of total deposits.

- *Insurance penetration and fee income.* As cross sale measurement is extended to other departments such as loans, additional indices of critical sales performance need to be included. Specifically for the loans area, the system should track loans eligible for insurance, the percentage of penetration of insurance sales for eligible loans, and the total insurance premium dollars generated.
- *Goals and peer group averages.* One of the most powerful motivators and management tools is to have individuals set their own targets and track their performance in achieving their goals. A state-of-the-art system enables goal setting and performance tracking for multiple performance measures. More importantly, these goals should be customized by individual, branch, and market segment. It is not fair or appropriate to compare teller sales performance with an average that includes new accounts and loan officers. For effective sales management, the system should compile averages and separately rank each job peer group with different sales responsibilities. Likewise, branch peer group averages should be calculated and compared with goals that are adjusted for different marketing potential.
- *Comprehensive incentive capacity.* Due to the limitations inherent in most early tracking systems, sales incentives have inappropriately been limited to SPIFs (Special Promotion Incentive Focus), which is a bonus per product sold. While SPIFs may be useful for selling specific products during promotional periods (such as IRAs), they are costly and generally not effective on a long-term basis. The tracking system should not limit the scope or nature of incentive compensation. A state-of-the-art system should enable the sales manager to cus-

tomize incentives on a variety of multiple indicators with the flexibility of changing rates so that commissions can be weighted to reward performance consistent with bank goals.

- *Point-of-sale marketing data.* A state-of-the-art system should be more than a cash register. It should truly become a sales management information system that collects critical point-of-sale marketing data. In addition to sales volume, the system should be able to track sales volume, sales value and sales ratios to new versus existing customers, the amounts and sources of new deposits, types of customers opening accounts, and age, sex, and zip code demographics.

Competing in the 1990s will require more than a cash register to track sales. Success in managing sales will be determined by the quality of a bank's sales management information system.

The positive results of measuring cross-sales performance is overwhelming. Typically, when the performance of customer service representatives are not being measured, their deposit/deposit cross-sale ratio will be in the range of 1.01. That is, for each one hundred deposit accounts opened, only one additional deposit cross-sale will be made. With sales training and performance measurement systems in place, that ratio can be increased to 1.30 within six months. The volume and profitability improvement is significant (Tables 8–1 and 8–2). For every 5,000 customer contacts an additional $12,375,000 of additional deposits are cross-sold. This will generate an additional $495,000 in pretax income based on a 4 percent spread. To relate this to activities in smaller organizations or individual branches, a structured cross-sell program that includes training, measurement, sales management and reward will generate an average $247,500 in additional deposits and $9,900 in additional pretax income for every 100 customer selling opportunities.

A comprehensive reporting format for cross-sell performance should have data and performance ratios for at least the following:

- Individuals.
- Employee peer groups.
- Branches.
- Regions.
- Banks.
- Holding company.

TABLE 8-1
Cross-Selling: Potential Additional Deposits and Profitability from Increased Sales Productivity

Number deposit accounts sold per customer	1.00	1.10	1.20	1.30
Customer sales opportunities	5000	5000	5000	5000
Number of deposit accounts sold	5000	5500	6000	6500
Additional deposit accounts sold	0	500	1000	1500
Additional deposits generated (national average of a second deposit account is $8,250)	$0	$4,125,000	$8,250,000	$12,375,000
Spread at 4% provides increased pretax income of	$0	$165,000	$330,000	$495,000

TABLE 8-2
Additional Pretax Income from Increased Deposit Sales

Use the following formula to project the potential deposit volume and pre-tax income improvement for increasing (just) deposit cross-sales

Example Bank	*Your Bank*	
5,000	________	Number of customers
0.30	× ________	Increase in deposit/cross-sell ratio
1,500	________	Additional accounts that would NOT have sold without cross-selling
$8,250	________	Average $ per additional account sold
$12,375,000	________	Additional deposits generated
4%	________	Average spread
$495,000	________	Additional pretax income

Commercial Sales Performance Measurement

Successful business call programs require many diversified skills and disciplines. However, only the measurement discipline is prerequisite to managing external call programs because, again, what cannot be measured cannot be managed. More importantly, to manage well, the measurement must be comprehensive, including effort, activity, focus, *as well as results.*

An inherent weakness is focusing on effort, not results. Programming the number of officer calls is essential in the early phases of selling efforts. Programming will provide tools, administration, and structure. However, call programs are, by design, able to produce one thing: calls. Typical measurement systems are limited to tracking numbers of calls. If the ultimate purpose is to develop profitable business, then measurement must focus on results as well as effort.

Some measuring systems also report the number of new accounts sold. However, developing new business is a long-term proposition. Typically, it takes five to seven calls over many months to develop a new piece of business. Therefore, reporting sales results by numbers of products sold by each call is not enough either. For example, doubling the line of credit on an existing quality loan may be safer and more profitable than developing a new line of credit with an untested prospect.

Finally, merely reporting numbers of accounts sold with opening deposit balances and lines of credit available provides a very limited view of business generated. To truly assess bottom-line profitability, management needs to know whether the accounts stay on the books, the average collected balance, the average credit balance, net interest margins, and relationship profitability.

The Benefits and Limitations of Mainframe Central Information Files in Tracking Sales Results

Successful management of business development requires a central information file (CIF) with customer portfolio analysis. In essence, what is needed for effective management and measurement of business development is a *true* CIF capable of profitability analysis of each customer's relationship and each officer's portfolio of accounts. With a CIF capable of customer portfolio analysis, it is possible to assess the long-term impact of an officer's efforts both to develop new business and to increase the profitability of key customer accounts. A true CIF yields multiple bottom-line performance measures, including increases in the number of accounts, average collected balance/net investable funds, credit balances, net interest margin, and customer portfolio spreads, as well as customer and officer portfolio net profits generated.

Unfortunately, there are very few mainframe CIFs that provide relationship analyses because, historically, CIFs were designed to perform accounting functions. Even a true mainframe CIF does not provide the relationship analyses necessary to manage sales, cross-sales, and referral results.

An actual client experience illustrates both the difficulty and the powerful potential of a microcomputer-driven portfolio management system. In this instance, the bank identified a prominent physician as a key prospect. The physician, who belonged to a group practice clinic, already had a personal checking account and a line of credit with the bank. The fact that a bank officer made four scheduled calls and eight follow-up calls on the physician's partners became irrelevant in light of the business developed, which included the clinic group's line of credit, two corporate demand deposit accounts, a commercial real estate loan for a new clinic facility, a substantial trust account, as well as refinancing the physician's home mortgage and making a car loan in his wife's name.

It is extremely difficult, if not impossible, to tie all of this business together on a mainframe CIF, and it is not necessary. On the loans, for example, the physician was not the primary signer on the note and, therefore, was not connected to the relationship by the (mainframe) personal identification number.

Likewise, it is extremely difficult to tie all of the business together via the calling officer's identification number. In the case of the demand deposit accounts, the calling officer did not, in fact, personally establish the account relationship. Yet, it was through the individual business development of one officer with the one physician that resulted in immediate new business with multiple relationships and tremendous long-range profit potential. Total results must be measured.

Benefits of Portfolio Business Management Systems

In addition to measuring volume results, a comprehensive portfolio business management system includes several critical components that offer distinctive benefits for sales management. Such a system offers

- Analysis of both sides of the profit equation: assets and liabilities. Officers can be given credit for "funding" their loans with deposits representing lower cost of funds. Likewise, officers can be given credit for maximizing spread on deposits by generating loans with a spread greater than the average rate for earning assets.
- Analysis of customer portfolio profitability prior to making calls to determine which customers have and will produce the greatest profit potential.
- Establishment of officer and team composite customer portfolios to track profitability and growth over time.
- Factoring in overhead costs, loan loss reserves, and capital requirements to determine net profit contribution to the bottom-line.
- Establishment of incentive compensation based on bottom-line results of extra revenues and profits generated by each individual or profit center.

Advantages of Microcomputer Portfolio Business Management Systems to Track Sales Results

The use of a microcomputer typically requires manual input of account data for key customer portfolios tracked. State-of-the-art microcomputer systems now enable downloading of critical information from the mainframe. Regardless of how account information is assimilated, the microcomputer has the flexibility and capacity to perform other functions that benefit sales management, including

- Establishment of call goals.
- Integration of referrals.
- Establishment of a schedule tickler system.
- Integration and customization of telemarketing.
- Evaluation of efforts in terms of profitable results.

The message is *do not wait for mainframe capability and capacity.* More effective and efficient options are readily available. In many banks, selling is compartmentalized by department or staff function. Call programs are implemented with officers; cross-selling with new accounts; and referral programs with tellers and other front-line staff. In successful environments, selling, cross-selling, and making referrals becomes everyone's responsibility. It *must not* be compartmentalized by department or staff function.

The measurement capability must also report bankwide activity. It must not be isolated by title or department. Everyone in the bank can make a significant contribution to business development, but each will contribute differently. Everyone deserves to be measured, and measurement must coordinate all activities.

In conclusion, a customer portfolio management system is one part of a total, integrated, bankwide sales management system. A comprehensive system must include officer calls, cross-sales, and referral tracking. Creating a customer portfolio management system for business calls is a vital element because it allows management to comprehensively measure effort, activity, focus, and results of building better business relationships. It serves as the very foundation of success.

Finally, performance measurement is important because your people deserve to know how well they perform. If people are not told what is expected of them and if their performance is not measured against these expectations, then how can they possibly know how successful they are? Sadly, after one year or five years or even forty years, if someone were to ask these people whose performance was not measured, "How did you do?" all they could reply is, "I really don't know. I guess I did okay. I think I survived!" A pitiful situation, but common in the banking industry.

To draw a parallel, let's look at a hypothetical example. Suppose that, rather than working for a bank, employees were part of a profit-making bowling team. Every day they went to work, setting short-term and long-term goals, enthusiastic about the future, and reflective of the past. As they perfected their skills, their enthusiasm grew. Some days their team would win and some days their team would lose, and individually, some days were much better than others. However, they always looked forward to improving their work.

Then, one day management, in all its wisdom, added a new element to the team's work environment. Upon arriving at work, the team members noticed that someone had hung a blanket in front of all the pins in their alley. Reluctantly, they went to work. But now they were aiming at invisible targets. Although they could hear (about) success, they never knew what they really accomplished individually, and the team never knew what it accomplished. They never again experienced success or failure.

How enthusiastic would that team be about coming to work in the subsequent days, months, and years. How enthusiastic would the team members be if they were unable to measure their progress and their success? How successful would they be in their attempt to enthusiastically transfer belief in their service and team they represented?

REWARDS FOR PERFORMANCE: INCENTIVES

The use of incentive rewards, feedback, and annual reviews to influence performance is the last, and most critical discipline, to be introduced in the nine interlocking, prerequisite steps to maximize a bank's potential in a competitive environment. Incentive concepts have worked with varying degrees of success within the industry. The degree of success results from management's understanding of how to construct and manage systems that reward performance. There are several critical pitfalls in designing a reward system.

Pitfalls

First, management should *avoid oversimplifying* the system. It has to be easy to implement and extremely accurate, which is why reward programs are comparably complicated to construct. Second, too often designers of an incentive program *think in terms of sales performance.* A sales activity and sales performance mindset is too short-sighted. Rather, the first question that must be asked is, "Does the organization have a commitment to reward for performance?" This is the issue. Will reward for performance become a critical element in our corporate culture? If yes, then design a program that rewards for all performance, not just sales. Design a program that will evolve to reward for sales performance, work flow, productivity, and bankwide profitability.

Too often, the designer of a reward program begins with the

question *"What can we afford?"* A good question but not relevant. Beginning with such an inescapable limitation as budget will doom the program to failure or, at best, result in unnecessary restraints that will prevent the organization from maximizing its potential. The biggest mistake a bank can make, and the one that puts the incentive system at risk, is to do a superficial job of analyzing the bank's particular situation and what it is trying to accomplish by installing a reward system. Analysis must come first. There are 19 other major considerations that each management team has to address. Then, the results of rewarding for performance above minimum standards will pay for the program.

Another pitfall is that many bankers *begin with an incentive program designed for individual customer contact people* or various customer contact departments. Incentive compensation must begin with the strategic analysis of what the bank needs to accomplish and the creation of a bankwide incentive pool that could be made available if the bank achieves some or all of its bankwide goals. It is important to recognize that overall bankwide goal achievement is the ultimate objective. Achieving or exceeding bankwide goals must be evaluated and a value placed on the worth to the bank of achieving or exceeding those goals. This is how the total bankwide incentive pool is first created. Only then can incentive pool values be allocated to the various divisions, departments, teams, and/or individuals.

There are very negative implications for a bank to begin to build incentive programs at the individual level. By the time it rolls up all the incentive rewards that are being paid out, the bank is usually paying much more in incentives than the performance is worth because any number of people influence and could be rewarded on each other's goal achievement. A total pool for goal achievement must be established and then allocated for pensions, profit sharing, sales performances, productivity, and bonuses. Goal achievement must be measured for the bank as a whole, as well as for divisions, departments, teams, and individuals. This is the only way to control the value of reward being distributed.

Another pitfall is that most managers try to build a reward system that is fair to everyone. However, a worthwhile reward-for-performance program must begin with the premise that incentive programs cannot be universally fair. The various jobs and opportunities for helping a bank achieve its business goals differ. If an absolutely fair system is created, the program will be diluted so much that it will not mean anything to anyone. It is perfectly acceptable—and even necessary and desirable—to offer different levels of incentive pay to employees in different areas of the bank. What has to be fair, though, is the administration of the incentive program, or you will put a hole in the bottom of your boat.

The program must be started with the premise that incentive opportunities cannot be equal to everyone. There are not many things that are equal in this world, and trying to make reward programs equal will prove to be an impractical exercise. Various jobs and opportunities for helping the organization achieve business goals differ. Therefore, an equal or even a near-fair system is totally impractical. Ensuring fairness ensures mediocrity, which is counterproductive when the very purpose of a reward program is to promote excellence.

Fairness is a very important consideration, however, in the design phase. Also, fairness must rule the program administration in measuring accuracy. There can be no tolerance for sloppy feedback or inaccuracy. The key is to communicate these assumptions to everyone *before* the incentive programs are introduced.

Another common pitfall with some incentive reward programs is that they can create a high degree of internal competition and tension among employees. In particular, they can encourage high achievers to run off by themselves without considering the implications of team or bankwide goals. It eventually will tear down the necessary sense of spirit among the participants. Incentive rewards can become divisive because the *emphasis* is on rewarding individual performance.

Individual reward is important, but the implications and probability for divisiveness is another reason why an organization must first stress, and then reward, bankwide and/or team achievement before individuals are rewarded. The emphasis on teamwork is very, very important. It is one of the great techniques mastered by Japanese human resource management, and it is one that deserves more attention in the U.S. banking industry. Always begin with team, group, or departmental goals, with rewards based on team performance.

Another pitfall is that designers of incentive compensation or reward programs often find it difficult to accomplish the very purpose of incentive reward: to encourage improved performance. Too often, people are rewarded for performance that they would normally achieve without incentives. This has been particularly evident in many banks. Banks have a tendency to reward an activity more than it is worth. They reward for selling rather than for improved sales performance, productivity, and bankwide profitability.

Similarly, too many programs are designed with too little thought made to the actual contribution to the overall bank goals. Often, inadequate measurement systems impose design limitations. For example, a multibillion dollar bank holding company recently experienced this situation. The bank was paying out rewards for cross-selling items that were not a priority and were not profitable. Management was enthusiastic about the upward spiral in cross-sell ratios from less than 1.01 cross-sell per customer contact to well over 2.5 cross-sells per customer contact. What perplexed management was that during a two-year period neither bankwide assets nor liabilities grew at an acceptable rate, much less than the overwhelming rate of improvement in cross-sell ratios. Investigation confirmed that everyone had improved their cross-sell ratios; however, the measurement system could not track the types of cross-sells. While ATM cards and safety deposit box sales were at an all-time high, asset and liability growth was at a standstill. The reward program had too much emphasis on doing things right instead of focusing on doing the right things—that is, concentrating on cross-selling the more profitable products. Rewards must be set for explicit objectives; what is being rewarded must be known as well as its value to the bank.

The bank holding company eventually switched over to a measurement system that was far more comprehensive, flexible, and practical and less expensive to operate. Within months, people were emphasizing customer needs fulfillment consistent with the bank's priorities. Cross-sell ratios of service products remained high, as cross-sells in loans and deposits grew at an astounding rate.

The last, but equally significant, pitfall is rewarding for singular goal achievement, such as profit, volume, quality, or fee income. There are two good reasons for implementing multiple-goal, rather than single-goal, incentive models:

- Because everyone's job description includes multiple responsibilities, reward mechanisms should parallel all priority activities.
- Rewarding one area of achievement, while ignoring other areas of importance, invariably results in de-emphasis of all responsibilities not included in the reward program.

An example is in lending where officers are, or should be, responsible for loan acquisitions, quality, spread, fee income, as well as cross-sales and referrals of other products. If the reward program is limited to acquisition (loan volume), quality, cross-selling, and referrals will suffer. The other side of the coin is a system that rewards only quality, with no counterbalancing expectations for volume. Loan volume will decline. In both cases, spread and fee income opportunities will not be realized, and no one will take the time to make referrals.

The professional approach is a comprehensive approach. Complex in design, simple to implement. The trick is to create incentive models based on multiple goal achievement and weighted to provide reward calculated to share explicitly from the value of improved contribution. Multiple-goal incentive models have been tested in banks throughout the United States since 1984.

Management must realize that effective incentive programs are not created by simplistic formulas to resolve major challenges. Effective rewards for sales and work performance depends on bankwide cultural changes. Offering commissions for sales will not equip a bank staff to sell.

Reward for Performance Strategies

The overall bankwide strategy is not to reward for sales or even to reward for multiple sales. The strategy must be to commit to reward for performance as a significant philosophy in the corporate culture. The objectives of implementing a series of incentive programs over a period of time include

- Staff focus on priorities
- Acquisition of quality assets and/or stable deposits.
- Increase in fee income.
- Reinforcing key objectives and explicit direction.

- Increasing work flow and accuracy.
- Reinforcing primary job functions.
- Providing salary administration flexibility.
- Stabilizing base salaries.
- Retaining high performance and productive personnel.
- Seeking staff support to discourage unnecessary new hires.
- And, overall, improving shareholder value.

Reward Prerequisites and Guidelines

To ensure that the reward program is managed effectively, several guidelines should be established and should include the following:

- Key responsibilities, including the function to be measured.
- Training to do the prescribed activity successfully.
- Strategies and specific objectives for each participant.
- Measurement systems.
- Communication systems to relate status.
- Supervision or sales management skills.
- Explicit rewards for goal achievement.
- Rewards to include group or team incentives to prevent divisiveness.
- Initial behavior measurement so that rewards are not given for business that would be acquired without a program.
- Incentives for specifically identified new performance.
- An initial short-term "test" period to allow flexibility.
- Performance rewards for supervisors or managers based on their team's results, not their individual contribution.
- Low starting rewards.
- Simple programs that are presented in writing to participants.

Management Versus Leadership

John Adehr has concluded[2] that few leaders do more than merely coordinate efforts. However, the most effective leaders create a sense

---

[2]John Adehr, "Leadership: The Special Talents that Set a Leader Apart," *International Management,* April 1985.

of team spirit that makes even the most arduous or hum-drum work exciting. The really great leader has exceptional organizational talents and also has the ability to inspire others to much greater effort than they would have expended had people been left to their own devices. Both organizational (management) and motivational (leadership) talents are needed in any true definition of leadership. Adehr thinks that "The best chief executives are both great managers and great leaders."

CONCLUSION

Every organization, from the smallest to the largest, is a reflection of its leadership. Maintaining a high order of truly excellent leadership is one of the toughest jobs in the business.

Sales and quality service leaders create a sense of family among all their players. The nine steps prerequisite to creating a successful sales and service quality culture are the very steps parents take in creating a successful family environment.

- Reward
- Feedback
- Measuring Achievement
- Setting Goals
- Training
- Organizational Rules
- Leadership
- Focus
- Vision

The very purpose of internal strategies is to establish management systems that will allow leadership to create an environment of belief and enthusiasm. From that ultimate purpose an environment can be created so that all employees will be as excited to come to work each morning as they are to return to their families at the end of each working day.

PART 3

EXTERNAL FOCUS

Successful external strategies can be developed only after the necessary infrastructure is in place. The approach to retail and commercial strategies begins with a reinforcement of the need to differentiate for *each* targeted market segment. *A market program that is not directed at a specific market segment is not a marketing program.* Various examples and formats complete the review of this discipline, which is characteristic of all successful companies and which must be mastered to compete successfully in a deregulated marketplace.

Subsequent chapters will deal with the application of market segmentation methodology. Unique approaches will be discussed to differentiate a financial services company in the consumer as well as the commercial services marketplace.

CHAPTER 9

DIFFERENTIATION: MARKET SEGMENTATION AND IDENTIFYING NEED

> If marketing is about anything, it is about achieving distinction by *differentiating* what you do and how you operate. All else is derivative of that and only that.[1]
>
> —*Theodore Levitt*

The most important lessons to be learned from Chapter 1 can be found in the examples of Federated Investors and SAS, two firms that followed through on their commitment to define an explicit market segment, identify the particular needs of their targeted segments, and then develop unique ways to serve those needs more effectively than *any* other competitor. To emulate their example, we must become the best at what we do for those we can best serve. That means we must *differentiate.*

Many banks are targeting priority market segments. However, most have targeted the same market segments because they are perceived to provide the greatest business potential. The more popular market segments are the

- Affluent.
- Professionals.
- Executives.
- Retired persons.
- Middle income individuals.

---

[1]Theodore Levitt, *The Marketing Imagination* (New York: The Free Press, 1983), p. 128.

Some banks have even become more creative by identifying targets with significant business potential that are virtually being ignored by financial institutions such as

- Early retired entrepreneurs.
- Female executives.
- Female entrepreneurs.
- Service companies.

Although targets are being identified, comparatively little is being done about identifying the targeted segment's explicit needs, training staff, and creating a product/service package to serve those needs more effectively than any other competitor. That's *differentiation!* The greatest opportunity for banks is to realize their potential to differentiate.

To differentiate a product or service for a market segment is to implement a strategy to attract and keep customers, which is the fundamental purpose of any business. To do that effectively, management decisions must be based on knowing what drives and attracts customers. Successful differentiation requires management to discern how customers differ from one another. Then, management must determine how the various differences it identifies can be grouped into market segments that can be served profitably.

It sounds easy enough! But why aren't banks doing it more successfully?

One challenge is that the concept of market segmentation is contrary to the traditional "full-service" mindset that banks have promoted and believed in for years. The second challenge is that managing by market segment is foreign to most bankers. Therefore, it might be helpful to clarify the process and expand on the implications. The third challenge is understanding the implications of market segmentation.

Definition: Market segmentation is the process by which a company explicitly divides its customer and prospective customers into groups that can each be reached with a distinctive marketing strategy (*differentiation*).

Target marketing began to be practiced in the late 1970s. The companies that first endorsed the technique are now champions in their industries, whereas the companies that were slow to react are now heavily involved in aggressive programs to recapture their market share. Those that did not respond are in long-term decline and are being consumed in the marketplace by companies that segment their markets and strategically plan to maximize the profit potential from the target markets they have chosen.

The traditional banking mindset of full-service banking (that is, being all things to all people) has been replaced by an approach that will bring greater success. Banking institutions, regardless of size, are most profitable when they identify the specific market segments they can best serve and then employ all their marketing resources on those targeted markets, thus optimizing scarce marketing dollars.

Contrary to the opinion of some, even the smallest financial institution in a limited marketplace can pursue its business more effectively through market segmentation. For example, one small bank that targeted certain customer groups via market segmentation was a $30 million dollar bank in an isolated rural community with a population of 35,000. The bank doubled its size during the height of the agricultural recession in the mid-1980s, when the community was experiencing an overwhelming out-migration of people and commercial businesses. It became a high performance bank because it explicitly defined its targeted market segments. Moreover, it competed with the best: an affiliate of a Minneapolis regional bank, two statewide holding companies, another local independent institution, one regional and one statewide savings and loan, and two very aggressive credit unions.

To excel in the marketplace, the bank chose to concentrate on serving small, locally owned businesses and early retired/retired consumers. Because the bank was able to direct all its available physical, financial, and personal resources to learn about and serve these markets more effectively, it captured an overwhelmingly high share of the market. In five years it grew from the smallest to the second largest of eight financial institutions and became the most profitable in the community. All the while, the bank did not ignore its other customers. Rather, it simply avoided actively seeking customers other than those it had specifically targeted.

This example raises a point that is commonly misunderstood. Target marketing does not mean soliciting certain customers while ignoring the rest of the populace. Effective market segment managers solicit their targeted markets with great enthusiasm and purpose, but they do not ignore clients who walk in the door. What they do *not* do is design their product and service packages and systems to become all things to all people. Those who pursue that strategy are going down the road to mediocrity.

Differentiation recognizes that different individuals and companies *need* to do things differently. The whole idea of market segmentation suggests that there are groups of individuals or organizations that have similar wants and needs. These groups can be identified into want/need categories through a series of techniques that will be discussed in a subsequent chapter. Thought of in this way, market segmentation becomes a powerful organizing principle that can be used in making decisions for the redeployment of available resources. Knowing how individual retail and corporate customers differ from one another and how those differences can be organized into segments that can be meaningfully and profitably managed requires comparatively sophisticated skills.

As most readers know, a marketing program typically encompasses a product or service that is packaged, priced, promoted, and distributed in a predetermined way to meet an identified need. *A marketing program that is not directed at a specific market segment is not a marketing program.*

A marketing program based on segmentation means that the organization is thinking about what drives individual customers, customer groups, or corporate organizations in making choices; it deals beyond the obvious. It goes far beyond the considerations relative to demographic, geographic, or user groups and buying practices.

MARKET SEGMENTATION STRATEGIES

It is important to understand that market segmentation strategies that work for one financial institution may prove disastrous for another. This is the reality of competing in a deregulated environment: there are *no* boiler plate solutions to complex strategic challenges. Each and every market participant must create its own strategies to differentiate itself in the marketplace. The more creative the differentiation, the greater the institution's ability to compete. Differentation in product design and delivery—and differentiation in the skills of the providing officers and staff—will make the difference.

POSITIONING

All financial institutions will eventually be positioned from one of three basic options as the financial services industry evolves into a free market. Each participating organization will evolve, very slowly into one of three overall strategic options shown in Table 9–1, the large money center, the low-cost producer, or the specialty boutique bank.

The *large money center banks* will have substantial resources to market their products and services nationally and internationally.

TABLE 9–1
General Market Strategies of Financial Institutions

	Large Money Centers	*Low-Cost Producers*	*Specialty and Boutique*
Market, primary	International and national	National and regional	Regional and community
Marketing focus	Many markets, organized by market segments	Price-driven	Limited number of market segments and convenience
Product line	Comprehensive	Narrow product basics	Limited, well-defined, unbundled or packaged
Product development	Internal	Some internal w/reliance on third parties	Customized and reliance on third parties
Pricing	Very competitive Complex, based on service quality and relationships	Discounted	Based on superior quality service Relationships, Fee-based
Delivery	Automated and personal	Low cost	Personal and automated
Management skills	Exceptional, particularly in marketing	Recruit from competitive institutions	Recruit from competitive institutions
Training	Internal	Recruit	External and internal

They will have superior management skills, particularly in marketing, and a key management focus will be on cost reduction and control. These banks will increase their market awareness by allocating substantial resources for marketing and promotion. In doing so, they will commit significant budget resources to training, including an internal training capability.

The second strategic positioning option will be to become a *low-cost provider.* Organizations that choose this option will create a narrow product line and provide minimal service. The management focus will be on line units instead of staff support departments. Prices will be discounted, and low-cost delivery systems will be dependent upon mini-branches. Promotional programs will emphasize price. The extensive training normally associated with deregulated banks will be replaced by a policy of hiring experienced people from competing institutions. Expansion will typically be accomplished by creating new low-cost offices that provide automated delivery services.

The third strategic positioning option is to become a *specialty or "boutique" bank.* This option will be selected mostly by existing community banks and some regional banks. Their marketing strategy, of necessity, will be based on market segmentation. These banks will offer an unbundled line of products that are not price-driven. The targeted markets will be convenience-oriented rather than price-sensitive. For some purposes, these specialty banks will emphasize fee-based services in an attempt to dominate their well-defined market segment or niche. Acquisitions of other banks will be made to deepen rather than to broaden their marketing capabilities. Image rather than price will be the theme of specialty banks' promotional messages.

Having analyzed the three alternative strategic approaches, it seems apparent that community banks will become specialty institutions with well-defined product lines that will be marketed to particular customer segments or niches. Some relatively large banks may be unable to find the product or market niches to support their current overhead. Such banks will face the choice of merging with other institutions or instituting drastic reductions in operating expenses and undertaking subsequent re-evaluations of their strategic options.

A very important parallel may be drawn at this point. The banking industry will follow the identical path of the retail soft goods industry. Each financial institution will eventually position itself into one of three strategic options: the large money centers (Macy's, Dillards, Bullocks, Federated Department Stores); the low-cost producers (K-Mart, Wal-Mart); or the specialty boutique banks (similar to regional and local specialty retail stores throughout the United States).

THE STARTING PLACE

Differentiation in the marketplace deals initially with identifying the market segments to be served. Target marketing involves delivering the right product or service to the right individual or organization at the right time, at the right price, and through the most appropriate distribution system. Obviously, few companies can get all these "right" things correct every time because they are confounded by various internal corporate pressures, the external competitive environment, and uncontrollable factors in the marketplace. However, the organizations that resolve the obstacles first will take the competitive lead. Target marketing's main purpose is to maximize the deployment of resources. The key is to direct all available resources to the targeted markets that can best be served—which means served most effectively and served at a profit. It begins with implementation of the market segmentation process. First, however, let us look at the major alternative to market segmentation—the mass marketing strategy.

MASS MARKETING STRATEGY

The mass market approach was satisfactory for financial institutions in a regulated market. However, the deregulated, more competitive market has created more sophisticated consumers. A wider variety of product options offered by a greater number of traditional banking and nonbanking providers now exists. This trend has caused the dilution of established values, such as long-term customer relationships.

Consumers are not becoming less loyal as some bankers lead themselves to believe. Rather, consumers now have such a variety of options, and *their loyalty depends upon who cares enough to identify their needs and serve them best.* The reason that many customers are no longer loyal to traditional banking environments is that they are being cared for more professionally by other financial service providers. The market trends of consumerism and multifaceted suppliers require that bankers become more sensitive to customer needs. That sensitivity must begin with a commitment to differential through market segmentation regardless of the size of the market or the size of the financial institution.

Nevertheless, the mass marketing approach is still pursued by many banks. The mass marketing approach basically involves aiming at the total market. Mass marketing does not recognize market segments. Instead, it tries to satisfy the greatest number of buyers with a limited number of products or even a single product. Figure 9-1 illustrates a mass marketing approach. Note that a single offering developed from a single marketing strategy is meant to appeal to the whole market. It is assumed that purchasers of mass marketed services do not differ from one another significantly or that the services offered are generic and so appeal to almost everyone.

A mass market "differentiation" strategy may be pursued, but it is often unrelated to the product or service being offered. This "unrelated to product" differentiation—used most often when the product is similar to everyone else's product or service—is a strategy that attempts to distinguish the company's product from a field of competing products by enticements not directly associated with the product itself. The banking industry used this technique for many years by offering gifts (toasters, for example) and unrelated premiums to promote their established product lines.

Mass marketing as a bankwide strategy is an outmoded approach that does not take into account the realities of today's consumers or the financial services marketplace. Therefore, successful banks will convert to market segmentation strategies. These basically

FIGURE 9-1
Mass Market Approach

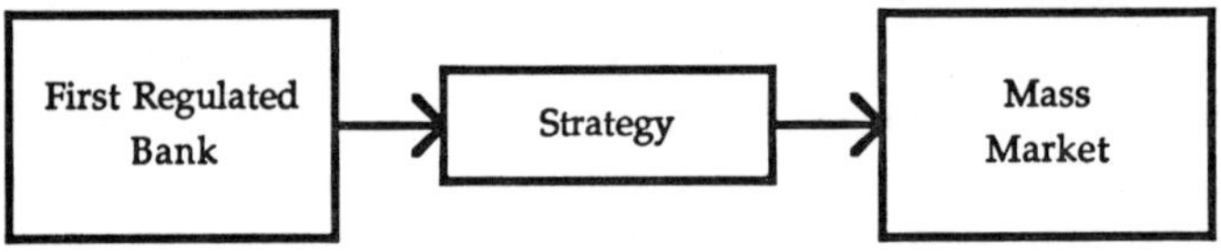

fall into two broad categories: multimarket segmentation strategies and market concentration strategies.

MULTIMARKET SEGMENTATION STRATEGY

The multimarket segment strategy allows the bank or financial institution to increase its share of the marketplace by recognizing the different wants of several market segments. Although additional costs may be incurred in planning, organizing, and creating product lines and by controlling the multiple offerings designed for different markets, the increased investment can be justified by the concentration of resources and the resulting success in the marketplace. Figure 9–2 illustrates the multimarket segmentation approach.

MARKET CONCENTRATION STRATEGY

The market concentration strategy focuses on efforts to serve one market segment among many. Several banks have found it to be efficient to pursue a large share of one segment of the market rather than expanding their resources across multiple segments (Figure 9–3). For example, a $200 million dollar bank in New England found itself competing with the money center banks and decided, therefore, that it could compete more effectively by organizing along a single

FIGURE 9-2
Multimarket Segmentation Strategy

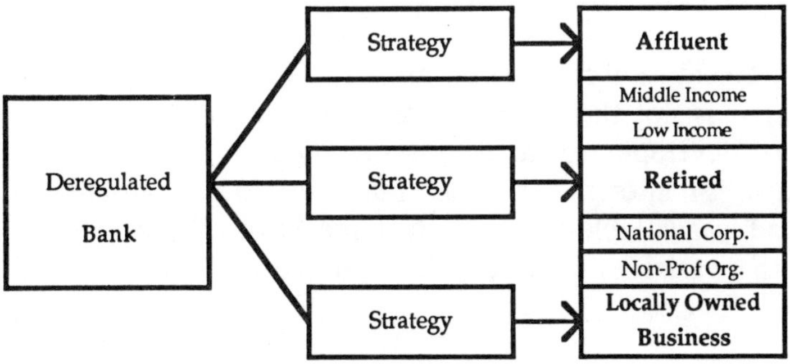

FIGURE 9-3
Market Concentration Strategy

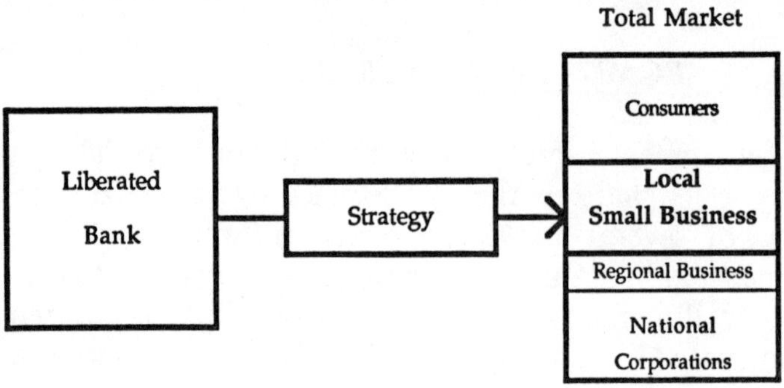

market concentration. Management literally organized the bank to serve only locally owned businesses, which constituted the bank's target market. The bank did not consider itself a retail bank; therefore, it did not create a strategy to serve the retail market. It did, however, have a funds acquisition team, which served to acquire consumer and institutional deposits from local and regional sources to fund the borrowing needs of its targeted market segment.

The funds acquisition team designed a very comprehensive and flexible marketing plan. The plan was directed toward a very clearly defined subsegment of the affluent consumer market segment. However, the plan did not respond to that subsegment's total financial service needs. The plan was designed to secure surplus funds. Period. And the strategy worked magnificently.

MARKET DATA ANALYSIS

Successful segmentation requires an analysis of the bank's local service market. It is not the intent of this book to relate the tactical techniques of developing or analyzing market segment data. However, it will be of interest for senior managers to understand that data are readily available to assist their marketing departments in evaluating the variables necessary in formulating a segmentation strategy.

Many banks and thrifts have acquired Standard Metropolitan Statistical Area (SMSA) data mainframe tapes and have downloaded the data to microcomputer software programs. The data base costs between $750 and $3,000, includes mapping, and contains more than 83 key market data variables with menu-driven software. The data base for each user-specified city or market area contains observations for 16 square block areas (cells), which allows greater accuracy than an analysis of the census tract at the zip code level. Users can also add data or modify the provided data by responding to easy request prompts. The data include population, ethnic background, numbers of families, number of wage earners and income, profession and skills, home ownership, employment, mortgage costs, occupation, education levels, and number of vehicles per household.

The demographic data can provide user organizations with a sophisticated site and market analysis calculation in a matter of moments. In-house marketing and site selection analysts no longer need to wade through stacks of census documents or wait for outside suppliers to provide the information. Examples of various analyses that have been undertaken using this type of demographic data follow.

- To support a bank charter request, the applicants wanted tabulations of families grouped into income categories and exhibiting 20 other market characteristics for an irregularly shaped geographic area that they had identified as their trade area and CRA for the proposed bank.
- A financial institution added data on competitor facilities to the data bases provided and then combined the supply information with other service demand variables to identify the best locations for new branch facilities. The institution's analysts also used the data to understand the market penetration of existing facilities and to create market segment profiles for each existing and proposed location.
- A bank used the data base to identify residents in the 30- to 45-year-old age group and families with incomes over $30,000 in an SMSA. The data specifically identified six priority areas where 200,000 or more people lived within a five-mile radius of a center point configuring to the age group and income requirement.

OVERALL ANALYSIS OF MARKET POSITION

The initial analysis of the organization's current position in the marketplace need not be exhaustive, but it must be comprehensive enough to take into consideration the various influences that must be analyzed in concert. A case in point is $2 billion dollar branch banking organization that had nearly 100 locations in a densely populated metropolitan area and out-of-state rural area. This particular case is not applicable to all management situations. Nevertheless, the though process followed in the initial analysis is critically important in the development of strategic market segment priorities. For this discussion, we have consolidated the total number of branches into a zone group of six branches, which was somewhat representative of the organization's overall challenges.

In the actual case, the management team perceived the bank as a retail banking organization. Over the years, the bank had acquired branch locations without setting target market priorities. Instead, the motivation in acquiring branches was to establish market presence and add distribution locations. As a result, the bank ended up buying locations that other banks had discarded. The analysis is comprehensive but concise (Table 9–2).

You will note in reviewing the first section of Table 9–2 that Branch #13 ranked first among 100 branches in the profit analysis relative to cost of funds. The branch carried a comparatively low (positive) liabilities and capital position compared with the other branches, and its overall rating on profitability, which took into consideration a number of other influences, was tenth compared with the other branch locations.

Section 2 of Table 9–2 deals with consumer demographic data. Sections 2a and 2b indicate that Branch #13 was, again, doing a pretty good job of penetrating the available customer base. The demographic profile of its customers was almost identical to the demographic profile of the market area. However, there was obviously no targeting going on in the marketplace.

Branch #14 shows a significantly different relationship with its market potential. Thirty-nine percent of the market was made up of upper-middle income families, and the branch served a clientele that was predominantly (47 percent) retired low-income families. The market demographic data relates that only 28 percent of the population was retired. Therefore, this particular branch was doing significantly well in penetrating that market segment, even though it did not have a defined marketing program to do that.

Branch #15 was doing a pretty good job of penetrating the market, consistent with the primary market demographic data. Again, however, no target market focus from the overall organization was evident. The customer base at Branch #12 was 77 percent blue-collar, and yet 40 percent of those residing in the market area were retired, 23 percent were in the upper-middle income category, and only 21 percent were blue-collar.

Section 3a of Table 9–2 indicates household penetration. None of the six branches had achieved a significant market penetration. Section 3b relates the number of each branch's customers who live within its primary market area. The data show that a significant number of blue-collar customers using Branch #12 did so on a pass-by basis because only 10 percent of that branch's customer base resided in its primary market area.

Section 4 of the analysis deals with the asset and liability mix, including total (general ledger) retail mix as compared with commercial and the volume necessary to break even. The data show some significant commercial deposit and loan activity in Branch #13, and some significant but very inconsistent commercial deposit activity in Branch #16. Otherwise, there is not much positive activity in commercial or retail relationships other than in Branch #12 (the pass-by branch) relative to the retail deposit base.

Section 5 of the analysis shown in Table 9–2 pertains to deposit growth, share of market, and the strongest competitor share of market. Some very significant implications are revealed from an evaluation of these totals. With the exception of Branch #11, this group of branches was competing with very strong providers of retail services. The preliminary analysis shown in section 5 of Table 9–2 also covers location and accessibility indicators and includes a brief preliminary rating (1 to 10) of each branch manager's strengths relative to 10 qualifying aptitudes. For obvious reasons, the rating values in line 6 of this text are hypothetical.

This very comprehensive but concise analytical tool had a significant influence on management's marketing decisions. Although the analysis of the six sample branch locations does not necessarily lead one to the actual conclusions that were ultimately reached, the com-

TABLE 9–2
Branch Location Analysis

Branch	*#11*	*#12*	*#13*	*#14*	*#15*	*#16*
1a. Profit analysis ranking by cost of funds	49	50	1	52	53	66
b. Total liabilities + capital	32	29	74	56	9	10
c. Overall rating	69	72	10	68	50	76
2a. Customer Demographics by Key Acorn grps and % of each Acorn grp*	I-47 B-23 G-21	G-77	I-36 B-18 G-13 E-10	I-47 B-22 G-13	B-66 I-13	B-42 I-30 G-18
b. Primary market demographic Key Acorn grps and % of each Acorn grp to 75%	I-36 B-22 E-11 F-10	I-40 B-23 G-21	I-39 B-22 F-11 E-10	B-39 I-28 C-10	B-73 I-15	B-38 I-25 G-20
c. Population growth % annual through '92	0.4	0.2	0.0	0.1	0.2	1.0
d. Median age	33.1	32.5	34.2	32.2	32.5	31.9
e. Household income median	27.2	30.6	29.0	32.9	41.2	34.6
f. $15,000 (% total)	27.6	22.4	26.1	22.3	12.7	17.9
g. $50,000 (% total)	17.4	21.2	20.8	25.7	35.0	25.6
3a. Branch: H/H penetration % in primary area	4.8	2.6	2.8	4.2	2.9	0.5
b. % Cust. w/i primary area	54.1	10.2	57.0	69.1	58.6	25.3

4a. Branch dep. (millions)—gen. ledger	9.1	8.8	33.0	17.8	5.7	5.7
Retail/coml.—marketing CIS	6.5/2.9	7.8/1.2	73./26.8	11.6/6.6	3.6/1.9	2.0/16.9
Needed to break even	7.7	7.5	15.3	15.1	4.8	5.3
b. Loans (millions)—gen. ledger	1.3	1.1	37.7	2.7	1.0	.9
Retail/coml.—marketing CIS	1.1/1.6	1.2/.5	6.7/20.1	2.2/1.4	1.0/.44	.6/.7
Needed to break even	4.5	4.5	11.3	9.1	2.7	3.5
c. Deposit growth 5 yrs. Market %	28.6	26.0	36.0	36.0	31.3	14.1
d. Branch %	(1.2)	2.3	6.0	6.3	19.5	6.7
5a. Deposits, branch SOM	3.6	15.2	3.9	2.3	2.7	2.2
b. Largest competitor SOM	4.91	43.8	48.5	48.5	25.9	32.6
c. Primary competitor #	(31)	(26)	(17)	(17)	(31)	(24)
d. Location analysis	8	7	8	8	7	6
e. Accessibility analysis	9	8	4	9	9	9
6. Manager Strength	6	4	8	6	5	5

**Note:* Acorn Groups: I=retired, low income; B=upper middle income; G=blue collar; E=Hispanic; F=Black.

posite analysis of all 100 branches was very convincing. The bank's management decided to rewrite the mission statement to serve the small business marketplace and close all retail locations. This strategic decision resulted in the organization selling or closing over half of its branch locations.

Having made the decision, the bank's management initiated a confirmation review during the subsequent 45-day period. The confirmation review included a projection of the bank's strengths and weaknesses in serving the small business segment (Table 9–3). As part of the confirmation review, the bank's management also looked at the potential of the small business market, further analyzed the geographic implications relative to branch locations, projected the resource and operational requirements of serving the small business market, undertook a competitive analysis of financial service suppliers already serving the small business market, and conducted a capital/cost risk analysis. The effort culminated in a rewrite of the bank's corporate vision.

TABLE 9–3
The Bank's Strengths and Weaknesses in Serving the Small Business Market

Strengths	*Weaknesses*
Senior Management expertise in serving target	Product needs: Trust/investment, transaction products, systems
Potential to draw on corporate officers	Recruitment, on-going training
Delivery system	Utilizing of marketing, marketing research
Branch locations: Zones 2, 6, 9, 11, 12	Branch locations Zones 1, 3, 4, 5, 7, 8, 10
Customer perception: Potential due to corporate division image	Organizational lines of responsibility
Capital markets, access	Operations, wire transfer
Market Research skills	Sweep, cash management
Network relative to target markets	
Concerted team effort and commitment	

The organization then set out to identify the specific needs of their new target market segment and to create a method to differentiate the bank from all of its competitors while meeting the unique needs of the targeted segment.

IDENTIFYING MARKET SEGMENT NEEDS

Most bankers believe in meeting customer needs, and that belief is sincere. What is often questionable is the degree of understanding that is required to ensure an appropriate level of commitment to meeting customer needs.

The process of defining customer needs can best be illustrated by a true story that occurred in San Francisco at a convention of one industry's top 5 percent of successful salespeople in the United States. Over 12,000 people met in the famous Cow Palace to share and congratulate each other for the great contribution they made through their profession of selling.

Typical of most sales meetings, the last evening of the event was devoted to a finale during which the most successful salesperson of all was named. That person was up against over 240,000 other sales professionals. The awards included an array of highly valued prizes: an automobile, a vacation trip, and jewelry. Most important, however, the salesperson judged the best would receive the coveted recognition of his peers.

As the moment grew near, the house lights dimmed and the orchestra began playing suspenseful strains as the spotlights searched the audience for the candidate about to be introduced by the master of ceremonies. With just the appropriate amount of fanfare to maximize the excitement throughout the great arena, the master of ceremonies identified the recipient, the spotlights centered on him, and the orchestra saluted the designee with a crescendo of music as the ceiling seemed to burst with balloons and the audience simultaneously exploded with applause. Suddenly, as the recipient made his way to the aisle, the audience became quiet, for they all noticed at once that the designee was moving cautiously with a white cane and was met by an escort on the aisle to be assisted to the podium. In that moment, everyone present observed that the man was blind.

Spontaneously, the audience again exploded in applause as they recognized their most successful peer, not only for his accomplishment but also because he attained excellence despite a comparative disadvantage. The recipient made his way to the podium with his escort as the applause grew louder and louder.

Finally, after the crowd had quieted and the master of ceremonies had presented the award, he turned to the recipient and said, "John, we know you have been successful all of your life. This year, you have been even more successful and you have no peer. Tell us—share with us—what is it you do that makes you so successful?"

"That has to be obvious," replied John. "I am successful because I must see the needs of my customers through their eyes."

When bankers internalize this great story and learn to practice its lessons, the banking industry, too, will experience unlimited success and have no peers!

Most managers and providers of financial services want to meet the needs of their customers. Many believe they do. The real challenge comes in implementation, because the pitfalls to successful needs identification are many.

1. Financial service providers commonly assume they know their customers' specific needs. This assumption has its roots in the regulated mindset that afflicts many bankers. The result of the assumption is that the bank's services are limited to available product lines. Compared with other industries in a competitive environment, banks do not commonly do enough market research that is focused on identifying the needs of explicit target market segments.
2. The industry is still primarily product-driven. Managers and providers continue to think in terms of traditional loans and deposits.
3. Bank managers have not yet focused on selecting and training staff to manage and provide unique services that are differentiated to meet specifically targeted markets. We're all still in it for a "serve 'em all" free-for-all. But the market is not free any longer. We can *not* be all things, yet we still try.
4. Too few banks research the level of customer satisfaction. No one can confirm customer needs without knowing the level of satisfaction their customers have with their bank's services and how their bank's services compared with their competitors' services.

To begin thinking in terms of market segmentation and needs identification, bankers have at their disposal numerous studies that define very contemporary marketing principles designed for use in the banking industry. For example, Thomas Thamara has identified 14 emerging high-growth market opportunities and the specific products and services necessary to meet the needs of that growth market.[2]

Thamara concludes that Individual and Family Financial Planning is probably the most important growth opportunity in the financial services market today. I agree! And, I have taken an advocacy position for personal financial planning (Pfp) since 1984.

Confirmed customer needs and benefits validate this high ranking with twenty-five percent of U.S. households willing to pay for the organization of their financial affairs[3] to

- Increase disposable income by reducing taxes.
- Convert taxes into savings.
- Increase investment income and redeploy investments.
- Increase after tax investment income: tax-deferred annuities.
- Manage estate planning.
- Increase credit availability.
- Ease debt burden by restructure or loan consolidation.
- Evaluate insurance adequacy.
- Find college financing alternatives.
- Establish financial peace of mind.

The changing makeup of the consumer profile and economic influences reinforce Pfp's priority ranking:[4]

- The ever-increasing number of two-income families with significant disposable income.
- An aging, upscale population with substantial purchasing power.
- Increased cost of higher education.
- Escalating cost of medical care.

---

[2]Thomas Thamara, *Bankers Guide to New Growth Opportunities* (Englewood Cliffs, NJ: Prentice Hall, 1988), pp. 5–7.

[3]Michael T. Higgins, *The Total Personal Financial Planning System* (Lincoln, NE: Michael T. Higgins & Associates,1984).

[4]Thomas Thamara, *Bankers Guide to New Growth Opportunities* (Englewood Cliffs, NJ: Prentice-Hall, 1988), pp. 29–30.

- Level of consumer installment debt.
- Complexity of financial products and services from an array of traditional and nonbank suppliers.

Because of rapidly improving technology and the complexity of available information and services, consumers need and demand to learn more about their financial alternatives. Now, more than ever before, consumers want to evaluate explicitly the implications of financial services as those services can meet their specific needs.

Consumers typically feel that the traditional banking institutions they once looked to for direction are not meeting their expectations. They are offered too many choices, which are advertised in too many different media through inconsistent promotional materials in a confusing financial marketplace. They need, demand, and deserve a more meaningful and concise organization of information to help them with comparison evaluations to better manage their money and their assets.

PERSONAL FINANCIAL PLANNING AS A MEANS OF IDENTIFYING NEEDS

Despite the growing evidence about the demand for Pfp services, a 1985 market study sponsored by the American Bankers Association concluded that "personal financial planning as a stand-alone product may make much less sense in community banks than relationship banking and cross-selling." Another study, this one sponsored by a state bankers association, concluded that personal financial planning ". . . would not prove to be a profitable product. Commercial banks should, therefore, look elsewhere for more timely services."

These myopic studies have done a great disservice to the banking industry. Pfp is not a stand-alone product, and it was never intended to be. Pfp services are a prerequisite—not a stumbling block—to cross-selling or relationship banking. Bankers, or any other financial advisor for that matter, cannot effectively cross-sell services or develop a long-term banking relationship without knowing the customer's needs, and Pfp provides that kind of information. Pfp is the source—the very foundation—for beginning to identify consumer needs.

When bankers attending a conference on Pfp compared their experiences in introducing the service to their clients, one CEO stated, "We charge $60 to $70 per hour to assist our customers in organizing their financial position and planning for their future. We have never experienced customer reluctance to our fee structure. However, as far as perceived value is concerned, our bank would be willing to pay our customers $60 to $70 per hour just to obtain the financial information they share with us."

Pfp provides the first real opportunity for bankers to see through their customers' eyes. Specifically, by offering Pfp services, banks and thrifts will

- Better understand the client's financial inventory and liabilities, as well as his or her financial goals, providing a perspective from which to cross-sell services.
- Attract additional accounts from customers who will switch from competitors who do not offer such services.
- Obtain a flow of income from hourly fees, fees as a percentage of assets managed, and commissions.
- Establish a reputation as a financial specialist interested in identifying customer needs and responding with objective solutions to fulfill those needs.

In a recent survey of medical professionals in one market area, over two-thirds said they were dissatisfied with their current financial institution and would switch to a different one if it offered more personal and comprehensive services, of which financial planning was considered an essential element.[5] A Pfp program was test-marketed, and interviews were conducted to elicit public reaction. The results strongly indicated that

- The consuming public prefers bankers to provide Pfp services, and that preference is very clear.
- Product introduction should start with financial organization and planning, with actual investment advice coming later.
- The service necessary to meet customer needs can be provided with limited training of existing bankers and trust officers.

---

[5]Michael T. Higgins, "Personal Financial Planning Is Not Just a Product," *Bank Marketing,* March 1986, pp. 32–34.

- The level of skill and sophistication demanded of Pfp officers parallels the customers' perceived needs for those services. That is, bankers can be trained to meet the current Pfp expectations and grow in that skill as the public's demands for more sophisticated advice evolves.

In short, the public wants Pfp, and customers are going to buy it. The question is, from whom? Who is going to identify their customer needs?

Banks and thrifts have the significant advantage of being perceived as more trustworthy and less self-serving than other vendors. For example, customers realize that Pfp services provided by insurance agents are mainly designed to sell insurance; brokers' programs are mainly designed to sell securities; and tax shelter programs are mainly designed to sell tax shelters. As part of their service as a Pfp consultant, banks may end up referring customers to other suppliers, but this is certainly preferable to ignoring a need and foregoing an opportunity to forge a strong, profitable relationship with the customer. Skeptics will conclude that Pfp will drive their customers to competing nonbanks. *Informed bankers will conclude Pfp will drive their customers to stronger and more significant long-term profitable relationships with their market-driven bank.*

CREATING PERSONAL FINANCIAL PLANNING SERVICES

The first step before offering Pfp services is to develop general objectives and create a strategic game plan to achieve the objectives. General objectives might include

- Penetrating a certain percentage of a target market or markets.
- Acquiring new customers.
- Creating more profitable relationships and serving the needs of the more affluent customers.
- Developing a new source of fee income.
- Emphasizing relationship banking by increasing a specified number of services currently being used by each Pfp client.

- Positioning your institution to become a leader in developing and providing contemporary financial services.

The potential market for Pfp services can be subdivided into four groups: (1) consumers currently being served by your bank or thrift; (2) consumers served by other financial institutions who are dissatisfied with their present relationships or who desire more extensive services; (3) corporate customers of your bank or thrift; and (4) corporate customers who are dissatisfied with or underserved by their present banks or thrifts.

The most effective method of identifying promising candidates already served by your own institution is to refer to a customer information file (CIF) or existing priority customer list. If neither is available, a good place to start is to identify the 20 percent of your current trust and retail customers who provide 80 percent of your business volume and profitability.

Exercise caution, however, in using other methods to identify your priority customers. Too often, bankers assume that a listing of customers with accounts having a $25,000 minimum deposit is sufficiently discriminating. This approach inadvertently excludes priority customers who have opened a large number of small investment accounts rather than a small number of large accounts. It also misses customers who have only a secondary relationship with your organization; such customers may have their money scattered among many financial service providers. The extra effort it takes to identify these important exceptions is more than worth the investment. Not only will it ensure that the top 20 percent have been identified, but it also detects those customers who are prime candidates for cross-selling the benefits of accounts consolidation.

One good system for identifying potential Pfp users is to list all accounts by type of account, followed by a cross-tabulation of potential clients' names. A referral program within the institution can also be very effective. The accounts can be divided up and assigned to account officers, whose responsibility is to determine what Pfp services his or her assigned customers might need. Each officer then submits a referral list of priority customers. All referrals are coordinated, and a schedule is developed for approaching the priority customers and introducing them to the advantages of Pfp services.

Consumers who do not currently have a financial relationship with your institution are another good source of prospects. Although tapping this clientele requires a concerted marketing effort, the potential reward for acquiring a new client relationship is well worth the effort. The availability or unavailability of Pfp services will be the catalyst for many changes in account relationships. Your customers, as well as your competitors' customers, are extremely vulnerable to the advances of institutions wishing to attract new accounts.

As already mentioned, a recent national market research study[6] concluded that a majority of medical professionals are dissatisfied with their current financial institutions and would switch to another if offered more personalized services, including Pfp. Furthermore, another study revealed that approximately 60 percent of households that want Pfp services from a bank or thrift would switch institutions to get the service.

A primary strategy in soliciting prospective clients is to target a specific market segment rather than scatter your efforts over an entire market. That is, the emphasis should be on selectively pursuing a limited number of prospects rather than on mass solicitation. Accordingly, you should identify and rank by priority those individuals who have the greatest need for Pfp services and who are most likely to switch to your bank for the purpose of establishing a Pfp account relationship.

Banks have an excellent opportunity to attract corporate customers by offering, for example, Pfp services as a "perk" or fringe benefit for upper- or middle-managers. These services can differentiate your institution from your competition. Offering executive Pfp services during a sales call to a corporate customer enhances the likelihood that the call will be successful because corporate clients will perceive Pfp as representing a valuable service for a minimal corporate investment. Your institution will profit by generating additional corporate business as well as securing new executive and professional consumer accounts.

As an example of how much success Pfp services can bring to an institution, one independent national Pfp service organization sold over 400,000 plans to corporate customers. Pfp not only pro-

---

[6]Michael T. Higgins, "Personal Financial Planning Is Not Just a Product," *Bank Marketing,* March 1986, pp. 32–34.

vides a valuable perk for corporate employees, it also serves the corporation itself by describing to employees the value of their fringe benefits. That advantage alone is worth many corporations' investment in Pfp services, considering that the standard professional fee for listing and defining fringe benefits ranges between $50 and $100 per hour. Pfp services will provide a listing as a mere entree to the service. However, the service will provide an overwhelming amount of additional financial management data that will prove invaluable to the bank and the client.

The benefits of personal financial planning vary among individuals within different market segments. Identifying your target market helps you decide how to design and promote your institution's Pfp program. For example, the promotion of benefits for middle market and emerging affluent customers should focus more on income stream than on assets. Conversely, when designing and promoting Pfp services for retirees, those with inherited wealth, and the high-asset affluent, you should emphasize assets and not income stream. High-asset individuals are also attracted to such benefits as estate planning. Overall, depending on the scope of the Pfp services offered, consumers may obtain some or all of the following benefits:

- Organization of financial affairs.
- Increase in disposable income through tax reduction.
- Increase in investment income.
- Conversion of taxes into savings via various instruments.
- Increase in after-tax investment income.
- Life insurance savings plans.
- Estate planning.
- Better credit availability.
- Lower debt burden through loan restructuring or consolidation.
- Insurance evaluation.
- College financing alternatives.
- Financial peace of mind.

PERSONNEL SELECTION AND ORGANIZATION

The selection of personnel to manage and provide Pfp services is the most important decision your organization will make. You must choose employees who care, that is, those who have the most potential rather than those having title or tenure. Assertiveness, empathy, and enthusiasm are important personality traits. Employees need assertiveness to get the job done and empathy to get it done properly. Enthusiasm is necessary to ensure that all business opportunities are followed through. Any profitable financial institution has employees who fit these staffing requirements. They can be found in your new accounts area, the personal bankers department, or the trust department. They may also be currently working in the teller group, investment area, or the loan department. The Pfp organization should be staffed to meet the demands and expectations of the primary targeted markets. It can be a separate department, or it can be part of a department that handles new accounts, personal banker functions, or trust activities. The only important consideration, however, in locating your department is, "Where will the service be managed most effectively?" In other words, "What area of the bank is most sales-oriented and customer-driven?"

There have been numerous success stories that demonstrate the timeliness and viability of Pfp provided by banking organizations. For example, consider the widow who, having communicated the complexities of her husband's estate to a banker, decided to transfer her assets to the bank's Pfp project. Why did she switch financial service providers? It seems that her husband, before his death, had asked his broker friend to manage the couple's assets, which the broker did enthusiastically. His management skills earned a 4 percent return for the widow on $1,150,000 over a five-year period while churning over $200,000 in fees. The widow was savvy enough to understand how the bank's Pfp program could help her avoid such a severe drain, so she transferred the entire estate to the bank.

There is also the story of the two retired postal workers, married for over 40 years, who related to a Pfp banker how cumbersome it was to go around to all their different financial institutions to reinvest their savings. When the banker successfully "sold" them its Pfp service, they were able to consolidate more than $700,000 from over 20 financial institutions in a two-state area. Moreover, under their own personal financial plan, a retirement plan and a program to finance their grandchildren's postsecondary education were created.

As these examples suggest, Pfp is not a stand-alone product. Rather, it is a sales vehicle that just happens to generate fee income and inherently provides the seller with an unlimited amount of data from which to identify customers' needs and generate additional business. Furthermore, Pfp services build stronger client relationships.

FOCUS GROUPS AS A MEANS OF IDENTIFYING CORPORATE NEEDS

Just as Pfp programs provide banks with a professional and accurate technique for defining consumer needs, focus group sessions are capable of defining accurately and professionally the needs of explicit market segments. Focus groups are particularly suited to identifying and confirming the needs, wants, and priorities of potential corporate customers. Of course, focus groups can be supportive in the consumer needs identification process as well. However, our experience has been that focus group analysis is most effective and expedient in defining corporate needs.

The techniques used in focus group analysis need not be so comprehensive or complex as to be impractical. For a corporate focus group, the first step is to identify representatives of people in the business environment who share similar needs and then to choose participants who are not reluctant to verbalize their preferences, priorities, and observations and to offer constructive criticism.

Focus group sessions can be facilitiated by outside specialists or by insiders who have some experience with the technique. We find both approaches to be beneficial, although our experience is that commercial focus groups tend to be more effective if handled by an inside banking officer. Accordingly, outside facilitators should probably be used only when the inside moderator is reluctant to play the role. The focus group discussion among corporate representatives is relevant to their day-to-day decision-making, so they are typically enthusiastic about expressing their opinions on how the bank can enhance existing products and services or create new financial services to serve their corporate needs. In the case of consumer focus groups, individual customers tend to be reluctant or sometimes have difficulty articulating their wants, needs, and expectations, and therefore the reliability of their feedback is often questionable.

Whether your focus group includes members of the corporate

or consumer communities, the discussion generally yields qualitative rather than quantitative data. Therefore, the focus group's input should not be the only consideration in evaluating the feasibility or applicability of a proposal. Another and equally important caveat is that reliable market research requires the scheduling of a number of focus groups representing a specific market segment to ensure that the conclusions are not influenced by an overzealous participant. Subsequent focus group discussions will improve, and the information you glean from them will be refined as you receive inputs that either agree with or clarify the views of prior participants. Finally, in the case of corporate focus groups, it is critically important to be sure that the participants are individuals who have significant decision-making authority in their organizations and who can articulate their needs rather than simply responding to a wish list.

Focus groups can be conducted in a number of different settings. For example, a group can be scheduled to take place during a business call on a client's management team at the client's location. Also, a focus group—which, under normal circumstances, should consist of not more than 12 people—can be scheduled in a location other than the participants' offices and preferably away from the financial institution.

The prerequisites to conducting effective focus group activities include the development of a structured agenda and design of visuals to effectively communicate the concept being proposed, features and benefits, and advantages and disadvantages. A series of objective, thought-provoking questions should be created and tested before the focus group session. The moderator must remain objective and avoid being argumentative. In addition, the moderator should be coached to ensure that any preconceived ideas he or she may have are not communicated.

Often, it is helpful to schedule a luncheon before the focus group session to allow the moderator and participants to become comfortable with one another, to discuss in general the purpose of the session, and to express the organization's appreciation for their commitment and time. A modest gift for participating is sometimes appropriate and, interestingly enough, may preclude clock-watching by the participants. The invitation to attend should convey the specific commitments of time that will be expected. The moderator should be capable of keeping the discussion on track and should possess the skills necessary to prevent any one participant from dominating the discussion.

Following the focus group activity, a decision should be made on how many subsequent sessions to schedule for the purpose of confirming the most recent input. Among the considerations should be the most appropriate timing for other sessions.

Focus groups provide a proven means of identifying client needs, and they are not so complex as to be beyond the wherewithal of most banks. For those with little or no experience with focus groups, resources are readily available to launch a successful program.

CONCLUSION

In creating strategies to maximize the bank's potential and achieve beyond survival, management must begin by assuming an overall marketing perspective and choosing one or more major segments of the market on which to focus. For most banks, the choices begin with commercial services, consumer services, or a combination of both. A few banks will opt for wholesale financial services.

The next step is to identify, within those broad segments, the specific market segments on which the bank will devote its energies and resources. At this stage, the bank needs to conduct an explicit needs assessment and define internal strategies to fulfill those needs. These analytical steps are necessary to understand the investment that a particular strategy requires in terms of personnel, facilities, and systems. Only then can a decision to proceed be pursued. Since most banks choose to serve the retail or commercial markets—or a combination of the two markets—Chapters 10 and 11 deal with the critical issues bank managers will encounter. If the choice is to serve the retail consumer market, then bankers have much to learn from other industries that have previously demonstrated that they can serve the retail market successfully.

CHAPTER 10

RETAIL STRATEGIES

> There are two sides to customer service: What goes on at the customer's rational level and what goes on at the non-rational level. To date, financial institutions have dabbled in the rational needs and have not yet begun to think about the non-rational needs of consumers.
>
> —*Mike Higgins, 1988*

A number of authors and speakers have likened contemporary consumer banking to retailing, thereby aiding bankers in gaining a clearer perspective on the marketing side of their business. In response, some bankers have gone so far as to emulate successful retail operations, while others have recruited managers who have prospered in the retail industry.

Prior to entering the banking industry, this author merchandized a group of better apparel stores. The lessons that can be learned in the retail world by creative trial and error, by observing the competition, and by the industry's role models are significant. However, the most meaningful lesson I absorbed as I made my transition into the financial world was that there are many retail management techniques that have absolutely *no* application in the new world of banking.

This chapter examines the five fundamental driving forces of retailing, the decision process that retail customers go through when making purchase decisions, and customer trends that will affect retailing in the 1990s. The similarities and dissimilarities between management techniques and leadership qualities in the retailing and banking industries are also carefully scrutinized.

Banking and retailing share a number of characteristics. They both:

- Exist in the same social, economic, and technological environment.
- Provide a service.
- Must respond to the same demographic and attitudinal changes.
- Conduct business in heavily competitive fields.
- Are characterized by increasing consolidation and growing centralization.
- Have depended, in recent years, on geographic expansion as their major growth vehicle.
- Are facing various forms of alternative delivery systems.
- Are confronted with nontraditional and discount versions of themselves.
- Recognize that identifiable customer segments exist and that target marketing is required.
- Depend on a successful customer interface to prosper.

There are also key differences between banking and retailing. In general, banking services—or, at least, funds storage, safeguarding, and retrieval—are a necessity, whereas much of the services provided by retailing is an option for customers. As a result, customers are likely to visit their banks more frequently and more regularly than they visit most retailers.

For many customers, handling money and furnishing information about personal finances are very private matters. It is also highly ego-involved—banking involves a rather introverted sense of self-identification. In contrast, the purchase and use of retail goods is often highly public and involves an extraverted sense of self-identification. Like banking, retail services intensely involve the customer's ego.

Owing to both the similarities and the differences between retailing and banking, there is a great deal to be learned by bankers through a close examination of retail trends, the example provided by leading retailers, and retail consumer behavior.

THE FIVE FUNDAMENTAL DRIVING FORCES OF RETAILING

Every customer tries to satisfy five requirements when visiting a retail store: *price, product, presentation, convenience,* and *service/informational standards.* All five requirements are equally important and all must be satisfied by providers of retail and financial services. While an individual consumer exhibits a normal range of behavior across all five dimensions, his or her standards are largely determined by the particular situation. For example, a normally price-oriented customer may find himself much more concerned with service and information when buying a technical or seldom-purchased item. Or a typically, high-net-worth, quality-oriented customer may find herself purchasing large quantities of goods at discounted prices because there is little or no ego or qualitative advantage evident in one product over another.

Price

In retailing, price can be interpreted as the lowest *price* for identical products or the *best (perceived) value* for products that will perform within an acceptable range and that are offered in a manner and with a service level that is also acceptable to the consumer. It is likely that in banking interest rates and service charges are considered by customers in the "lowest price" sense, whereas the supporting services and other banking products are judged on their perceived value.

Product

Winning retail strategies often employ some form of product dominance strategy. Given their busy schedules, the proliferation of stores, and the virtual absence of store loyalty, consumers tend to shop where they are reasonably certain they will be able to find the products they seek. Product dominance can be achieved by offering a full range of products or through specialization. Dominance—that is, being thought of first by consumers as the most reliable source of a product or service—cannot be attained by dabbling in a wide array of products and services.

Presentation

Stores must exude a level of ambiance appropriate to the products and prices they are trying to sell and to the type of customers they wish to attract. In addition, specific products must be presented in a way that brings them to the customer's attention and that highlights their features and benefits. As the array of stores and products has grown, the presentation area of retailing has become very sophisticated. To differentiate products and increase market share, it is essential to respond appropriately to customer logic, a concept that will be discussed in detail later in this chapter.

Convenience

There are, of course, many examples of retail concepts built on the premise of convenience. Seven-Eleven and other so called "C" stores trade almost entirely on convenience and can, therfore, place less emphasis on price, product, and presentation than other, less convenient, retailers. Convenience, however, enters the consumer equation on every shopping trip. Is the chosen store convenient to work? To another required errand? Is it easy and quick to shop once inside? Are the hours convenient? Does it offer a full range of wanted products? Is it a one-stop shop? Is it too large for easy shopping?

The convenience element on any one particular shopping occasion depends on what information the shopper requires, the product he wants, and his familiarity with the desired category of products, as well as the amount of time he has available.

Service and Information

In a retail setting, the amount of information consumers need depends on their level of familiarity with the product sought. For example, the first-time, do-it-yourself house painter may require a great deal of information about surface preparation, prime paint, oil versus latex, trim colors, tinting, and so on. The same do-it-yourself painter may later need just one more quart of sash trim to finish the job and, on that trip, requires no additional information.

Service and information are considered together because much information comes from the store's staff and because consumers' knowledge can be enhanced through the delivery of superior information by means of signs, presentation, and audio and video devices. Discussing service and information together also reinforces my precept that selling and service are synonymous because selling is nothing more than the activity of gathering, disseminating, and agreeing on various relevant information.

THE DECISION PROCESS OF RETAIL CUSTOMERS

Customers go through four specific and identifiable steps in deciding to purchase retail products or in selecting banking services and institutions.

Step one in the customer's decision process is the *Product Need Decision.* Consumers recognize their needs or desire for a particular product, for a solution to a problem, or for the "tools" to realize an opportunity. This recognition may be sudden, such as what happens when a household appliance breaks unexpectedly, or it may be a dawning realization, such as a growing awareness that one's wardrobe is becoming outdated. The needs/wants recognition step can be accelerated or fostered through planned "interruptions" in the consumer's normal recognition procedures. The methods used to accelerate or foster the needs/wants recognition process of consumers include advertising, store window displays, special events, sales, locational convenience, and tie-in promotions, as well as more subtle events such as charity sponsorships and community participation. In addition, an emerging body of retailing practice works on the principles of consumer logic, prompting needs/wants awareness at a subconscious level. Consumer logic will be discussed in more detail later.

Step two in the decision process is the *Source of Purchase Decision.* This step involves attracting consumers to a specific product or institution by arresting their attention. In retailing, this is done with store design, signs, displays, information, service, packaging, and convenience. In arresting consumers' attention, the retailer interrupts the normal purchase cycle and inserts some new information. Essentially, the retailer says, "Stop and think. Wouldn't you really rather have a __________?"

The same tools of communication apply in banking. To use the tools effectively, it is important to clearly and precisely understand what each mechanism of interruption communicates to consumers. Multiple messages may work in concert as intended, but it is also possible that they may inadvertently cancel one another out. Each interrupter should be evaluated and the overall message orchestrated for maximum impact.

Step three is called the *Specific Product Decision.* Having attracted consumers, the seller has several techniques to help direct purchasers to a specific choice within the range offered. In retailing, interrupters that influence the decision include ease of handling, compatibility of products in a line of products, price, value, quality, delivery, after-sale services, and guarantees. Again, these same interrupters apply in banking.

A relevant question at this stage of the purchase cycle is: should your product or service offer "something for everyone" or should it be targeted to a particular type of customer? To answer the question, it helps to know that most consumers find it easier to move *incrementally* among product choices than to leap from one possibility to another. In retailing, for example, it is easier to move a customer up one price point on an item than to persuade him or her to jump from budget items to high-quality items, bypassing moderately priced goods. This is why department stores are departmentalized by price and fashion as well as by product category.

The most successful banks will become department stores of financial services, not only departmentalized by product category but also by price/value and possibly fashion (risk) level. Obviously, successful specialty stores/boutique banks need to target a narrow audience and compete with a single or limited number of areas that are part of a department store/full-service bank. For example, a private bank that caters to affluent customers typically competes with the trust and personal banking departments of a full-service bank. In many cases, branches of full-service banks would become much more successful if they were designed to provide specialty or boutique bank services targeted at explicit market segments in the immediate target area.

Step four in the consumer's decision process is the *Performance Decision.* Having prompted a need recognition and interrupted the purchase cycle at both the source of purchase decision and specific product decision steps, the retailer must be able to deliver the implied promise of those earlier efforts. Do you have in stock or ready for delivery what was promised? Does it perform as promised? Does it have the effect of making the customer want to return for that or related products? The seller's success in the final step not only influences individual customers but also, through word of mouth, the entire community. Further, the positive result at the final step can be amplified through a postdecision advertising campaign, which not only informs potential customers of the seller's delivery capability but also reinforces the confidence current customers have in the institution.

KEY CONSUMER TRENDS

Several key trends will affect retailing and retail banking in the 1990s. Banking institutions must be prepared to develop aggressive but flexible marketing programs to respond appropriately. The trends include demographic and attitudinal considerations. Obviously economic trends are paramount in banking and in retailing as well, but these are already well-tracked and usually of a shorter duration than are demographic or attitudinal trends.

Demographic Trends

It is beyond the scope of this book to identify and evaluate all the key demographic trends. Rather, it is the purpose here to challenge conventional wisdom about the observation of and response to demographic trends. Most demographic "wisdom" is based on averages and national trends. An aging population, migration to the Sunbelt, and marriages later in life are all examples of demographic phenomena identified through data analysis.

A careful analyst, though, assesses demographic data by looking behind the numbers for meanings. Does an increase in the number of later marriages mean that everyone, everywhere is marrying later, or does it mean that people on the East and West coasts are marrying later, while those in the Midwest and South have not changed their pattern? Does it mean that some couples are marrying much later, while the majority marry at about the same age as did their parents? The rapid movement from blue-collar to white-collar jobs would, at first glance, suggest that more highly paid, executive-level jobs exist. In fact, a large number of white-collar workers are simply doing routine work in an electronic age that requires a white-collar and pays less than a blue-collar job. Many "office" workers are, in fact, machine operators. Other demographic data that must be examined carefully by retailers and bankers include working women, income trends, multiple incomes, proportion of population in each age group, education, mobility, and birth rates.

Above all, beware of journalistic conclusions drawn from superficial observations of demographic data. For example, the great yuppie hoax of the mid-1980s would have readers believe that all baby boomers (those born between 1946 and 1964) were yuppies—Young Upwardly Mobile Professionals. The truth is that such "yuppies" account for only about 10 percent of the baby boom population and, thus, less than 5 percent of the total population. Yet they dominated the media characterization of baby boomers for several years.

Attitudinal Trends

Just as it is beyond the scope of this book to discuss readily available demographics, it is also not possible to identify and evaluate here the many social trends that have affected retailing in recent years. These changes in attitudes are well-documented in both the popular press and in academic writings and include such things as the emphasis people now put on their health and appearance, the attractions of a simpler life, and the tendency toward self-indulgence. Retailers and bankers both must understand and adjust to attitudinal trends if they are to successfully promote and sell their products and services over time.

Intrinsic Value Recognition

The characteristics behind the success of McDonald's is consistency and known value. This is achieved by quickly cooking and serving an adequate hamburger that the customer knows will be uniform in quality from visit to visit and from restaurant to restaurant. Costs are kept down; the customers are pleased; and a reasonable unit profit is made.

The purpose of consistency and known value in retailing is to create a more efficient distribution system. Unfortunately, however, these attributes also create some negative side-effects, for example, limited choice of product, sameness, and, ultimately, boredom. This has led to what some call the "plasticization" of America and of American tastes.

There is a growing backlash to uniformity and boredom among consumers. People who grew up in the mass culture now want things to be different. They seek personalization through *differentiation.* People—now more reluctant to merge into the mass of society—wish instead to emphasize their uniqueness. This does not mean that they shun mass market retailing. It simply means that they increasingly are seeking relief from highly predictable and often boring product and service offerings.

This shift is based on some fundamental changes in customer values. In general, consumers are moving from a willingness to be led by authorities to a longing for independence; from a desire for quantity to a desire for quality; and from community orientation to self-orientation. The maturing of the population will intensify these shifts and tend to cause consumers to "divisionalize." This means that some products and services will continue to be sought for a price, while others will be set apart by consumers and held up to a standard of quality and service. This, in turn, will cause consumers to reject authority and make product and store decisions based on their perception of intrinsic quality in goods and in quality of service.

The desire for greater clarity in intrinsic values in products and services is spurred, in part, by a higher level of consumer knowledge. The increase in consumer knowledge is attributable to better education, better communications, a belief in consumer rights, and the emergence of a more mature and experienced consumer base. Retailers themselves have accelerated the process through the proliferation of self-serve retailing, beginning with supermarkets and now including fast foods, gasoline stations, and automated teller machines (ATMs).

Sense of Adventure

Among many consumers, a growing sense of adventure comes as a reaction to traditional and parochial values. An increasing number of consumers, going beyond differentiating themselves, now try to stay one step ahead of others by discovering new goods, new services, and new ways of doing things. The old attitude that shopping itself is fun is no longer prevalent; however, the discovery of new shops as well as new products and services can support the consumer's desire for adventure. Further, new and better ways of conducting the business of life, from dry cleaning through lawn care to banking and money management, are sought by time-pressed and hurried consumers.

A grocery shopper may go to a specialty food store to look for guest or party foods or unusual spices or herbs. Open to new products and ideas, this shopper is more likely to disregard convenience and price for exotic, high-quality foods such as imported cheeses and coffee beans, specialty packaged foods, gourmet vegetables, and special cuts of meat. Ideally, the store is fun to shop in and provides surprises and "something different" for the adventurous shopper. The same shopper may purchase more mundane food items at a warehouse type outlet or other "price-promise" outlet to satisfy price desires, and the same customer might occasionally pick up a few items at a convenience store. Nevertheless, the shopper also enjoys the adventure of occasionally visiting a specialty store.

The sense of adventure is often communicated, not by the product or service itself but by the end use that will be made of the product or service or by the setting in which it is sold. An adventurous shopper might buy a $2 ice cream cone if it is sold on a terrace that overlooks crowds of fashionable people listening to a jazz band or watching yachts docked in a harbor. The same person wouldn't dream of paying $2 a dip at the neighborhood dairy store, and he or she might not buy an ice cream cone at all in an everyday setting. *Adventurous shoppers are willing to pay more for goods and services if the environment in which they make their purchase fosters a feeling of escape from the routine.*

Using bank services can be an adventure too, as long as the ultimate benefits of the service are communicated. For example, if a vacation savings program is promoted in terms of the vacation and not just the savings program, the customer is likely to enjoy opening an account. The adventure must be easy and fun for the customer—he or she must view it as choosing a service that enhances personal life-style, not as choosing among complex systems that benefit the bank. Obviously, the "adventure" must be relevant to the consumer, and it must be believable.

Banking services are deemed by consumers as very important and, often, very personal. For the most part, however, banks primarily provide only support services. In most cases, consumers take little or no pleasure from the functions a bank can provide, although they may well enjoy the *results* of those services.

Interest in Activities Rather than in Acquisition

Closely related to an adventure orientation is the shift in consumers' focus from acquisition to activity. What motivates the consumer's decision to purchase has changed—from needs to desires and now to style. The current interest in life-style places more emphasis on the activity an item allows the consumer to experience than on the item itself. As a result, an appeal must be made on the part of retailers to the activity in peoples' lives. *A simple focus on merchandise itself is too limiting.* In a parallel manner, the activities that a banking service can facilitate are more appealing to contemporary consumers than are the services themselves.

Today's consumers do not buy imported food processors, foreign cars, handmade dinnerware, or video cassette recorders because they think they actually need any of these items. They buy the *use* of the objects, in effect, the experience the object allows them to have, whether it be preparing gourmet food, doing some serious road driving, impressing dinner guests, or being entertained. Consumers believe these experiences will help realize or facilitate an actual or desired style of living.

Just as more and more money will continue to be spent on services such as travel, adult education, and food eaten away from home, the goods that will increasingly gain in popularity will mostly involve activity, for example, sporting equipment, cookware, and nonfiction/how-to books. Likewise, more money will be spent by consumers on banking services that free them from the routine duties of everyday life and allow them to participate in fulfilling activities or allow them the peace of mind that comes with resolving their anxieties about financial stability and attaining their hopes and dreams for the future.

Desire for Superior Service Quality

A growing change among consumers is their shift away from being placid, accepting, and loyal to being unforgiving, demanding, and easily straying. The greater importance placed on intrinsic value, plus a higher level of knowledge among consumers, has created a need for a fine-tuned, no-mistakes product or service delivery operation. In today's highly competitive marketplace, there may be no second chance.

Consumer loyalty and acceptance are eroding as a result of the dissatisfaction consumers continue to experience when dealing with virtually all kinds of service organizations. This growing level of dissatisfaction arises partly because of diminished delivery systems and partly because of the higher standards demanded by consumers. Higher standards are the key; higher standards established by the all too few retailers who care enough to ensure service quality.

Time-pressed consumers, when confronted with long or slow-moving lines, difficulty in understanding programs, employees who are rude or unconcerned, and what is perceived as false advertising, most likely will go to another institution rather than put up with such imperfections in the old one. However, as competition forces further refinements in operating procedures and services offered, consumers will defect for even less cause than true dissatisfaction. Further, as more unique offers arrive on the scene, even long-term consumers may be lured away.

Life has become complex. There are new machines to learn how to operate, computers to program, automobiles that are complicated to repair, highways and interchanges that are confusing, phone bills that are indecipherable by many people, and a multitude of other complexities. The last thing consumers want is a complex and confusing banking transaction or procedure. Customers welcome any system or procedure that is refreshingly easy.

The clear implication for bankers of this "longing for a simpler life" is that operations should be simplified, at least from the point of view of the consumer, as much as possible. The simplification must reach not only the queuing system and the account statements, but the counter and platform arrangement and decor, as well as the placement of ATMs—everything should be done for the customer's benefit. Services should be easy to understand, logically presented, and presented in a way that helps consumers choose among them. Hours should be as uniform as possible throughout the week. Policies should be simple, easily understood, and minimal.

Today's self-confident consumers want to have a voice in their service selection and in their actual transactions—an attitude that has led to their preference for efficiency, better value, and control.

In retailing, these preferences have given rise to self-service operations. At the same time, there is a more recent back-swing toward a desire for full-service, luxury operations in certain situations. The preference for self-service or full-service largely depends on the type of product or service involved; that is, full-service is most likely to be a desired feature in all types of adventure shopping, whereas self-service will probably continue to hold strong appeal in most other types of shopping. Banking services are mostly thought of as commodities, meaning that they simply support other activities; however, some can be considered in the adventure category, meaning that they facilitate the activities and aspirations of the consumer. Commodities are best sold in a minimalist style with maximum efficiency, whereas adventures must be "romanced."

Demand for Efficiency

Similar to the desire for superior service, the demand for efficiency in retail and banking operations is fast becoming a foundation to continuing success. Two-income families, with no extra time for relaxed shopping or browsing for fun, will not tolerate a slow or inefficient operation, nor will they bank with an institution that wastes their time (any more than they would with one that wastes their money).

Time-conscious customers will not exchange "unedited" broad assortments of products and services for time. Instead, they will find the stores that have "edited" their assortments down to the things they want, so that they can quickly buy the goods and services they need. It is not unlikely that these same consumers are seeking "edited" banking services; that is, they seek out banks that understand their needs and offer superior services that meet those needs—and only those needs. An efficiently run operation that offers selected services, which can be put together in various ways according to a particular customer's needs, will save time and keep the customer happy and returning.

Willingness on the Part of Buyers To Perform Seller's Role

A major trend in retailing has been the shift of functions from retailers to consumers. The first great change from full-service to self-service was the conversion of the grocery store to the supermarket.

Through supermarkets, retailers trained consumers to select, assemble, and transport their own orders. Now the customer goes through the store with a cart and does most of the work. In so-called warehouse stores, customers go one step further, bagging their own groceries, often with a bag or box they have brought from home. In a short time, customers will probably check out their own orders using scanners. In many supermarkets, driver-salesmen stock the shelves. Thus, many functions of the old grocery store have been shifted forward to the customer and back to the supplier. The retailer offers a meeting place for supplier and customer. As an attraction, food retailers may offer high levels of service on selected categories of goods such as in a delicatessen, bakery, and butcher shop.

Since the advent of the supermarket, we have witnessed an increasing number of self-service operations. Dominating the "food-away-from-home" business are fast food restaurants, where the customer stands in line to place his order at the counter and carry his own food to the table. Curiously, many, if not most, fast-food restaurant customers bus their own tables as well. If customers choose a salad or a "Sunday Brunch," they happily assemble their own order. Service stations offer self-service, credit card–driven pumps, which are popular for speed of service as well as reduced price.

In the banking industry, ATMs are another self-service operation offering 24-hour banking privileges. There are, in addition, other services that could be shifted to the consumer or to "suppliers." Banks can conceivably also become meeting places for consumers and financial services.

Some consumers have never experienced full service in retail banking. They are ripe for an introduction in selected categories and situations. However, when functions are shifted to consumers, they may well be thinking,"Okay, I will serve myself. I will bus my own table, assemble my own order, pump my own gas, be my own teller, but only in exchange for something else: lower prices or rates, faster service, better selection, more efficiency, and more convenient hours."

There is, of course, strong evidence that, given something of value in exchange for fewer services, many customers not only are willing but prefer to perform certain services themselves. The two main reasons for preferring self-service to full-service operations are time saved and more perceived control over the transaction. This is the age of the involved, independent, and time-pressed customer. However, there are occasions in which the customer wants full, gracious, and informed service. In effect a bimodal demand is emerging. On one hand, a willingness to perform traditional functions is pervasive; on the other hand, an appreciation of truly good, full service continues. There is no profitable market for inadequate, self-delivered service.

Need for Information

Modern consumers have become more self-confident than consumers of the past. The combination of good communications available through radio and television and a higher percentage of the American population able to read means that more information about products, stores, and services is available to consumers. Moreover, more aggressive laws have been designed to protect consumers and give them the right to obtain product and service information. Consumers have become legislatively enabled, and through "Nadarization," their consciousness has been raised. Informed consumers become self-confident shoppers.

Self-confident consumers, used to receiving clear information about products and services from suppliers as well as from the media, expect good, simple, plainly expressed information. Small print, gimmicks or other tricks are not tolerated by many consumers anymore. Self-service and partial self-service operations are enjoying widespread popularity among shoppers, in large part because consumers believe they are more capable of controlling the transaction (be it gas, fast food, self-serve banking, or whatever).

There must be knowledge on at least one side of the counter. Increasingly, it is the customer who knows most clearly what he wants and what products or services a store or bank offers. It is not uncommon, in fact, for the customer to know more about a product or a service than the person offering it to him. Because of this unwelcome functional shift, a retail operation or bank that goes out of its way to hire knowledgeable, interested employees able to tell the customer something about the service that he does not already know will find greater favor among the new breed of demanding, self-confident, educated, well-informed consumers. Providing honest information at the point-of-sale or through take-away materials reinforces an even more positive response from the consuming public.

These trends and attitudinal factors are the underlying forces behind the formation of a multitude of consumer clusters or groups. Clearly the differences between "consumer groups" outweigh the similarities. Furthermore, the environment today presents consumers with many, many options. While we can predict with accuracy the outcome of certain, one-dimensional, fixed-choice situations, such as election results, it is far more difficult to predict the behavior of consumer segments. Clearly, marketers must move beyond using simple demographic and attitudinal profiles to develop a competitive advantage in today's marketplace.

BEYOND SIMPLE DEMOGRAPHIC AND ATTITUDINAL PROFILES

There are two dimensions to customer expectations: what goes on at the customer's rational level and what goes on at the nonrational level. Traditional retailers and bankers have been successful in understanding and predicting the *rational* needs of consumers (products and services), while only dabbling in the mysteries of (and attempting to second guess) the *nonrational* needs of consumers.

On the rational level, a bank may understand the types of financial services their customers want and how they want them delivered in terms of banking hours, drive-up windows, ATMs, and so on. On the other hand, there seems to be no way to predict what makes a customer change banks or shop the "competition" or what motivates a customer to look into a financial service never tried before. Such behavior might be considered nonrational on the part of the customer, and there seems to be no way of knowing why, when, or under what circumstances such deviations occur. Yet, of course, they do happen. Customers who have been loyal do change loyalties; customers who tend to use a bank for the same services for years do seek out a service that is different or unique; and customers who tend to use a bank for one purpose do change banks and use it for their other needs.

If it were possible to identify, analyze, and understand the nonrational behaviors of customers, bankers would be able to introduce strategically more effective motivations to which customers could be responsive. That is, it would be possible to reach customers, not just with the "right merchandise at the right time and the right place and the right price" but to get them to come back more often and acquire more banking services for reasons that *defy* logic, enticing them to use services regardless of price or place or even product.

Information that would allow the banker to appeal to the "nonrational reasons" for buying would be incredibly helpful, for it seems that the *real* basis for consumer purchases is *far* from logical. Why else do people spend (on average in the United States today) $13,000 for a car and $100,000 on a house, when basic transportation and housing can be had for much less? The same is true for financial services.

CONSUMER LOGIC

The value of understanding nonrational needs (or what we will refer to as consumer logic) lies in the fact that a very tight retail market exists in the United States today. Any retailer, including a bank, without a competitive edge of some kind is a company that is heading for problems. All bankers have sought a competitive edge in the areas of product, place, price, or promotion, and few can afford to offer more expensive, traditional services. In today's market, however, that is not enough. Something more is required to provide that competitive edge. The concept of consumer logic provides insights into offering services with a competitive edge, that is, customer service with some strategic and tactical advantages.

Nonrational services that appeal to customers' nonrational level, if appropriately applied, typically

- Cost no more than current services (that is, it is more a matter of *how* you offer the services than what services you offer).
- Make current services more appealing to both customers and noncustomers (more people come in, they stay longer, and they buy more).
- Are hard for the competition to copy since they involve structured changes at a subconscious or nonrational level and are not obvious to consumers or competitors at the conscious level (the strategies work, but no one outside the company knows why; the competition cannot successfully duplicate them, and, therefore, strategic *differentiation* is realized,

which is the very essence of strategic marketing in a competitive environment.

Most bankers, like most retailers, know (or can find out through traditional research methods) what their customers need in the way of tangible products and services. Therefore, we will focus on something fewer bankers have a grasp of: how to provide nonrational services. The information has been gathered from three years of studying consumer logic. What we have learned from retailers can be applied more specifically to bankers.

The observations and conclusions are divided into sections covering the three basic areas of selling services:

- Attention, or how to be noticed by the customer at the nonrational level.
- Benefit, or how to appeal to the customer's nonrational interests.
- Convincer, or how to motivate the customer to buy at the nonrational level.

Attention

Three aspects of getting the customer's attention work at the nonrational level: (1) sensory preference, (2) level of detail, and (3) degree of change.

Sensory Preference

All of us gather information selectively. We may pay more attention to visual information, auditory information, information that we read, or information we obtain from touching or handling an object—that is, through our senses. It is important when communicating to customers that you do so through all four sensory modes, thereby ensuring that you reach all customers. Whatever you put in writing, also *tell* the same story graphically. Let your people know how to say it in words and, ideally, have something for them to give customers—something the customer can actually handle (for example, ask the customer to sign something, hand the customer a booklet, and so forth).

Note that, for both practical and psychological reasons, it is important to separate out what we *see* and what we *read*, as two different sensory modes. We handle visual and symbolic information (that is, letters formed into words and sentences) differently in our brains. "Seeing" is a nonlinear sensory mode—we see everything in a picture all at once. Reading, on the other hand, is linear—we read one word at a time. People who are very "visual" are not necessarily readers, and vice versa.

While it is safest to communicate through all four sensory channels, if you can also find out which is the preferred mode of a majority of your customers, you can stress that mode as a way to get the most attention from the most customers. For example, if the preferred mode is visual, the following rules of thumb apply in advertising:

- *Photographs versus line drawings.* A photograph rather than a line drawing makes any product more realistic, which is more compelling to the visual customer.
- *Color versus black and white.* Again, pictures in color are more "real" than black and white.
- *Larger versus smaller.* The larger the picture, the more compelling it is to the visual person. We hear the phrase "big as life," and the bigger the picture (which includes close-ups and photographic blow-ups), the more life-like it appears.
- *"Event" settings.* Pictures showing the product as part of a typical event that is real in the minds of customers are effective for visually oriented people. Several levels of effectiveness can be attained when showing financial products or services to be visually "real":

  —At the least effective visual level are ad pictures that show just the products. The rationale is that shoppers can identify with items.

  —At a more effective visual level are ad pictures that show products in use (for example, pictures of models using the financial service or reaping its rewards).

  —At the most effective level are ad pictures that show products in use in an appropriate *setting* (for example, a business meeting at which the service is being discussed).

In bank layout and design, visually oriented customers respond well to the following:

- *Angled displays* that face the customers as they walk by are more visually attractive than displays the customers approach at a 90-degree angle. In other words, the more a display reaches a customer face-on, the more compelling it is visually.

- *Contrasts.* The use of contrasts has a wide variety of applications, whether it is achieved through color contrasts in display or signs, contrasts in display heights, or contrasts in flooring to set off clearly defined departments.

Other techniques exist to appeal to customers' other sensory modes. For example, Hear/Read/Do displays or literature appeal to the sense of touch. When attempting to cater to the sensory preferences of customers, bankers often obtain assistance and advice from various types of creative services. The main thing to remember is that any or all of the four sensory modes can be stressed in both advertising and bank layout and design.

Level of Detail

Getting customers' attention at a nonrational level requires introducing them to your offer at a level of information detail with which they are most comfortable. Suppose two people are shopping for a watch and they want to know how it works. One of the two prefers a general level of detail and so may want to know only whether the watch is battery-operated or stem-wound. The other person, who prefers a more detailed level of information, may want to know much more about the product: Does it have a tuning fork or crystal driver for a battery watch? How many jewels does it contain if it has a wind-up mechanism?

Applying this concept to banking services, we know that some customers need a lot of detail about what the bank has to offer; others want only the "big picture." The bank's promotions should be designed to accommodate both preferences for level of detail. For example, a product pamphlet should provide a general overall introduction followed by the details. A table of contents and the use of headings within the body of the pamphlet allow people to decide how much detail they want to absorb.

When describing a service verbally, it is important to "sound out" the customer to find out how much he or she wants to know about a service, and then communicate the information only at the level of detail he or she appears to want. This requires being sensitive to cues from customers that indicate whether they continue to be interested. Knowing what the customer wants to know about a service is the first and most important step in identifying customer needs.

An example from retailing may help to make the point. A pharmacy chain on the West Coast needed something to bring in increased traffic. The stores were dealing with heavy competition and were not meeting it very effectively. The new owners decided to take advantage of a series of opportune buys to obtain gift items, seasonal goods, and imported packaged food products. The idea was to devote the front center section of the store to a number of tiered tables, crowning the area with huge banners announcing, "Everything on our Center Stage, 50-70% off." A great deal of time and effort went into rearranging the stores to open up the space for the new merchandise. In addition, the chain undertook a massive advertising campaign offering "Center Stage Merchandise." Because the items changed from week to week, it was not possible to detail the offer in the ads and not all the stores had the same items.

The program was a flop. It was a mystery to management why the products did not sell since they were of excellent quality in most cases and were priced at truly deep discounts. To save the Center Stage campaign, the company took a profile of the customers' nonrational needs. It found that most customers, when shopping in the pharmacy, were attracted to small pieces of information and not "big picture" concepts.

The Center Stage idea, with its generalized banners, did not tell the shoppers enough detail to get their attention. They did not want to see tables piled with "stuff." Instead, they wanted some indication of the subcategories, an idea of the old prices versus the new prices, and information about how long the special promotion would continue. None of this was clear. With its newfound insight, the company created subdepartments (gifts, food, seasonal, and so on) in the Center Stage area, and marked each item to show the original price and the new price. Signs and advertising let the customers know that the promotion was an ongoing feature of the store. Customers started moving into and through the Center Stage area, rather than around it, and they began to buy the merchandise. Apparently, they simply needed more *detail* to feel comfortable trying out the new department.

The concept of level of detail applies to banking as well as to retailing. The following pointers will help you use level of detail preferences to your bank's advantage:

- *Signs.* By comparing the signs in your bank, determine whether some of them present a lot of information and some only a little. Ask yourself whether they should be more uniform and whether different services call for more or less detail.
- *Departmentalization.* Are some departments in your bank huge and some small? Should some big departments be divided into subdepartments or should the smaller departments be consolidated to help them achieve more visibility? Consider the case of an apparel chain with small (2,000 sq. ft.) stores, each of which had tiny accessory displays throughout the stores containing such items as belts, jewelry, shoes, hats, and scarves. The accessory displays had nowhere near the impact of a full-fledged department, such as the Junior, Misses, and Women's departments. To bolster accessory sales, an accessory department was organized from the bits and pieces of accessory displays around the store. This organization matched the customers' preference for detail and made it easier to sell add-ons. The lesson for banks is that they should consider the size of a department when trying to respond to customers' preferences for level of detail.
- *Advertising.* In your bank's ads, are there too many small items of information and no expression of an overall concept? Do too many of the ads convey one big idea but provide insufficient detail to help potential customers determine whether they are interested in a particular product or service? By studying your advertising from the perspective of level of detail, it is possible to improve the attention-getting power of your bank's promotional efforts.

Degree of Change Over Time

The degree of change that an institution undergoes varies. It used to be that banks changed their services very infrequently. In more recent years, however, many banks have begun to alter their image, with some banks still considered conservative but others becoming quite progressive. Much of a bank's progressive image stems from how often it changes its services, advertising theme, interior decor, and so on. Banks need to study how fast they should change their image, products, and services to match the preferences of targeted customers.

From a traditional retailing point of view, a clothing store selling to junior-sized women needs major new fashion items in the store every *week.* Change is important to customers who shop for this category of clothing. The very same customer, shopping in a grocery store, does not want such frequent change. If the brand of milk or butter or cheese were changed weekly, she would shop somewhere else. Such change would be frustrating. Finding the appropriate degree of change is an essential aspect of getting the customers' attention. How to determine that appropriate degree of change for bank customers will be explained later in this chapter.

There are typically three types of customers if you categorize them according to the amount of change with which they feel comfortable. Each group likes to be communicated to with a different "language." Some examples:

- With regard to *Sameness* customers, it is important to talk about a new service as having the *same* qualities they have always counted on and to discuss the ways that the new service is like the old one. To appeal to this type of customer, an insurance agent might say, "This Universal life policy is *just like* the old Whole Life policy, *and* you can determine how much of it will be insurance and how much will be savings."
- On the other hand, when dealing with *Sameness with Exceptions* customers, salespeople are apt to make them feel most comfortable when they point out how the new product is the same but better than the old product. Our agent might say to this customer, "This is just like the old one, *except* . . . ," and then introduce a new feature. That is, "This Universal life policy is just like the old Whole Life policy *except* you can determine how much of it will be insurance and how much will be savings."
- When encountering *Difference* customers, it is important to focus on the new features and how the product is the latest or most unique of its kind and has become available only recently. Our agent would change the approach to this type of customer and say, "Universal Life is a *totally new concept—unique* to the financial field."

Generally, bank customers tend to like "sameness language," but a few like "sameness with exception" or "difference" language.

Using the right language makes the bank's customers feel more comfortable and, thus, more apt to buy products and services. Therefore, it is important to train bank personnel to listen to customers with an ear to determining whether they tend to talk about things remaining the same, things changing a bit "to keep up with the times," or things being new or unique and different. It is then possible to use the most appropriate words in conversations, ads, and promotional materials. A message can be delivered in any of the three ways, but it is most powerful when the customers' preferences for degree of change over time are taken into account.

Benefits

Benefits is the second area of consumer logic that must be understood if a seller wishes to appeal to the customer's nonrational interests. There are three factors that contribute to a customer's nonrational sense that he or she can benefit by conducting business at a particular bank:

- Speed of services
- Degree of routine/choice
- Banking orientation

Speed of Services

The first benefit customers perceive at a nonrational level concerns the "pace" of an establishment. There is a Korean delicatessen on 34th Street in New York City that offers a streamlined "salad bar format," with over 100 varieties of foods, ranging from traditional, to ethnic, to exotic. The food is all delivered self-service and sold strictly by weight. The deli is geared to quality and quantity—and quickness. One does not feel rushed when eating there, but one does not tarry over the selection either.

By contrast, a fine jewelry store or an old and respected bank would, comparatively, seem to move at a glacial speed. Yet this is what most customers want of these types of establishments. To understand the appropriate speed preferred by your customer base is to understand a nonrational benefit your customers need.

Note, however, that the desirable speed can change with the service being offered. Most bank customers, once they step up to the teller window, want the transaction to be swift. On the other hand, customers working out the arrangements for a loan may want things to move more slowly so that their personal situation can be thoroughly understood. Trust arrangements usually need to take place with even less speed, because of the sensitive nature and complexity of the relationship. Decide how fast or how slow various services need to move, and make sure that the pace is understood and met in terms of customer needs.

Those who work with the public can be trained to observe and match the speed preferences of individual customers. Some businesses are naturally fast-paced. For instance, a valet parking attendant at a hotel or airport or the mall gets the biggest tips if he hustles. This is because his customers prefer to be taken care of quickly. In contrast, salespeople in optical shops do best when they allow customers to take ample time to choose new frames for glasses. Customers prefer not to be hurried when their appearance or other personal matters are affected by their purchase decision.

Most retail establishments, including banks, have to work with a wide range of customer speed preferences. Some people are in a hurry, and some people want to take their time. This important difference in preferences can be mitigated by training staff people to convey the nonrational benefit that your bank is a comfortable place to do business.

In addition to matching customers' speed preferences, it is also possible to build almost instant trust and rapport by matching other subconscious behaviors of customers. Because people tend to like (and trust) people who are like themselves, the more a staff person seems to be like the customer, the more comfortable the customer becomes. For this reason, a customer-contact employee needs the personality trait of *adaptability* to be most successful. If the ways in which the staff person is like the customer also happen to be at a subliminal level, the customer feels good about the staff person but does not know why. The customer just gets a good feeling.

An additional bonus that comes from teaching customer-contact personnel to accommodate the customer's pace and/or adapt to the customer's business/social style is that, to do so, employees must focus on the *customer* instead of on themselves and instead of how they themselves look or feel. This focus on "other" rather than "self" is communicated to the customer at a nonrational level, and it "feels good" to the customer. This is a critically important skill that can be learned. When customers perceive such empathetic treatment, they tend to come back more often.

Degree of Routine/Choice

The second aspect of appealing to customer logic with regard to perceived benefits is degree of routine/choice. What does this involve? If your customers make lists, use your services "on the way" to something else, or "fill out your forms with precision," they are routine seekers or procedural shoppers who want to do the "right thing." For such customers, finding ways to involve them in procedures makes them experience your bank as a benefit rather than as a hassle. This area of benefits perception affects such areas as bank design, sales training procedures, advertising layout, and location.

Other customers are not seekers of routine. Instead, many of them like to choose among alternatives or seek ways to get around routine procedures. Such customers are happy, for example, to go out of their way to an off-beat location. They also want a great deal more services from which to choose.

It is important to have fixed procedures in a bank for security and other reasons, which is fine with procedural customers. For them, it is important to discuss the "right" way to invest their money, for example. However, for customers who like options, you need to offer several ways to invest or several loan programs. You also need to offer them options that they perceive as giving them a "special deal." Even banks can negotiate terms, and it is important to know that some customers are happy only if they can negotiate. Procedural customers do *not* want to negotiate but want to know the "correct" way of doing things. If your bank has one type of customer and not the other, it is easy. If there is a mixture, which is the case for many banks, it is important to offer both types of nonrational benefits.

Service Orientation

The third type of benefit perceived at the subconscious level is service orientation. Some customers find benefits in things (products and services) and the systems the bank use, whereas others deem more beneficial the relationships they develop ("I visited my banker today"). This person and/or thing orientation is an important consideration. Thing-oriented customers want to focus on the services they receive, and they view the banker as being there to help them through the maze—and that is all. The person-oriented customer, on the other hand, comes back because he is greeted at the bank—ideally by name—and enjoys a comraderie with tellers and officers.

The implications of this difference among customers' perceptions means that your staff might be considered "helpful" by some customers and "pushy" by others. It is important to sort out whether your bank needs to focus on a person orientation or a thing orientation. For example, small banks and/or small departments are expected to be more intimate or person-oriented. If confronted with an impersonal clerk in such an environment, customers may feel uncomfortable. The reverse can also be true when, in a large bank, a staff person gets too chummy with a customer too soon. Decide where the emphasis should be in your bank and hire and train employees to be either more thing-oriented or more people-oriented.

Convincer

Convincer is the third area of consumer logic that must be understood if a seller wishes to appeal to the customer's nonrational interests. Four nonrational factors affect the decision to use a financial service:

- Source of decision information.
- Direction of the motivation.
- Basis for decision-making.
- Final convincer.

Source of the Decision Information

Your customers may sense that they are making a good decision or they may be confident with a decision only if they know that some trustworthy source other than their own judgment makes the decision for them. In the retail world, many customers who shop at variety stores and food stores can accept the price of a product as a real bargain only if they can compare it with the price charged by other stores. Otherwise, they have absolutely no idea about value. On the other hand, other customers know immediately if an unbranded apparel item, for example, is a good deal by inspecting the seams and feeling the material. These customers do not need an outside comparison or source of advice. They just "know' whether or not they have a bargain in their hands, just as some clothes shoppers "know" an item will fit (and they are usually correct) without trying it on.

In banking services, more often than not, people tend to want bankers to tell them what they should do with their money. This is particularly true if the service is new to them. By providing the external source of the decision, bankers can actually help people make decisions.

However, if the decision is related to something a customer feels comfortable with, and he or she has made such decisions independently over the years, it is important for the banker to defer to the customer, taking the attitude that "It is your decision; we will do whatever you think best." If a suggestion is made to this type of so-called internal customer, it can be a turn-off. In reality, most customers respond amiably to a suggestion, but it is important to spot those customers who want to decide for themselves and allow them to do so. The opposite is true for so-called external customers. Telling them that they have to decide independently when they want the banker to decide what is best for them is not the right approach. Instead, making constructive recommendations is the best way to satisfy the external customer.

In a bank setting, at the close of a sale, customers are more likely to buy if they hear a statement that matches their decision source needs.

1. Internal customers respond best to a statement that lets them know that the salesperson will leave the decision up to them. This requires that the salesperson make a statement like: "What do you think? It's your decision."
2. External customers respond best when the salesperson tells them what decision to make, such as "I think you should buy this one because . . ."

If the salesperson uses approach 1 on an external customer or approach 2 on an internal customer, there is a good chance the sale will be lost! Customers who are experienced in buying a given product or service tend to be internal. That is, they know what they want when they find it. Customers who are inexperienced in buying a product tend to be external. They need guidance. Note, however, that the reverse can also be true, although it is less common.

Some banks serve only internal or only external customers, and it is possible to train staff to approach them appropriately. When it is not clear whether internal or external customers predominate, the solution is to use another approach that appeals to everyone:

3. It is possible to appeal to both internal and external customers by using a statement such as this one: "I think this product is the best one for you, but you have to decide." The customer, who may be of either type, is given both a recommendation and permission to make a decision. The internal customer hears the "you have to decide" part, while the external customer hears the "I think this is the best" part, and everybody wins.

Direction of Motivation

The second nonrational factor that helps convince a buyer to make a decision is direction of the motivation. Many customers are goal-oriented, meaning they have a "toward" motivation. The language of advertising and the benefit statement a salesperson makes about services are rendered most powerful with goal-oriented people when couched in "toward language," which indicates what the service will do for them and how it will help them fulfill a goal.

Many bankers are "toward" people, and much of the ad copy they like explains what the customer will gain or attain. Some customers, however, are not "toward" but "away-from" people. That is, their motivation does not come from what they will get, but what they will get away from; in other words, what financial problems will be solved. Knowing when to use "toward" and when to use "away-from" language can make the difference in convincing a customer whether he or she should take advantage of your financial services.

The following are examples from retailing of both "toward" and "away-from" language. Study the list and decide whether "toward" or "away-from" phrases would best appeal on a subconscious level to the customers of your bank.

Toward	***Away From***
Buy today for the best price	Buy today before prices go up
Come to where the value is	Get away from high prices
We have what you want	Solve your problems here
We offer the best	You best the others cold with us
Get the most value	Why pay more?
Small down payment	No large down payment required

To appeal to customers who have both "toward" and "away-from" needs, use phrases that contain both "toward" and "away-from" statements:

> Get the best price without the worry of poor quality
> Largest selection in town to solve your every problem
> No waiting—Immediate service
> If you don't find your size, we will order it for you

While some retail stores are mostly problem-solvers (for example, hardware stores) and some stores are mostly goal-fulfillers (for example, fine jewelry stores), the majority of retailers deal with both kinds of situations. By the same token, it behooves most banks to make "toward" and "away-from" statements together in ads and bank signs. That is, banks should offer to solve a problem in a way that gets a customer closer to some goal.

In a selling situation, staff people can be trained to ask cus tomers what they hope the product they are seeking will do for them. The customer will either give a "toward" answer or an "away-from" answer, and the salesperson will know whether to stress the goals the customer wants to achieve from the purchase or the problems that will be solved by the purchase.

How do you determine a particular customer's direction of motivation? A good way to do it is by asking questions. For example:

- A customer's "toward" answer to the question, "What do you want the insurance you're seeking to do for you?" might be something like: "Earn money in a forced savings program."

- An "away-from" answer might be more like: "Take care of my family if I can't be around."
- A combined "toward/away-from" answer might be: "Earn money without worrying about what will happen to my family when I die."

The first answer means the insurance agent should concentrate on the financial growth of the policy. The second answer tells the agent to concentrate on the security aspect of an insurance policy. The third answer indicates to the agent that the customer is interested in both financial growth and security. Armed with this information about the customer's motivation, the agent can adjust the sales call to the nonrational needs of the customer and thereby convince him or her to buy.

Basis for Decision-making

The third nonrational factor that helps convince a buyer to make a decision is the basis for decision-making. Most shoppers have a set of criteria when they seek financial services. By criteria, we do not mean product specifications, but rather a complex set of feelings that a customer needs to have about a product or service before being convinced to buy.

There is no way to know exactly what this feeling is for every customer, but interestingly, many customers who use the same bank agree on specific words that both describe *and evoke* the feeling they seek. In retailing, when shoppers of off-priced merchandise were asked what they wanted when shopping in a discount store, almost universally they used the word "bargains." However, what they buy and what they consider to be a bargain vary greatly. Again, the customer's response is defined by perceived value. If customers are convinced it is a *bargain,* they will buy. This means that such stores can use the term "bargain" in ads and in the store and be much more successful than if they used a word like "value," which may seem to mean the same thing but, in fact, does not evoke the feeling the customer seeks. The promotional verbiage used has more to do with perceived value than the literal definition of the verbiage.

Knowing the criteria words that are the basis for customers' decision-making can help close the sale at the nonrational level. A good way to tap this nonrational aspect of consumer logic is to ask your employees to list the words customers frequently use in their conversations and what words seem to evoke good feelings when they use them. Use the same words in your advertising, information booklets, and conversation with customers.

Final Convincer

The fourth nonrational factor that helps a buyer to make a decision is the final convincer. This can best be explained by means of an example from retailing. A furniture store in Miami has a reputation of closing more sales than most furniture stores. Its success is attributed to a system of "endless TOs." If the customer will not buy, the sales is turned over (TO) successively to as many salespeople as it takes until the shopper buys something. While this method can be terribly offensive (it may make the sale, but lose the customer), there is a germ of wisdom in this process. That wisdom relates to the fact that half of all shoppers in the United States, when making what they consider a difficult consumer product decision, need more than one exposure to the item before they feel convinced. Some people need two or three exposures; some people literally need five or six exposures!

Such multiple exposures can come not only from a TO method but from using the same ad over and over to convince a customer to come to your bank. It is important to know that a customer may have to come back to the bank several times before he or she is comfortable making a decision on a major investment or service. This sometimes causes problems. If the customer hears your offer and then goes to a second bank and hears its offer, the second offer becomes the second exposure. Having been exposed twice, the customer may feel comfortable enough to go ahead and ge the loan (or whatever) from the second bank. To deter this possibility when the customer is unsure, a specific second appointment should be set up to give him or her another exposure.

The concept of final convincer gives insight into why tracking referrals and developing follow-up systems are so critical. If a referral and follow-up system is lacking, customers who need a final convincing are likely to be convinced by your competition.

OVERVIEW OF CONSUMER LOGIC RESEARCH METHOD FOR A BANK CASE STUDY

Identifying which of your customers are influenced by various nonrational factors can be accomplished by a combination of strategic priorities, training, and primary research. The research project described in this case study was conducted following a strategic planning retreat. Its purpose was to identify the nonrational influences the bank could use to entice a large market segment that had been lost to more progressive competitors.

Current Situation

In 1984, the pricing strategy of the Bank was changed in an effort to strengthen its financial position. The new policy caused an unprecedented number of account closings (at the level of 1,000 per month, rather than a more normal 50 per month). The customer attrition was not, at first, viewed with alarm, because it was assumed that the accounts lost were small and unprofitable. Once the smoke cleared, however, it turned out that the pricing policy had aggravated many good customers to the degree that large numbers of the city's residents took their bank business elsewhere. Most of them never returned, even after the pricing policy was later addressed.

The new policy also resulted in a rather skewed set of market segments. This is what the Bank's market looks like:

On the retail side:

- The largest customer segment is made up of senior citizens. This segment is the envy of other area banks, which also seek the business of this clientele. The Bank is favored by older residents who have been long-term, loyal customers and who believe that the Bank can do no wrong. This, along with recent marketing programs that have provided senior citizens with services they find very desirable, has made this a large segment.

However, the Bank has not done so well with three other market segments:

- The credit union segment was one of the weakest. This is made up of people in the 25- to 45-year-old age bracket, with incomes in the $25,000 to $75,000 range—often families with children at home or in college. The Bank's limited market penetration of this segment is due, in part, to a local credit union, which provides many of the services these customers need for less. Ironically, credit union customers regularly visit one of several of the Bank's offices, but only to use ATMs that serve both institutions. They did not use the Bank's services at all.
- The upscale group was not a large part of the Bank's clientele; some stayed with the Bank, and some left when the pricing policy change was instituted.

On the commercial side:

- This end of the Bank's trade is made up primarily of small businesses in the local area. There is growth potential here; seeking out business from this group also fits the original aim of the Bank, which is to a "good citizen" of the city in which it operates.

Bank Objectives

The objectives of the Bank are to take the business to $270 million dollars in total assets through a 10 percent annual growth, along with a 15 percent return. This is a challenging objective in view of the fact that bank growth has been flat for the last 10 years. However, it is a very realistic goal if the consumer "code" can be cracked, which will convince previously loyal customers to bring their business back to the Bank.

Project Objectives

Relative to the Bank's objectives, the purpose of this project is to gather appropriate data and then to develop a strategy that will bring back a substantial segment of the customers who had taken their banking business elsewhere. Ordinarily, this would be a most difficult objective. With the approach outlined next, it is highly probable.

Approach

Traditional marketing research gathers data in terms of (1) what customers consciously tell us (the Text), (2) while discussing a specific situation (the Context)—in this case, banking services.

By adding customer logic to this methodology, we can also gather data about customers' nonrational decision-making processes. This means that, not only can we understand *what* they want *when* they are in a given situation but also *how* they need that information packaged. That is, we can understand how they think while they are (3) within a given motivational framework (the Subtext).

These data will provide us with what is often the missing link in traditional research: the key to what motivates the customer beyond the basics of price, product, promotion, and place. The approach, then, will be to use all three forms of data to understand why customers continue to stay at the Bank and what it would take to create a turnabout for those who left. This translates into the model shown in Figure 10–1. This "triangulation" approach provides the level and quality of data needed to fine-tune the Bank's existing services and

FIGURE 10–1
The Triangulation Approach

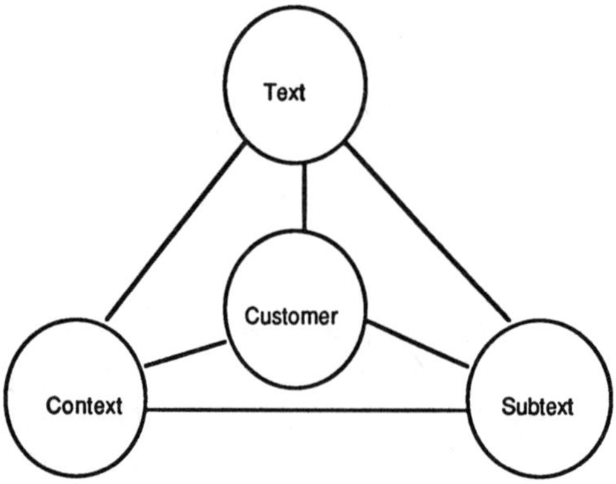

marketing approaches to match both the conscious and unconscious needs of the customers.

Research Process

To gather the data needed, there are five steps:

1. A review of existing consumer research and details of the current banking services offered on the retail side of the business.
2. A screening process to reach both current and past customers to be sure the Bank reaches the right market segments for the study, as well as gathering basic shopping behavior and demographic data.
3. Telephone interviews to obtain the basic information needed to establish the consumer logic profile of each segment.
4. Group interviews to obtain the necessary detail regarding how customers go about choosing and/or switching from one bank to another.
5. Data analysis and recommendations.

The screening process will be accomplished through telephone contact using lists supplied by the Bank. We are assuming for now that there will be two target market groups: current satisfied customers and past satisfied customers. Note, however, that we recommend that the sexes be kept separate. If the Bank is interested in understanding how to reach *both* males and females within the findings of this project, it would mean looking at four market segments:

- Current satisfied male customers.
- Current satisfied female customers.
- Past satisfied male customers.
- Past satisfied female customers.

However, the final number of market segments can be decided at a later date.

For each market segment, we will be screening for 100 respondents—50 of whom will be interviewed by phone. From the 50 interviewed, 20 will participate in a focus group (two groups of 10 each).

CONCLUSION

As a banker seeking a truly competitive edge in the retail or consumer marketplace, it is useful to understand how all the factors discussed in this chapter tend to operate in your particular bank.

- Get your customers' attention by communicating in all four sensory modes: See/Hear/Read/Do, while stressing the mode that has proved most effective for most customers.
- Keep the level of detail in your bank's information and ads consistent.
- Keep the degree of change in your bank and its ads consistent.
- Train staff people to move and talk at a speed that matches the pace of your customers (and probably speed up somewhat at the point of transaction).
- Be consistent in the degree of "procedures" or "alternatives" built into your bank.
- Focus on the things or the relationship, whichever is most important for your customers, and be consistent about it.
- Offer a balance between suggestive selling and letting the customer feel he or she is making his or her own decision, to appeal to both external and internal customers.
- offer a balance between "toward language" and "away-from language" in promotions, to reach a broader audience.
- Learn the most appropriate criteria words to use in your promotions and with customers.
- Find ways to offer customers products and services a number of times, rather than just once, to help make them feel comfortable about being convinced to buy.

The key is consistency in your offer. Most bankers are unknowingly using an array of marketing concepts covered in this chapter, but frequently the application of the concepts is inconsistent and therefore not as powerful as it could be. By learning the most powerful combination of marketing factors and using them consistently, you can make your bank more compelling for current customers. You can also entice those noncustomers who have the same subconscious needs as your customers but who are unaware of the bank's specific services that could meet those needs. Providing the right service level is crucial for a bank to gain a competitive edge in today's market. How the service is provided is just as important as what service is provided.

CHAPTER 11

COMMERCIAL STRATEGIES

> People are unhappy, not because their standards are too high, but because they know their performance has been, and is, too low. The solution is not to lower the aim, but to increase the accomplishment.
> —*William Glaser*

Although commercial banks are improving their overall profitability, the banking industry is not growing as fast as the economy. The obvious conclusion is that banks are losing significant market share to other suppliers of deposit and loan services. Also, current profitability does not ensure the long-term viability of the banking industry. In fact, if banks become complacent and do not have a sense of urgency to recapture market share, the industry's current profitability will have a negative impact on its future fortunes.

A significant majority of banks have traditionally focused on the small to medium-sized closely-held businesses. In fact, 90 percent of most bank loan portfolios consist of credits to this very critical market segment. With the exception of regional and money center banks, financing small to medium-sized businesses has always been the heart of the banking industry. Even regional and money center banks have begun to recognize that small to medium-sized businesses are a very viable part of American enterprise. Why? First, they are the only significant growth segment in the commercial business economy. Second, they provide acceptable profit margins that no longer exist with larger corporate borrowers. Third, banks have the opportunity to build personal banking relationships with small to medium-sized commercial organizations. Contemporary banking goes way beyond the traditional focus on corporate borrowings. Developing business relationships adds up to greater opportunities for the bank to identify client needs and sell products. This, in turn, results in much greater profitability. Commercial relationship banking benefits the banker as well as the bank client. Finally, there is reason to believe that the risks of small business loans can now be rationalized. More sophisticated monitoring and training of commercial account officers have reduced the inherent risks of lending to comparatively less mature businesses.

In today's competitive environment, small to medium-sized businesses provide unlimited opportunities to bankers who can look beyond mere borrowing needs. By serving a small business through professional selling—in which needs are identified and a relationship is created—a bank comes to know the business intimately, which goes a long way to resolve unknowns and to reduce credit risk. Of course, technology and contemporary techniques in loan analysis reinforce the ability to reduce risk.

WHY BUSINESSES DO BUSINESS WITH A BANK

Commercial businesses do not choose their banks on the basis of price. Unfortunately, too many bankers feel that this is the case. Nothing could be further from the truth.

Rate

I have never talked with a corporate customer who even hinted that the interest rate charged for a loan (or the interest rate charged for a loan after being adjusted for compensating balances) has *ever* been the most important reason for establishing or changing a banking relationship. Nor have I ever read a research study that made such a claim.

Since 1975, most of our data compiled from any variety of research projects and interviews consistently found that *personal relationships* and *banker understanding the commercial business* are the most important factors. Reliability as a source of credit, responsiveness, timeliness, and service variety also rank ahead of low borrowing rates.

More recently, research by the *American Banker* related that the most important issues in a banking relationship are quality service, timeliness, personal relationship, and credit availability. Similarly, the American Bankers Association study found that poor service, low interest rates (paid on deposits, not charged for loans), unresponsiveness, and credit limitations or credit refusal were the most important reasons why corporate customers switched banks (Tables 11-1 and 11-2).

These observations are consistent with strategic assumptions in nonbanking enterprises. The only reason a client or prospective client considers expanding or developing a banking relationship because of price is when the bank has nothing else to offer the client. People buy perceived value. Perceived value deals with relationships, not rate. The only time decisions are made based on rate or price considerations is *when there are no other considerations presented.*

Rates typically do not vary much from bank to bank. One-quarter of a percent, and in some cases even one-half of a percent, is not that significant when a quality relationship is established. Rate becomes crucial only when there is no relationship.

Astute bank clients recognize that the lowest rate does not always mean the best deal. Perceived value is thoroughly understood among contemporary business managers. They recognize that financial institutions need to charge a premium if they are going to give exceptional service. Successful business managers consistently rank service as the number one reason for picking a bank and establishing a banking relationship.

TABLE 11-1
What Is Most Important in a Banking Relationship?

	Middle Market	*Large Corporate*
Quality of service	27.3%	31.2%
Timeliness	15.1	17.8
Personal relationship	14.6	13.0
Credit availability	12.7	9.1
Service variety	10.2	9.6
Knowledge of company's business	6.8	3.8
Interest rates charged	3.4	6.3
Rate of return	1.5	.0
Service fees	1.0	3.4

Source: "American Banker Corporate Survey," *American Banker,* March 1988, p. 10.

TABLE 11-2
What Would Make a Company Switch Banks?

	Middle Market	*Large Corporate*
Poor service in general	25.9%	31.6%
Nothing would cause a switch	17.8	10.5
Interest rates too low	17.3	7.4
Bank unresponsive to company's needs	11.4	19.5
Credit limited or refused	10.3	7.4
Fees too high	7.6	14.7
Bank instability	7.0	3.7
Dissatisfied with personnel	2.2	2.1
Better deal elsewhere	1.6	3.2
Company expansion	1.1	0.5
Other reasons	8.6	14.7

Source: "American Banker Corporate Survey" *American Bank,* March 1988, p. 10.

The critical issue is that the cost of borrowing money has very little to do with establishing a successful banking relationship. The cost to the corporate customer to do business with a bank consistently ranks near or at the bottom in importance. The message is clear: successful business people rely on service and understand they must pay a price for good service. The challenge for bankers is to learn to sell professionally—that is, to sell perceived value based on service quality.

Competitive battles in a deregulated marketplace cannot be won with strategies to undercut a competitor's price. One need not look any further than the airline industry to see that a low-rate strategy in the big leagues is a strategy for failure.

Responsiveness

The second most important issue, as ranked by commercial customers, is responsiveness, both in reaching decisions and in bringing innovation to the market. The tempo of today's business environment is such that successful entrepreneurs and corporate managers just do not have the time to wait around for a weekly loan committee meeting. The one unique advantage the community and community-related regional banks have over their money center competitors is that they can be more responsive. Corporate financial officers who have changed their lead bank consistently cite lack of responsiveness as a major factor in their decision to look for a different supplier of financial services.

The small to middle market and the large corporate market hold different opinions relative to the responsiveness of new product innovation. Very large companies are more interested in innovative products. Small and middle-market companies just do not have the need for innovative or creative product lines.

Referrals

A vast amount of new business can be acquired from existing customers. Referrals from existing clients are consistently the number one source of new business, regardless of the size of the company or the size of the financial institution. Yet, many banks do not take advantage of this source. The opportunity for new business from existing customers is so great that we have a place "engraved" on our client call reports to specifically record the answer to a specific question asking each customer for referrals and to document to whom the customer referred the bank.

Internal referral programs are another important strategy. Figure 11–1 shows the number of referrals per participant made and closed as a source of new business in a 15-month period following implementation of a referral program. The group of banks had between $200 million and $1 billing in assets. This includes referrals from existing clients and from other departments in the bank.

The results of a referral program strategy can be significant and are almost immediate. Chapter 12 details the results of a structured referral program, including the number of referrals by department and the volume of new loans and deposits created by a structured referral program.

Small Business Market Potential

Businesses with sales of less than $500,000 are another very lucrative market. These businesses are infrequently attended by their primary bank.

Businesses with sales of less than $500,000 create 60 percent of

FIGURE 11-1
Referrals/Participant/Month

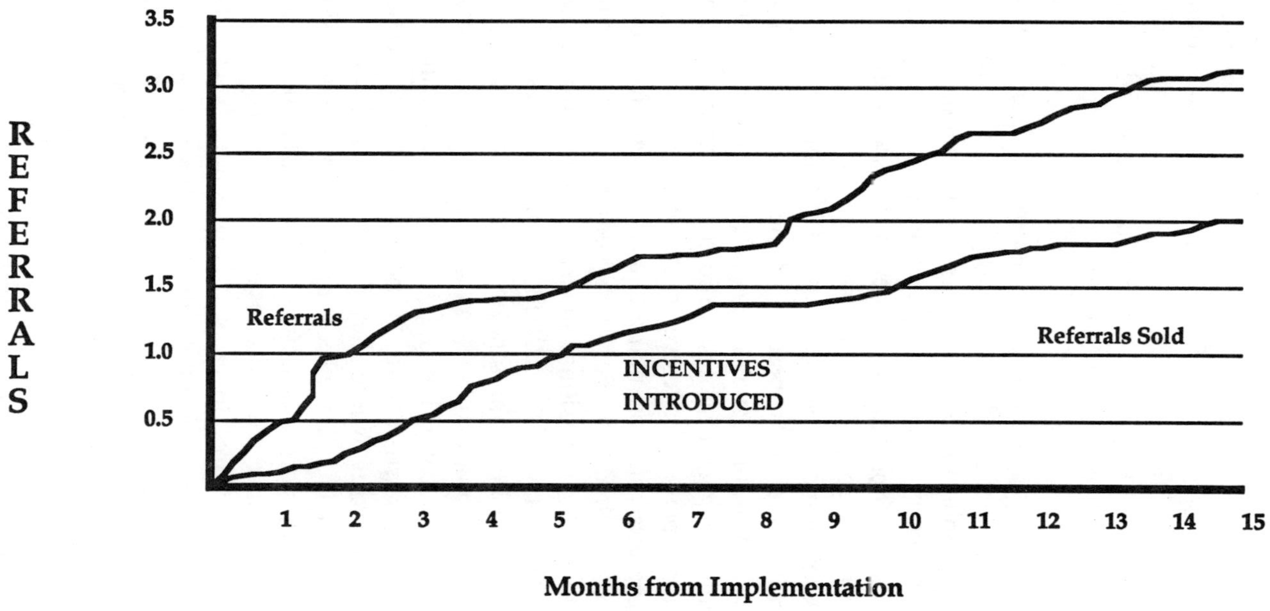

all new jobs and comprise 92 percent of all new businesses in the United States.[1] The small business market, although risky, is a significant player because it offers so much potential business and is an excellent training ground for young commercial service officers. In addition, small businesses are typically heavy borrowers.

However, the risk of lending to a small business does not have to be that great. If a bank focuses in on a subsegment of the small business market and conducts the appropriate kind of research, it can almost be assured of providing commercial financial services to risk-free applicants. For example, early retired and retired entrepreneurs currently make up 17 percent of all new businesses.[2] After three years, 99 percent of the new businesses started by early retired people are successful.

Another market subsegment is the female entrepreneur. Women currently make up 46 percent of the new business market and are represented in all business categories. Female entrepreneurs have a substantially higher success ratio than their male counterparts, yet less than 1 percent have ever been called on by their bank.

The small business market has other significant players that provide very limited risk. For example, contemporary banks that have truly targeted professional subsegments—such as doctors, dentists, accountants, lawyers, certified public accountants, or engineers—have become better at serving those subsegments than any other bank in their marketplace. As a result, they walk off with a loyal client whose account has the potential to grow into a total banking relationship. Furthermore, 90 percent of the professionals do their personal banking where they do their business banking. They are much less likely to have secondary banking relationships.

The key point, however, is that different strategies must be created for each bank because differentiation is the only critical strategy. Therefore, different strategies must be established for each of the various professional subsegments.

Westinghouse Credit, Prudential Bache Securities, Inc., American Express Company, Merrill Lynch, and many other nonbanking

---

[1] "American Banker Corporate Research," *American Banker,* New York, NY, March 29, 1988, p. 10.

[2] Art Lucy, ABA CEO Conference, February 1987, Scottsdale, AZ.

organizations have already targeted small to medium-sized corporate businesses with explicit strategies. In addition, the big three automobile credit companies have designated the professional marketplace as their target for 1992. To date, banks have done little more than identify professionals as their target and then circle the wagons to ward off the impending attack. However, banks must recognize that their current product line and their position in the marketplace provides them with an enviable opportunity to attack. Banks should not be on the defensive.

STRATEGIES FOR THE COMMERCIAL MARKET

The key to success is segmentation. Segmentation defines opportunity; it allows managers to set specific strategies for maximizing market potential by becoming the very best in serving that particular market segment or subsegment. The key strategies for success in dealing with the small to medium-sized corporate client is quality service, responsiveness, and building personal relationships. How each organization does that must be significantly unique to ensure differentiation.

There are other critical issues to be inventoried by each individual bank. Each bank's management style and skills are always very different from its competitors. Therefore, there can be no boiler plate strategies because it is impossible to standardize solutions for different banking environments, even within the same marketplace. Outlines and checklists for defining individual market segment needs and determining the market's priority needs—and, therefore, the bank's opportunity—are provided in Appendix D.

A recent Greenwich Report[3] suggested that there are only two critical areas that bank management must consider in today's competitive environment when attempting to deal successfully with small to medium-sized businesses. First, the selling effort must be strategic—that is, targeted at very specific companies. As a result, it becomes critically important for calling officers to understand the com-

[3] *Benefitting from a Buyer's Market: Commercial Banking 1988* (Greenwich, CT: Greenwich Associates, 1988), p. ii.

panies they call on and to know how to listen closely to learn how to serve their clients better. Second, account officers must have a structure to their calling activity to ensure that they are consistently calling on their priority customers and priority prospects, which is critical to retaining and building relationships.

Calling should be consistent, not only to maintain contact with the client or prospect but also to identify a competitive vulnerability and look for opportunities to propose or create new ways of serving and providing financial services to the targeted company. Our experience suggests it takes five or more calls to create a new business relationship or to expand an existing one. Yet, over 80 percent of banking officers never call on a prospect more than twice and rarely call on an existing client more than twice a year.

While clients may perceive no value in the bank knowing a lot about their businesses, it is *critically* important for banking officers to understand the businesses they are serving. It is the most important element in successful professional selling because it is absolutely impossible for a banker to identify needs without first having a clear understanding of the businesses with which they are dealing.

The situation is quite different in a regulated environment when the only service to be provided is a loan, and the bank is the only act in town. In that case, all the bank has to do is evaluate assets, analyze financial statements, and draw some conclusions about the borrower's character. Banking is just not that easy any more—not when there are relationships from which to build and profit.

RELATIONSHIP MANAGEMENT

When a banking organization commits to customer service, nothing is more important than recognizing the importance of relationship building and knowing how to build relationships. In business, *the only thing that counts is continuing business with existing customers, creating additional business with existing customers, and having existing customers become a primary source of referrals.*

Relationship management is absolutely essential for the viability of all banks because it explicitly relates to getting the customer to come back over and over again. This is what business is all about. To build relationships with each and every customer, a bank must emphasize selling, product design, product reliability, quality service, and distribution systems. Moreover, the bank must get the people from the back office and the customer-contact area to listen to the customer.

Listening is the key. You must understand what the customer needs and wants before you can begin a relationship. As Yogi Berra once said, "You can observe a lot by just watching." That is pretty good advice for starting a new commitment to identify the unmet wants and needs of your customer base.

If you take a look at the most successful organizations in the country—whether it be Apple Computer, IBM, McDonalds, or Domino's Pizza—you find that they are constantly finding bigger and better ways to build relationships with every customer. Each of these successful companies explicitly targets its efforts and activities to one or a very limited number of market segments or subsegments.

The concept of relationship management affirms that a customer is, in effect, an asset. That asset has to be managed or its equity will be dissipated. Bankers are normally rated and rewarded by the number of client relationships they control. These relationships, like any other asset, can appreciate or depreciate. The maintenance and enhancement of relationships are not a matter of public relations. Rather, relationship management requires a company-wide commitment to maintain, improve, and, most important, understand the implications of managing each and every relationship.

Relationship management is the cumulative management of all things, both large and small, throughout the organization. Building partnerships between corporate entities is a prerequisite to successful relationship management. Also, the corporate partnerships must be stronger than individual relationships to ensure that bank officer promotions and turnover do not have a negative impact on the bank. Relationship management values are, therefore, a major part of the corporate culture and strategy.

Managing a business relationship requires very special care. Even good customers with strong relationship ties with their banks often think, "What has my bank done for me lately?" *A mismanaged relationship, which includes not calling on the client, leaves a bank vulnerable* to a competitor who can merely walk in and claim, "I can do more and do it better!"

This vulnerability is supported by our research on small to

medium-sized businesses. As many as 70 percent of the primary customers of community banks would change financial institutions if they could be assured that some other banker would take responsibility for their account relationship. They want to know who is really responsible for decision-making at their bank for their account. Is it the individual banker with whom they believe they have established a relationship? Is it an unknown group of people who make decisions in a closed committee meeting? Is a computer in a distant city really the decision-maker? *Responsiveness, the key to sustaining relationships, has much to do with knowing who really makes decisions.*

Banks' reliance on high-technology capabilities, indeed, has caused customers to demand more personal attention. More personal attention requires better training to orient banking officers to understand the implications of financial client relationships. Therefore, there is a definite need to incorporate relationship management skills throughout the banking organization.

Theodore Levitt states that there are some very explicit things that should be done to establish and reinforce business relationships.[4] Adapted for the financial services industry, the actions that adversely or positively influence relationships are shown in Table 11-3.

The checklist shown in Table 11-3 is a good one. Ask each of your customer-contact people to rate themselves on a scale of 1 to 10 on how they typically deal with their customers, with a rating of 1 indicating a very negative influence and a rating of 10 indicating a very positive influence. Total all of their scores to determine your bank's relationship-building capability. Many banks rate very high!

"Relationship" is the key word. Think relationship and you will achieve beyond survival. Tom Peters, the author of books on excellence, tells the story about the retail wonder of the decade, Nordstrom, which grew to become a multibillion dollar retail success story. Nordstrom achieved its growth without acquisitions. When it comes to service, Nordstrom's customers literally make social evenings out of sharing Nordstrom's service stories. At one of Tom

---

[4]Theodore Levitt, *The Marketing Imagination* (New York: The Free Press, 1983).

TABLE 11-3
Actions Influencing Business Relationships

Negative Influence	*Positive Influence*
Contact only to sell services or respond to problems	Schedule & prepare for contacts
Dictate formal letters	Send handwritten notes or use telephone
Tell them what they want to hear	Be honest and up-front
Take relationships for granted	Show appreciation
Respond only when problems have occured	Anticipate possible problems
Ignore personality conflicts	Discuss possible conflicts
Refuse to be accountable	Accept responsibility Use "we" in solving problems
Refer to contracts or agreements	Offer service solutions
Wait for requests for service	Initiate recommendations Follow through
Respond only to the client's questions	Anticipate and plan for the future
Wait for follow-up call	
Recount what you have done for them	

Peter's seminars, a skeptical participant resented all the talk about Nordstrom because he assumed that the only way a store could offer the kind of service Nordstrom was noted for was to charge premium prices for the apparel. (He was probably right because customers buy perceived value; that is, price is less important than perceived value.)

One day this individual found himself in desperate need of a new suit and remembered the Nordstrom advertising commitment of same-day alterations. Ironically, on this day of desperation Nordstrom was having a sale on its business suits, although the advertisement stipulated that the semi-annual sale would result in next-day alterations. Reluctantly, he went to the closest store and not only purchased a suit on sale but also ended up buying another suit for full price.

Because the suits needed to be altered and would not be ready until the next day, it was not until late the following afternoon that he arrived at the store to pick up his suits. The salesman, who had only met him one time before, identified him by name—a Nordstrom tradition. The salesman reluctantly informed the skeptic that Nordstrom had made an error and the suits had not been altered as promised. Obviously upset, the skeptic left for home knowing his trip to Dallas the following day would be without his new suits.

The following evening he checked into his Dallas hotel. In his room he found a message that a package was in the lobby waiting to be delivered. Nordstrom had spent $98 to send his two suits via Federal Express from California to Texas. He opened the package to find two complimentary $25 silk ties, which perfectly matched the suits. On top of that was a handwritten note from the clerk, apologizing for the oversight and hoping that this consideration would at least restore his confidence in Nordstrom.

That's differentiation. And, that's quality service. The key is to look around to find ways that you can be better than your competition. It's how to win customers and keep them. It's what brings customers back and has them enthusiastically refer their friends to you, without asking them to do so. *Service quality goes way beyond training*. It deals with the very heart of responding to customer needs: accessibility, location, packaging, signs, environment, attitudes, inventory, friendly service from a caring provider, and a commitment to identify customer needs through the eyes of the customer.

Some traditional bankers might be skeptical about applying that kind of analogy to commercial financial services. However, this is exactly the reason for this book. No matter what the industry, if you operate in a competitive environment, the disciplines are always identical. It is the strategy that must be *very* different.

When I became president of a community bank, the organization had just gone through a very traumatic period. The bank had four different CEOs in six years and had lost a significant amount of money on agricultural loans during good times—the 1970s, when the agri-economy was at its peak. Also, there had been some improprieties that had a very negative impact on the bank's image in the marketplace.

Shortly after I arrived, a Fortune 500 company announced that it would open a large plant in our community with 1,200 employees and plans to grow to 3,600 employees in three years. Within six months of the announcement, 22 executives would transfer into our area.

Because I was new to the community and had not yet been involved in its industrial development, we were the last to learn about this new business opportunity. However, I promised our entire staff that we would get all of the new accounts if they would work hard and commit to learning how to differentiate, commit to learning how to be better than anyone else in the marketplace, commit to identifying customer needs rather than to try to push loans and deposits, and commit to learning how to plan and execute professional business calls.

Shortly after I made that promise, our enthusiastic staff helped plan the best business call that I had ever experienced in a banking environment. I called the president of the Fortune 500 company to schedule an appointment. His reply was, "Don't bother flying 1,000 miles to visit us, Mike. We have a corporate policy *not* to show preferential treatment to any bank in any town or city where we locate a plant. You'll get your share of accounts."

I was determined to make an appointment. I was determined for two reasons. Number one, I had promised the entire staff that we would get all of the accounts if they worked at it. Second, I had belief! I was confident that if we could just get a few minutes to visit with the president, our business call plan would break his corporate policy because we had identified the company's needs by looking through their eyes. We developed a call plan proposal the prospect couldn't refuse. And he didn't.

During the initial phone call, the president asked me to limit our presentation to 20 minutes. We did. However, after he heard our proposal, he asked if we could stay longer to discuss the details. Six and one-half hours later he drove us 45 minutes to the airport and literally walked us to our airplane. Six months later, our bank acquired all of the corporate accounts and 20 of 22 of the personal accounts of the transferred executives. Three months after the plant opened, a member of the company's founding family joined our bank's board of directors. Corporate policy was not to show preferential treatment to a local bank, but we prevailed. Why?

We began by disdaining traditional tactics. We did not push deposits or loans. Rather, we approached the sales opportunity by anticipating and confirming needs through the eyes of the prospect. We knew that if we could differentiate our service and show that we really cared about the prospective client's priorities, we would deserve and get more than our share of accounts. We did—because we took the time to plan a professional business call.

The plan included some traditional considerations. First, we focused on their people: newcomer's kits, a structured meeting with the transferred executives and their spouses on their first trip to their new community, an introductory subscription to the state's activity publication, and temporary office space to recruit their employees. We then introduced some very nontraditional ideas:

- A seminar for all the company's new raw material suppliers so that they could learn about the company's quality standards.
- A comprehensive 1,100-page list of all end users of the company's products, including who to contact, phone numbers, addresses, and volume and type of product used.
- A bank deposit premium promotion to publicize the company's product (the promotion was so successful that it was extended by two months).

The entire cost of implementing the program was minimal because the company subsidized the expense of the promotion and paid for the seminar. We acquired the user's list at no cost. However, it took time to plan the business call, to create the proposal, to identify needs, and to execute the proposal.

PROFESSIONALISM STRATEGIES: PLANNING THE BUSINESS CALL

Professionalism requires planning. Many bankers do not perceive the need for an aggressive sales organization. They view aggressive sales efforts as counterproductive to maintaining the professionalism that is necessary in a banking environment. In reality, the degree of sales aggressiveness has little influence on professionalism. The two are linked, however, because being professional is a necessary condition for successful selling to a financial client.

Too often, bankers feel at a loss as to what to discuss or what questions to ask during a commercial sales opportunity. I find it helpful to list the different types of questions relevant to different circumstances. The questions should not be prepared like a script to be read from. Rather, the questions should be developed and presented in concept. Each banker must construct the questions to fit his or her communications style.

For example, when a commercial business moves into a new market area, there are six preliminary questions that must be asked before the banker proceeds to determine more about the prospect's specific financial needs. When commercial clients or prospects are already in the market area, there are 13 questions that need to be clarified relative to business operations and management styles. Further, there are eight questions dealing with the client's product or services, four critical questions dealing with the client's competition, and at least seven questions relative to the client's financial stability and profitability.

Equally important, each calling officer should have very explicit objectives developed and written *before* the business call is made. Each call plan and its objectives must be different because each client is different. However, there are certain things that must be accomplished during every business call if it is to be considered a professional, quality call.

I discourage "Howdy-Doody" calls. Calls in which nothing more is done than stopping by to say hello or thanking the customer for the business are a waste of the customer's time, a waste of the banker's time, and an insult to the customer. However, maintenance calls on priority clients are very important. The key is to execute meaningful objectives. There are at least 10 specific objectives that can be accomplished during a maintenance-type call. The primary objective of a maintenance call is to compliment the customer, reinforcing his or her feeling of importance to the bank. This objective must be accomplished *every* time a maintenance call is made. Strategically, planning for business calls and executing carefully planned calls are the very foundation for success in creating and developing new commercial business.

Professionalism requires preparedness. Preparedness requires planning. Planning requires that a major effort be made prior to each business call. Being thoroughly prepared requires more than knowledge of the technical requirements, benefits, and features of the bank's products. Preparedness in selling bank services requires a complete understanding of the client's past and current financial relationships, business, trends, needs, and personal idiosyncrasies.

Preparation takes work. The banking officers must learn as much as possible about the prospect or client, the company, and its needs. Finally, written objectives must be developed to execute a professional call. Preparation assures professionalism.

In financial institutions throughout the United States, it has been found that, for the most part, bank officers do not appreciate the need to plan a business sales call. The result becomes, ironically, a "Catch-22." A bank officer who does not plan for a business call is inadequately prepared. Being inadequately prepared results in the bank officer not achieving an acceptable level of success, which causes the banker to think poorly of the experience. This inefficient use of the banker's and client's time reinforces the perception that there are more productive things to do than making business calls.

To experience success in sales calls, there must be an appreciation of professionalism in selling. Professionalism creates an environment of trust. Caring enough to plan for a business call is the first step toward establishing that environment of trust. Preparation provides immediate results. It installs an attitude of confidence because preparation resolves the fear of the unknown. A banker who has resolved the fear of the unknown can proceed with a clarity of purpose. The banker will be rewarded by a newfound confidence that creates that environment of trust.

STRATEGIES: WHO TO CALL ON

Today, most business calls are not made on priority customers and prospects. Also, too many business calls are unnecessarily repetitive. Untrained, disorganized bankers frequently call on those who offer the path of least resistance and greatest comfort. Therefore, ranking clients and prospects to be called on and implementing controls to ensure that priority clients are called on are prerequisites for success.

The number of times a banker calls on a business varies significantly among banks and the clients being called on. This is because each client has different needs and, therefore, has significantly different requirements relative to how often a business call should be made.

Suffice it to say that the banking industry does not call on its clients often enough. Unfortunately, there are not enough banking officers in the industry to call on the priority clients to allow the bank and client to maximize their potential. This is why it is so important to incorporate nonofficer customer-contact people in the job of calling on maintenance customers.

My experience confirms the 80-20 rule in dealing with commercial business development. Consistently, 80 to 85 percent of all the business volume and/or profitability of a commercial banking department are provided by 16 to 21 percent of all commercial clients. This leads to the next point: there is a need to target and to structure the entire business call system to ensure that all targeted priority clients and prospects are called on.

The need to target the top 20 percent of existing clients or potential clients is reinforced by the fact that, on average, only 8 to 15 percent of small to medium-sized companies add a new bank to support their financial services needs each year. The variance depends upon the type of commercial business and/or the current economic conditions of a particular area. The goal is not just to get people involved in professional selling but rather to get them calling on the most appropriate businesses. First, however, their inherent resistance to selling must be resolved.

Resistance to Selling

The problem in the past has been that people have been asked to participate at levels of selling beyond their current skill level—that is, beyond the level at which they know they can be successful. For example, many financial organizations have required all or most of their officers to make a certain number of calls per month, with a percentage of those required to be calls on prospects.

Everyone can contribute to the sales process, and most will contribute in a very significant way. However, the first step is to know what they can do successfully, because people will not participate in things they know they cannot do successfully. Management activities must be directed to ensuring that each participant can be successful doing those things they have been asked to do.

In the past, well-intentioned bank managers have wasted tremendous amounts of time and effort trying to convince officers to call on prospects, and all the while the officers were convinced they could not be successful. As a result, the officers were not successful, leading management to conclude that no one can contribute and no one can sell.

The way to get everyone to contribute is to convince them to contribute at the level at which they are comfortable—because they know they can be successful at that level. How do we find out what the level is at which each person can contribute? Psychological testing will not do it. Past experience in making calls is not the answer either. Why? Because they did not want to do what they knew they would be unsuccessful doing, and they fulfilled their own prophesy. The reason people fulfilled their own prophesy is because they are successful only when they think they will be successful. This concept must be understood by all managers who are strategically planning for the future.

This strategic management issue begs another question: "In order for you to be as successful as you possibly can be at the level you want to begin, what can I do as a sales manager to give you the tools?" "What tools—whether training, materials, or information—will reinforce your effort to be as good as you possibly can be at the level you want to contribute?"

I am convinced that people really want to participate. They really want to contribute. However, they want to contribute at the level they know they can be successful. Everyone can contribute and most will contribute in a very significant way, but we have to start with asking them to do the things they know they can do. Therefore, our sales management activities should be directed to ensure everyone that they can be successful doing things that they have identified they *can* do and that they *want* to do.

Just as a successful football team looks for players with specific skills to fill certain positions, a successful sales organization selects players with different skills to accomplish different objectives. Everyone cannot be a quarterback or a halfback. Blockers and receivers are necessary. Most important in today's competitive environment, strong defensive players are required to retain priority customers who are vulnerable to aggressive, sales-oriented banks and other financial institutions. Therefore, how we employ individual skills becomes most critical.

Call Participation

Customers generally fall into one of three categories, whereas professional salespeople can be classified according to one of four sales call skill positions (Figure 11–2).

A good number of participants have the defensive skills that can be employed in calling on maintenance customers. Banks have more maintenance-types of customers than any other. Maintenance customers are those who have a strong relationship with the bank, but they do not have a great capacity to expand their relationship. Most priority deposit customers are maintenance customers. Interestingly enough, the number of loan officers, new account officers, and other customer-contact people who have the skills to call on maintenance customers are generally proportionate to the institution's number of maintenance customers.

A smaller number of participants have the skills to deal effectively with priority growth customers. Growth customers have good relationships and/or have the potential to substantially increase their business relationships. Normally, the bank's number of growth customers and the number of participants with skills to identify needs and cross-sell growth customers are also proportionate.

A third group of participants, likely to be the smallest in num-

FIGURE 11–2
Business Call Participation

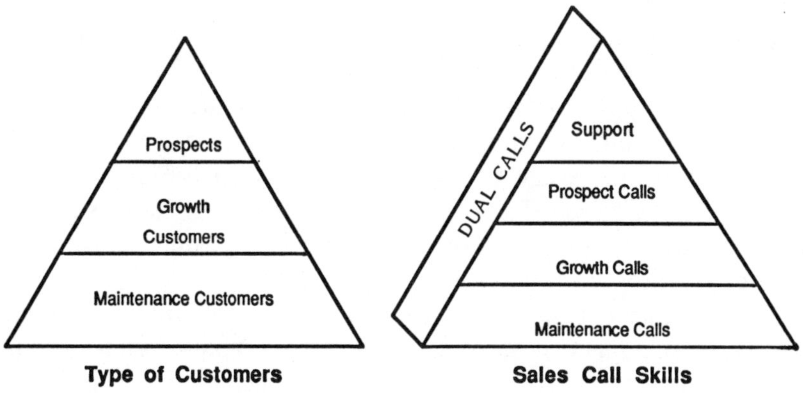

ber, has exceptional skills in soliciting prospective clients. Comparatively, banks should be working on a very limited number of prospects and should never encourage anyone to call on a prospect unless the individual has *exceptional* prospecting skills. Obviously, many people involved in calling on prospective customers also have the skills to call on growth customers. It is a very fine line that must be determined by the person who will be initiating the sales call.

A fourth group of participants has the skills to contribute in a support role. They are likely to be technical or operations specialists who serve best as backups to the officer of accounts. They can also be other types of specialists learning about customers. Salespeople can always learn to listen to and observe the client if there are other bank representatives on the call. Dual calls provide an exceptional training ground for people to learn product and sales skills and to gain confidence. Dual calls are also very important because the customer interprets them as a compliment—as an acknowledgment of his or her importance.

Interestingly enough, a bank's participants in the selling process normally match up to the styles and needs of the bank's clients. Training reinforces that balance. There is no such thing as a natural salesperson. Selling can be taught and it can be learned, but it requires patience and reinforcement.

Management has the responsibility to recognize employee strengths, train to build on those strengths, and assign the appropriate business development responsibilities to maximize potential. Everyone can contribute, but everyone will not—and cannot—contribute in the same way.

To reinforce this concept, assume for a moment that we do not care whether or not our people have the skills to sell. Consider for a moment that "aptitude" and "skills" to sell are not relevant. Rather, assume that everyone in our organization—every customer-contact person and every backroom person—has the potential to contribute to the sales effort. If we can acknowledge that, we must accept the obvious: that each of us will contribute, but we will contribute differently.

If we can accept the notion that everyone can contribute, then we, as sales managers, need to know only two things: What do our salespeople need to contribute at the level at which they feel comfortable? What do they need to maximize their potential, that is, to become even more successful by stretching to that next level of participation.

SALES MANAGEMENT

Successful sales organizations designate and hold individuals responsible throughout the organization for sales management. In a competitive financial institution, the president or CEO is the *ultimate* sales leader. Depending upon the size of the organization, the CEO assumes and facilitates that role, or the role is delegated to the individual who has the time and can better master the specific responsibilities. If the role is delegated, it must be delegated to the number two officer in the organization or to an individual who is a peer with the second level of command in an organization. Regardless of who serves as the active sales manager, it is important to recognize that sales management functions exist throughout the entire organization. Among those who are involved in sales management are division managers, market segment managers, branch managers, customer service representatives supervisors, and, in some larger organizations, the district and/or regional managers.

Sales Manager's Role

Even though sales managers must set the example and serve as role models for the salespeople under them, their own sales performance is not the most important thing for which they should be rewarded. First and foremost, sales managers must be rewarded for the performance of their people who produce sales. Second, sales managers should be rewarded for their own specific sales performance, but only as a secondary responsibility. Preferably, achieving group goals should be a prerequisite to receiving a reward for individual performance. Therein lies the clarification for successful sales managers. A successful sales manager must be an exceptional role model, but should be held more accountable for managing the people who create sales than for producing sales.

Managing a sales organization requires skills and attention to planning, organizing, administrating, recruiting, directing, and measuring the activities of the sales participants. It is the sales manager's responsibility to work with the individual participants and teams throughout the financial organization to accomplish the goals of the organization, division, department, or team.

Each sales manager's main goal, then, is to achieve a level of sales in a predetermined mix of profit and growth. The key factor underlying the manager's success is the ability to influence the behavior of all the other participants. The key to success is the sales manager's ability to influence salespeople to do things they would not do on their own. Successful sales managers assist their people in:

1. Planning individual goals to meet the organization's overall objectives through prioritizing specific target markets and providing the tools necessary to maximize the potential of those targets.
2. Providing an organizational and administrative system necessary to support the sales activities without burdening the sales participants.
3. Training and/or recruiting the type of individuals who have the skills and aptitudes to achieve and participate successfully.
4. Orchestrating the individuals and teams toward maximizing their potential. The most important question a sales manager can ask is, "What can i do for you to help you be more successful?" This might include additional sales tools, specific sales training, or research to help salespeople identify specific targets.
5. Coaching with sales measurement systems to manage and improve results. If you can't measure it, you can't manage it. The measuring systems have to be simple to administer, yet comprehensive enough to provide all participants with the information necessary to maximize the opportunity in their areas of responsibility.

Sales managers throughout the organization—whether the branch, CSR, regional, or market segment manager—must also be held responsible for each of these five executive sales management responsibilities.

Reinforcement

Reinforcement is implemented in several ways. Administratively, there are 39 prerequisites in a successful sales organization to ensure that nothing falls through the cracks. All employees need reinforcement, but salespeople need it desperately. Pats on the back and other forms of recognition can spur people on to greater heights or push them over the edge into exhaustion. It is the quality, quantity, and timing of reinforcement that determines whether or not it is a positive or a negative force.

Successfully providing reinforcement to employees involves a series of strategic considerations. Providing the proper amount of stimulation is a question of energy and adaptation. Seasoned athletes have the advantage of years of experience and training. They have learned how to pace themselves in order to win. Your people will not all have the same experience or perspective. Consciously or unconciously, they rely on their sales manager to set the pace that enables them to become winners.

Learning how to set a proper pace for subordinates requires determining where each person's stress "comfort zone" lies. Up to a certain point, performance increases by increasing stress, and it is effective to "push" people with deadlines, incentives, or other forms of pressure. However, a point is reached beyond which increasing the stress causes performance to drop sharply. A manager then will be able to improve performance only by decreasing the pressure. Too little reinforcement can be just as great a problem as excess pressure.

Managers who want to ensure that their people achieve levels of peak performance must learn exactly where each participant's "comfort zone" lies. In addition, managers must understand that the effect of stimulation or motivation, or lack of it, varies with each individual because the confidence and commitment of each individual are different. Being aware of these differences enables managers to help people hit high achievement levels. This is why it is so important to have people set their own goals. Some input and parameters should be applied by the unit manager. However, the best motivation is individualized and should be tied to individual goals. It relates to the specific job a person is performing and is linked with measurable outcomes. Appropriate, well-managed stimulation is the stuff that makes winners.

CONCLUSION

The number and complexity of issues and techniques in building successful commercial strategies are as great as the number of opportunities. However, if an organization is committed to achieve beyond survival in the commercial services arena, 10 issues must be addressed. They are, in order of priority

1. Communicating that management is committed to holding people responsible for sales performance. Sales performance becomes a critical influence on participants' annual reviews.
2. Constantly reinforcing the idea that professional selling is a top priority.
3. Recognizing sales training and product training as an ongoing, never-ending process, not an event.
4. Having participants sell to the types of customers or prospects that they are capable of handling successfully. A successful program requires calls on only priority customers and priority prospects.
5. Placing a priority on quality calls and results rather than on the number of calls made.
6. Reinforcing positive motivation rather than negative motivation (for example, job insecurity is a negative incentive.)
7. Involving everyone in the development of the program, the definition of their role, and the formation of their expectations.
8. Putting into place measurement systems that track bankwide referrals—cross-sales as well as direct business sales from external selling.
9. Instituting comprehensive incentive and reward-for-performance programs.
10. Ensuring that successful sales management becomes a bankwide management process.

PART 4

UNLIMITED OPPORTUNITIES

The challenge is great, yet the opportunities are unlimited. This final section relates that the investment to create and sustain a sales and service quality culture is significant. However, success stories have proved that the pay back is overwhelmingly positive, and they also reconfirm the most important theme of this entire text:

The challenges are internal,
not external,
and the internal challenges are management,
not staff.

Every bank and thrift currently has the resources to compete successfully. The *only* difference between those who will compete successfully and those who will not is the CEO's decision that the issue is important enough to do something about it. The issue will become important enough when the CEO realizes that the cost of not making the commitment is greater than the cost of making the necessary commitment.

CHAPTER 12

THE OPPORTUNITY

> Corporate performance is the result of combining planning and execution. It resembles a boat race. No matter how hard each crew member rows, if the coxswain doesn't choose the right direction, the crew can never hope to win. Even if the coxswain is a perfect navigator, you cannot win the race unless the rowers strive hard in unison.
>
> —*Kenichi Ohmae*

It has been over a decade since the banking and thrift industries began thinking seriously about preparing to deal with a deregulated, more competitive marketplace. During that time, a myriad of activity and much discussion have ensued about how to become market-driven, how to create a sales culture, and how to ensure service quality. Nevertheless, relative to the ultimate goal of becoming more competitive, very little progress has been made.

Those few who have made exceptional progress have several common characteristics. They have

1. Recognized the transformation to a market-driven sales culture as an *opportunity* of unlimited proportions.
2. Enthusiastically demonstrated their *commitment* to professional selling throughout the entire organization.
3. *Resolved the internal resistance* to change and have introduced management skills and techniques to manage change as an ongoing, opportunity-laden process.
4. Implemented and *reinforced the nine prerequisite disciplines* required to sustain a successful sales and service quality culture.

In 1961, Theodore Levitt introduced the concept of contemporary marketing concepts to the banking/thrift industry. His much referred to paper, "Marketing Myopia,"[1] concluded that the regulated banking industry would not prevail and that a contemporary marketing environment had to evolve if the industry were to survive. By the 1970s, the buzzword became "market-driven"; banks had to become market-driven. By the early 1980s, "sales culture" was the buzzword. For the 1990s, "service quality" is in the forefront of everyone's mind.

All along, bankers were being told about the importance of market planning, market segmentation, sales training, sales measurement and reward. The prerequisite disciplines were always the same, they just became more sophisticated as the participants matured.

This is not really atypical. Fads have come and gone in management circles for years. In the 1950s, it was Theory Y and Management by Objectives; the 1960s brought matrix management and managerial-sales grids; during the 1970s, zero-based budgeting and participatory management were touted; and in the 1980s, Corporate Culture, Theory Z, Streamlining, and one-minute everything gained notoriety. However, the prerequisite disciplines were always the same.

As various concepts were introduced, things may have improved for a time. For the most part, however, companies reverted to their former behavior because the goal of improving long-term performance became secondary to the priority of improving short-term performance. Failing to change was not life-threatening. However, failure to change the way a financial institution is managed for a more competitive environment is life-threatening. *And, we must build on long-term priorities; the penalty for maintaining the status quo is certain death.*

SUCCESS

There have been some real success stories in banking's effort to become market-driven and to create and sustain a sales culture. Individuals, bank departments, and even entire banking institutions have experienced great levels of success. Organizations that have implemented and reinforced the nine prerequisite disciplines to sustain a

---

[1]Theodore Levitt, "Marketing Myopia," *Harvard Business Review: On Management* (New York, Harper and Row, 1975), p. 37.

successful sales and service quality culture are experiencing dramatic improvements in service quality and achieving impressive results from quality calls with priority customers and prospects (Figure 12–1). It is not unusual to expect key players to generate 120 quality calls per year while maintaining a commercial services portfolio. Many banks exceed those goals while managing a $15 to $20 million loan portfolio.

Activity of such a high caliber can be expected to bring in substantial new business (Figure 12–2). Again, it is important to think in terms of *new* business created by sustaining a successful sales and service quality culture. A group of medium-sized community banks experienced significant improvement in pretax earning per participant as a result of their new business program. Year 1 results were modest; however, in Years 2 and 3, the banks demonstrated marked improvement in additional gross income per participant (Table 12–1, p. 263). The results would not have been acquired in the absence of the program.

This experience puts into perspective the relative financial return

FIGURE 12–1
Commercial Services Officer Calls

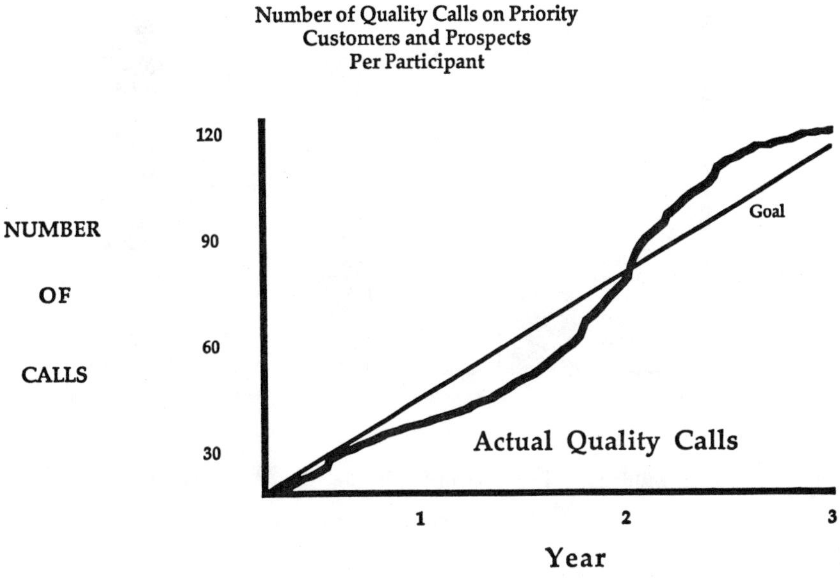

possible when a bank invests in sustaining a successful sales culture. A typical $200 million bank with 120 employees must make a substantial investment in training and systems. On average, it requires the level of investment in training, program and systems per officer and staff person shown in Table 12–2, depending on the size and affiliations of each bank.

FIGURE 12–2
New Business Call Program

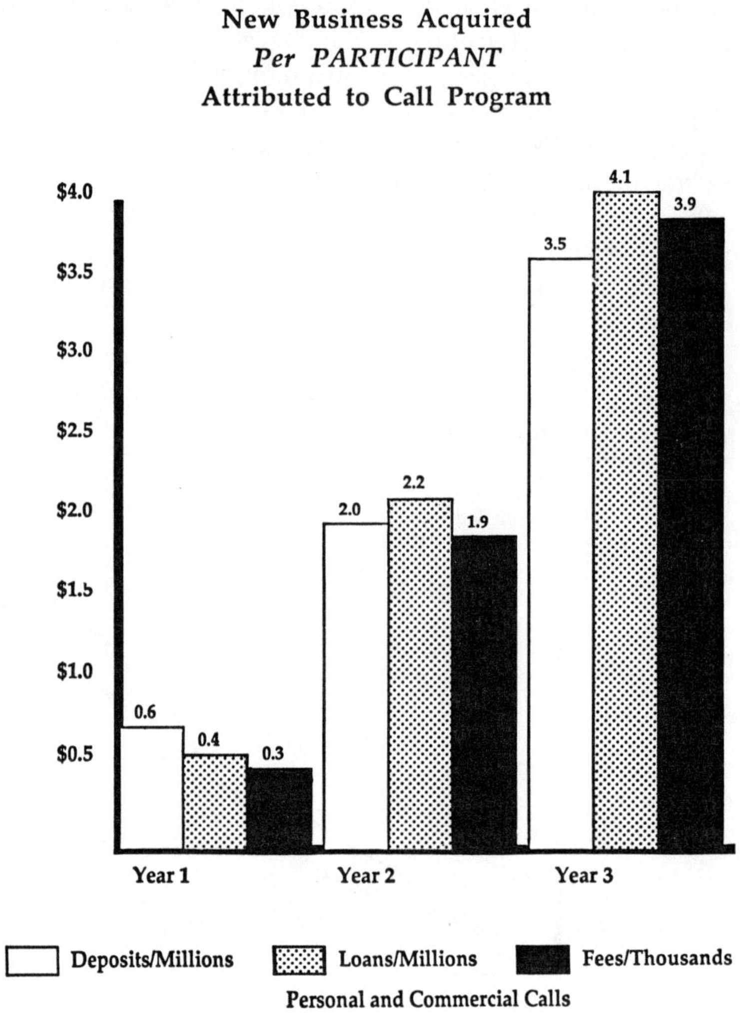

TABLE 12-1
Gross Income Per Participant From Acquired New Business

	Year 1		*Year 2*		*Year 3*	
Deposits (millions)	$0.6		$2.0		$3.5	
Spread	× 2%	$12,000	× 2%	$40,000	× 2%	$70,000
Loans (millions)	$0.4		$2.2		$4.1	
Spread	× 4%	$16,000	× 4%	$88,000	× 4%	$164,000
Fee income		300		1,900		3,000
Gross income		$28,300		$129,900		$237,900

Trust/investment officers not included.

Table 12–2 puts everything into perspective. It relates the investment required to create and sustain a sales culture. When the numbers are compared with those in Table 12–1, it confirms the unlimited opportunity to which banks have access to maximize their annual return on that investment. For example, an officer with lending responsibilities would require an investment of $750 to $1,200 in Year 1 and approximately one-half that investment in each subsequent year. The officer should, on average, return $28,300 in additional gross income in the first year, and $237,900 in additional gross income in the third year of the program. In other words, one offic-

TABLE 12-2
Investment Required to Create and Sustain a Sales Culture

Size of bank	$50 million		$150 million		$300 million		$1 billion	
Each officer	$1,200 ×11	13,200	$875 ×33	$29,535	$800 ×66	$52,800	$750 ×200	$150,000
Each staff	$750 ×19	14,250	$500 ×57	$28,500	$450 ×114	$51,300	$400 ×400	$160,000
Investment								
Year 1		$27,450		$58,035		$104,100		$310,000
Year 2		$15,000		$30,000		$ 90,000		$260,000
Year 3		$13,500		$27,000		$ 81,000		$240,000

er's contribution will pay for a small bank's total investment in creating and sustaining a sales culture. It will take less than two officers to cover the investment required of a $150 million bank and just over three officers to cover a $300 million bank's total investment in sales culture, as economies of scale improve dramatically.

A customer service representative (CSR) will require, on average, an investment of $750 in systems and training in Year 1, and approximately one-half that amount in subsequent years. Yet, a CSR who improves his or her cross-sales ratio on deposit accounts (not including loan referrals, trust referrals and cross-sales of nonasset or liability services) from 1.01 to 1.35—a not uncommon feat—will contribute greatly to pretax income, as the following figures show:

Customer contacts per day	4
Number of working days/year	245
Customer contacts	980
Deposit cross-sell improvement	0.34
Number of new deposit accounts	333.2
Average balance of additional deposits	$8,750
New deposits	$2,915,500
Spread	2% to 4%
Additional contribution to pretax income	$58,310 to $116,620

There have been even more dramatic success stories than this. A $200 million midwestern community bank invested approximately $75,000 in systems, market research, and training during its first year of commitment to a sales culture. Forty-five days after the program was ceremoniously "kicked off," the CEO, who served as sales leader/manager, reported the impressive results shown in Figures 12-3 through 12-6 to his board. The results were for new business created by referrals only. The referrals were reported by numbers made and loan/deposits acquired. The pretax income contribution of the new business was calculated as follows.

New Deposits	$2,500,000	
× Fed-Funds Spread	×1.50%	$37,500
New Loans	$2,700,000	
× Spread	×4.38%	$118,260
Annualized Contribution		$946,080

Figure 12-3
Referrals Made by Peer Group (First 45 Days of Program)

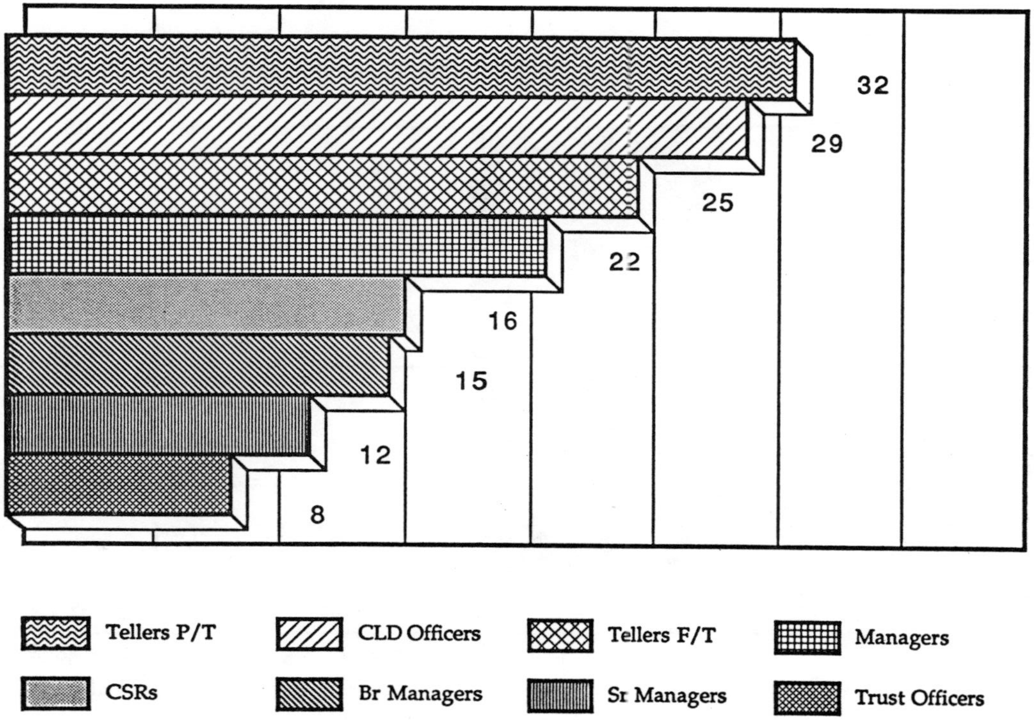

FIGURE 12–4
Amount of Deposits Sold (First 45 Days of Program)

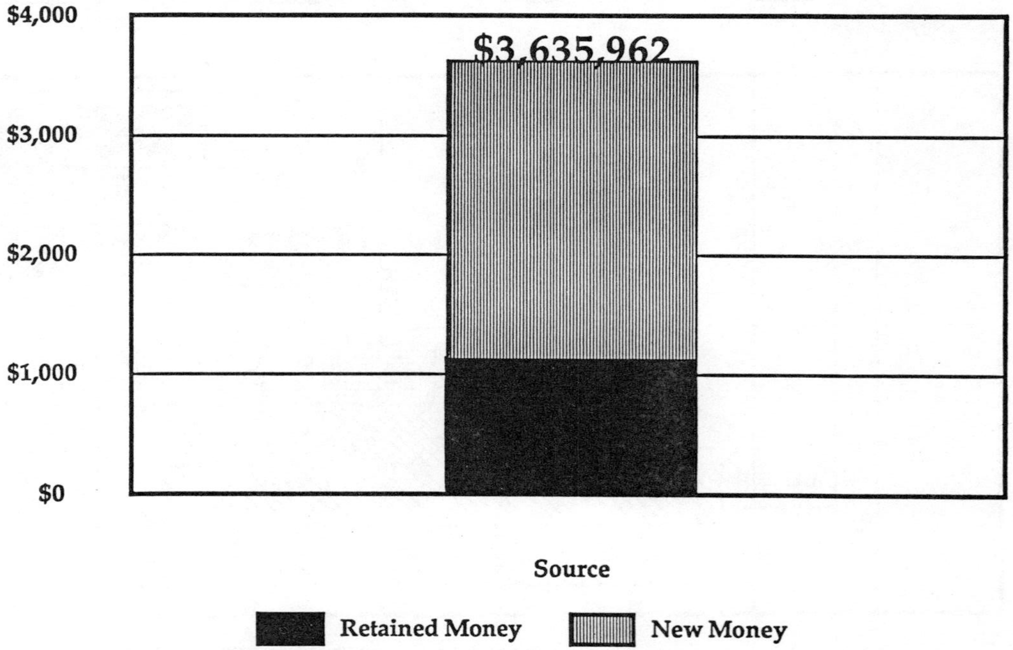

Average Deposit/Sale = $10,478

FIGURE 12-5
Amount of Loans Sold (First 45 Days of Program)

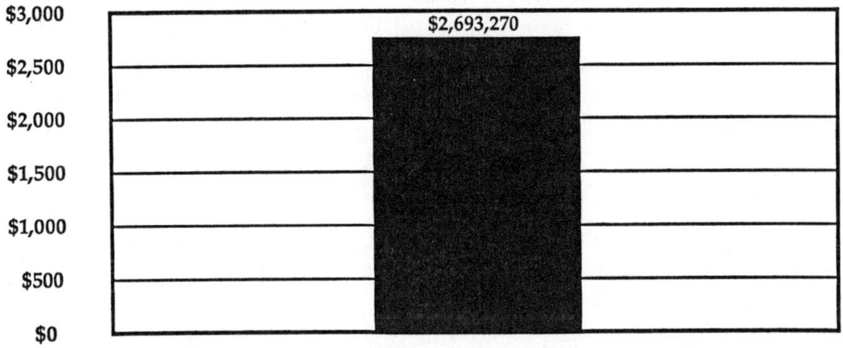

In this example, even if the new deposits were used to support the new loans, the investment required to create and sustain a sales culture for the next three years was paid for by the new business acquired in the first 45 days of the program. Referrals increased substantially by the end of the fourth month. More importantly, the closure of referral sales increased from about 25 percent in the second month to 55 percent in the fourth month.

Corporate transformations like the one just described reinforce

FIGURE 12-6
Bankwide Referrals Made

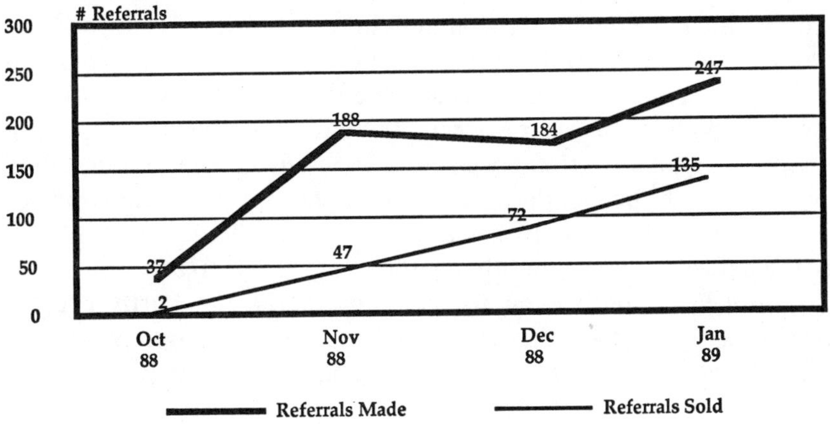

the potential to get employees to behave differently. The only way an employee or team of employees will respond appropriately is if they can be inspired by creative, visionary executives functioning as leaders as well as managers. Managerial leadership is required at every level. However, every leader needs a structured program to deliver and reinforce the message, and his or her arsenal of techniques must include the nine steps necessary to sustain a successful sales and service quality culture.

Therefore, it is not what's hot; it is what's relevant. What is relevant is management's awareness and a sense of urgency; however, systems won't change the way people do things, and systems by themselves will never change corporate culture.

The lessons learned from the two success stories presented in Chapter 1 are very important. The lessons reinforce that all successful companies in a competitive environment, although they may have significantly different situations, require identical managerial-leadership disciplines to be successful. However, each organization's strategies must be tailor-made. To reiterate, only the disciplines that are required to compete successfully—beyond survival—are the same for all competitors. The disciplines are the nine steps in creating and sustaining a successful sales and service culture. The disciplines begin with creation of *vision* and *focus.* Unique strategies then must be designed to serve the priority *market segments by differentiating* the service company from its primary competitors.

Both Federated Investors and SAS—the two companies described in Chapter 1—were consistent in mastering the prerequisite disciplines. Each avoided the temptation to become all things to all people. Each recognized the immeasurable value of defining and making a commitment to serve an explicit *market segment.* This self-limiting focus allowed them to achieve their unlimited potential by employing all available resources toward becoming the very best among many in an extremely competitive environment. *Service quality,* then, could be clearly defined by the needs and expectations of their designated targets rather than becoming diluted and confused by the expectations of an all-encompassing marketplace.

Both Federated's Glen Johnson and SAS's Jan Carlzon recognized that the president's role in a market-driven company must be as *sales manager.* However, the new responsibilities involved in heading a financial institution are not limited to managing; *leadership* is equally important.

Research has shown that too few companies that engage in strategic business activities experience an acceptable level of success. The challenge will lie in the ability to lead an organization through the changes necessary to *differentiate* in order to compete successfully. This takes *commitment* and *persistence* to master *change* as a process and thereby to take advantage of an opportunity-laden marketplace.

The successful management of change as a process entails ensuring that all participants implement priority action plans and achieve objectives within a scheduled time and an agreed upon budget. Successful change management can be sustained *only* if those affected are convinced that the present way of doing things is more expensive than the price of the transition. Therefore, management's only real responsibility is to educate key players that the pain of maintaining the status quo will be too severe. Therefore, the anticipation of an unacceptable level of pain will serve as a prime impetus for movement into the future. Communicating the high cost of mismanaged change is the key to releasing people from their present state—the status quo—and moving them toward the desired state characterized by unlimited opportunity.

Officers and staff desperately want to understand the purpose of their work in a sense deeper than as a way to earn a wage or improve shareholder value. They want to contribute, and they want to contribute something meaningful. A properly communicated vision will serve as the very foundation from which bankers can become enthusiastic about their important responsibilities to their banks and to their customers.

Don Mengedoth, Chairman of Community First Bankshares, recently shared the importance of vision:

> "Vision is the glue. It is the statement of perception about how we will bring all of our stakeholders to a common understanding. Every stakeholder—employees, stockholders, customers, and our regulators—must have a common understanding about our purpose: what we stand for, where we are going, that is, how we will differentiate our company from our competition. I can't believe an organization can function without it."

Differentiation is the key. The only purpose for taking time to create strategies is to give focus to how the organization will *differentiate* itself from its competition. If there is little or no competition, there is no need for strategies because there is no need to differentiate. If the number of competitors is increasing, the organization cannot survive without being different. This differentiation must be communicated and clearly understood as a strategic focus by all those involved in implementation.

The entire staff must understand the organization's priorities. Only then will they become enthusiastic about the vision and, by virtue of their enthusiasm, commit to improving the organization's position in the marketplace and pursuing its prioritized market segments and objectives. Everyone must have a thorough understanding and acceptance of his or her role in bankwide and individual goal achievement. The management effort consists of communications; the result must be an understanding and an enthusiastic endorsement of the focus and strategies formulated to bring that focus alive by all who are involved.

The evolution in organizational leadership extends to other areas as well. In medium-sized to large organizations, the CEO, and possibly the executive vice president, should be viewed exclusively as leaders, not managers. Their responsibilities should not be concerned with doing the everyday activities right but rather doing the right things—that is, defining the organization's basic purpose, focus, and goals and then leading the organization in that direction. The switch in emphasis from manager to leader is a new approach in banking, one that envisions a future. Ultimately, vision gets translated into the organization's performance as a responsible and viable player in a relatively limited marketplace. In the days of a regulated, product-driven environment, the focus was on numbers and volume. Vision was not necessary.

ACCOUNTABILITY

Once the leader sets the direction and goals for the organization, skilled personnel need to be attracted so that the vision is brought to fruition. All personnel must share this vision and assume responsibility for achieving it. This sharing of responsibility is called "alignment," which is present when every employee is working at full capacity and in concert with his or her co-workers. In other words, alignment is the extent to which a group of people function as a team. It is very important to recognize that organizational alignment is limited to the extent of each individual's alignment. Once aligned, people can become accountable.

One of the most significant challenges senior management teams will encounter in the 1990s will be to translate vision into daily practice. While senior management's vision, commitment, and leadership are all essential prerequisites, they are not sufficient to produce or sustain the organizational change necessary to move beyond survival. Until the vision and organizational mission permeate the fabric of daily management practices at every level of the organization, it remains only a vision in the minds of senior management.

The hundreds of strategic plans gathering dust across America are adequate testimony that expectations, and even detailed action plans, are not in themselves enough to ensure meaningful change. Strategic plans are like the architect's blueprints. They are essential for visualizing results and guiding progress, but they are useless unless everyone on the team understands his or her role and accepts individual accountability for achieving excellence in his or her own area of responsibility.

Organizational change does not happen by decree. Nor is individual accountability established by distributing copies of a mission statement. There are at least 10 major conditions that must be established in the organizational infrastructure to create the collective accountability necessary for producing the organizational change required to move beyond survival. The conditions are that

1. Senior management is committed to the organizational mission.
2. Managers agree about the organization's vision and focus.
3. Organizational and individual success is defined in terms of critical results.
4. Managers have accepted individual accountability for producing specific, critical results.
5. Managers are empowered with sufficient authority and re-

sources, and they are backed by an effective organizational structure necessary to support their accountability and to achieve results.
6. Coworkers follow through on commitments to support each others' work.
7. Managers set and team members agree about their performance expectations and goals.
8. Performance critical to achieving results is regularly measured.
9. Everyone receives timely feedback on their performance.
10. Successful achievement of results earns significant rewards.

Organizational change requires individual behavior change. Herein lie two inherent challenges. The first is obvious—old habits die hard. Managers are easily caught up in daily routines built upon precedent and reinforced by yesterday's reward systems. Staff members quickly return to what is comfortable and familiar unless an organizational infrastructure and culture are present in which new behaviors that have significant benefits for both the organization and the individual are valued and rewarded.

The more salient and significant challenges, however, are to establish and manage the critical performance of each senior manager and thereby sustain the change necessary to make a difference. The challenge is really one of defining new expectations and behaviors that must replace old habits. The importance and difficulty of this challenge cannot be underestimated.

How many CEOs attempting to establish a market-driven sales and service quality culture have explicitly identified their expectations, set specific goals, and measured what the cultural change will produce in terms of real measurable, bottom-line results such as additional pretax income and return on investment? How many managers have worked with their staff to measure and manage the critical performance that must be consistently executed to achieve the necessary results? *It must begin with senior manager accountability.*

Microcomputers have lent a new meaning to measurement. Systems are now readily available to target and measure senior and middle management accountability for all aspects of every job responsibility. It is now quite easy to measure, both quantitatively and qualitatively, sales, referrals, work flow, quality, and productivity. Everything can be measured and should be.

Accountability must be the focal point. The critical challenge lies in creating individual accountability through performance management. Accountability must be monitored throughout the organization. When each individual in the organization can clearly identify the performance changes he or she must make on the job and can understand how certain behavioral changes will produce measurable results that have both personal and organizational benefits, we will achieve the individual accountability required to produce the change necessary to move beyond survival.

COMMITMENT AND CONSENSUS

Accountability will clarify and reinforce commitment. This is very important because the most significant difference among successful and unsuccessful organizations are the senior management team members' varying perceptions of commitment. Management's commitment is the issue, and until that is resolved, there are no other issues. Most CEOs obviously think they have made a commitment. However, their senior managers may not perceive that the CEO's commitment is sufficient to make things happen, that is, to change the current environment enough to become competitive.

There must be consensus among the management team members in order for the organization to be successful in creating a sales culture and ensuring service quality. Many bank management teams are making a concerted effort to become more competitive. The real challenge, however, is internal. If a serious difference of opinion among senior management team members exists, it will result in a lack of consensus about where they are and, therefore, what must be done and who is responsible for what. The inconsistencies are a result of different perceptions about the internal implications of sales culture, service quality, and marketing in general. Therein lies the basic premise for this book: *the prerequisites for competing successfully in a deregulated environment are internal challenges. Banks must focus, organize, and then truly commit. The real challenges do not primarily involve products and systems. The major challenges involve people, and the people challenges that first need to be resolved pertain to management, not staff.*

The consensus among senior managers must include a fairly consistent agreement on where the organization is currently with regard to state-of-the-art sales culture. Moreover, the managers must be able to agree upon the critical disciplines that need to be introduced or reinforced. Strategies specifying how those things can be accomplished must be agreed upon. A clear definition of who is responsible for what tasks then should be formulated. These steps are critical in reaching an understanding of the most important priorities and activities that will be emphasized in moving the organization to maximize its potential. A consistent understanding throughout the management team is necessary before the organization can pursue specific *internal strategies* that are *prerequisite* to creating *external strategies.*

The issue of consensus about the prerequisites for success must be focused internally. They must be in place *before* external challenges can be dealt with successfully. Once implemented, the internal strategies will also solve other management inconsistencies, and that consensus will help resolve and expedite the ability of the organization to resolve external challenges.

If an organization is committed to creating a sales culture to ensure service quality, the culture must permeate the entire organization. Sales culture becomes the corporate culture. There is no room for conflicting cultures. Therefore, the very organization of the traditional bank must evolve from a product- and operations-driven orientation to a market-driven orientation headed by senior officers who manage market segments, not products.

SALES LEADERSHIP

The very function of the leader is to convert large problems into opportunities, to inspire people to meet difficult challenges, and to stimulate creativity and purpose. Yet, change and the overwhelming number of everyday events make it difficult for a leader to spend the time necessary to think about and pursue visonary goals. Not long ago, leaders were allowed to give high priority to their ideas. Today, the traditional functions of leadership are being diverted by the tremendous amount of change going on and the complexity of events.

The daily agendas of leaders preoccupied with managing day-to-day activities are overloaded with situations that threaten to unsettle the entire organization. Almost every level of leadership is in danger of being destroyed by unimportant interruptions and having to attend to what is expected rather than what is necessary. We must resolve those barriers because our great organizations and wonderful people demand and deserve our leadership.

A critical precept of sales leadership is that people tend to participate only in activities in which they can assure themselves they will be successful. *Self-concept equals performance. People rarely perform beyond their level of self-concept.* Therefore, we must manage people with a thorough understanding of their perception of their ability to be successful. People who sell successfully want to. They want to because they know they can be successful. Those who think they will not sell successfully will not be successful. Because they do not think they will be successful, they will find every excuse imaginable not to participate.

Therein lies the key to the lock on improved sales performance. We must identify people's perception of their own abilities to engage successfully in professional selling. We then must look at what each employee can do best and build on that capability. It is impossible to impose one's expectations about another's ability to perform at a certain level if that person does not feel he or she can perform successfully.

Successful sales culture leadership begins with the selection of a marketing director with expertise and clout. Finding the right marketing director is one of the five most critical challenges facing a bank. The failure to install effective sales leadership is one of the most important reasons underlying the banking industry's less than satisfactory progress in creating a sales culture and reinforcing service quality. It also explains why many CEOs have become so disenchanted with the results of their marketing activities.

CEOs serve as sponsors for sales and service quality culture. Their verbal directives influence the entire staff. However, unless the CEO's agent—the marketing director or the sales manager—has the clout and the ability to reinforce the sponsor's directives, nothing new will happen. Therefore, the selection of a sales manager or marketing director who has neither the expertise nor a significant position of influence in the organization means that the person will be powerless to influence the necessary change. As described in Chapter 2, unless the targeted audience is reporting through the agent or unless the sponsor (CEO) gives the agent unequivocal sponsorship, there will be no influence to change anything.

Typically, a traditional bank environment exhibits a triangular relationship, as depicted in Figure 12–7, in which both the targeted audience and the change agent report to the CEO (sponsor). The advocacy role between the agent and the target is nothing more than wishful communications. If there is no clout and no influence, there will be no change! If there is no significant change about to take place, there is no reason to manage sales. This is why a sales manager or marketing director serving as an equal to the second in command is so critical.

The goal of performance management in a sales culture is to ensure that the entire sales function is measured against objectives for achievement on a bankwide level and at the level of individual divisions, departments, teams, and individuals throughout the organization. Therefore, the sales measurement system must be able to measure external selling as well as internal and external cross-selling and referrals *throughout* the organization, including at the advisory board and board of directors levels. If the bank can afford it, the measurement system should be managed in-house so that it can be flexible and responsive to changes in organizational priorities. Sales performance measurement is a critical component of accountability.

FIGURE 12-7
No Change

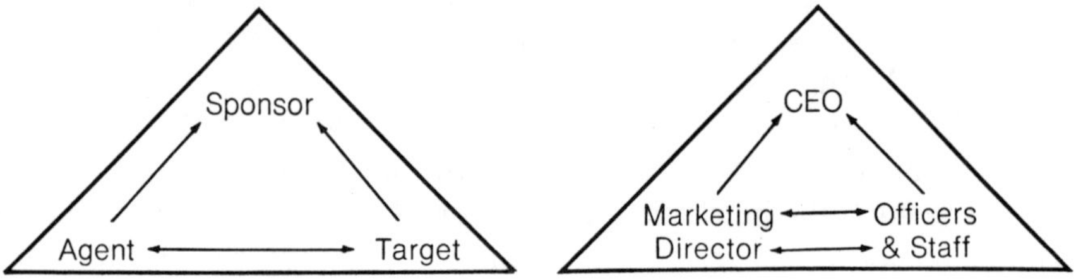

REWARD

Reward for performance is as important as any other of the nine critical disciplines that must be implemented to create and sustain a successful sales and service quality culture. People do not improve performance because someone has asked them to or because they are receiving a fair wage for their day-to-day activities. People make the extra effort when there is reason to make the extra effort. Reward and recognition are the reasons. Compensating people for tenure and/or experience does not serve as an incentive for the recipient, and it tends to serve as a disincentive for high performers.

There are many pitfalls to creating a successful incentive program. A successful program must begin with a reference to bankwide goal achievement, *not* to individual sales activity or sales performance. Rewarding only for sales performance is too self-limiting. At issue is the challenge to reward for improved *performance* and improved *productivity* in support of long-term *bankwide profitability*. Incentive programs for sales activities cannot stand alone. Furthermore, incentive programs designed for individual or small group sales activity tend to be counterproductive because they create divisiveness and may unnecessarily reward people for performance that would likely be achieved without incentive programs.

Management must realize that effective incentive programs are not created by simplistic formulas to resolve major challenges. Effective rewards for sales and work performance depend on bankwide cultural changes. Offering commissions for sales does not and will not equip a bank staff to sell.

MAKING CHANGE AFFORDABLE

The investment required to become competitive and to sustain a competitive position in the marketplace is significant. Financial institutions must streamline to be able to invest in the systems, disciplines, and skills necessary to compete in a deregulated, highly competitive financial services environment. High performance profitability will also ensure that the organization can provide the level of service quality necessary to remain competitive. *Twenty percent* return on equity will become the norm. *Twenty-five percent* should become everyone's goal. However, management cannot just pursue short-term profitability. *The key for success beyond survival is to parlay profit improvement into expanded opportunities for additional profitability through targeted growth.*

Streamlining requires a significant commitment to a whole new way of doing things. It involves the fundamental improvement of personnel efficiencies, work flow productivity, and measurement systems. *High achieving, productive personnel*—the kind of people necessary to maintain an organization's competitiveness—*will be attracted only to those institutions that meet the challenge.*

A bank's management today is faced with demands that never had to be considered before deregulation. At the very heart of this challenge for improved productivity is the need to make fundamental changes in an industry that has been—and continues to be—"fat." Banks compare unfavorably with other service industries in this respect, and the need to improve should not be taken lightly. No area of the bank can be exempt from the benefits gained through improved productivity.

A critical issue that must be addressed is that *competitive advantage is based solely on differentiation.* Every traditional financial institution, however, offers more or less the same products and services. The only difference between one institution and another is in the *delivery* of products and services. The institutions that invest in contemporary marketing strategies and allocate resources to create systems to train, reinforce, and reward their people will acquire the advantage. The good news is that the resources to pay for implementation are currently within the reach of institutions who have made the commitment to streamline. It is not unusual for banks with the commitment to become competitive to reduce noninterest expense by as much as $500,000 per $100 million in assets. These savings are realized year after year and can be invested in creating a successful, competition sales organization.

It is essential, however, that streamlining *not* result in reduced service quality to the targeted customer. The banking industry has already done a pretty good job of running customers out of the bank by improving various operational efficiencies. These operations-driven marketing schemes include drive-in windows, automated teller machines, and bank-by-phone services. In some respects, these services are welcomed by the consumer, but they have limited the bank's capacity to market by reducing the number of times a bank deals directly with its customers. On the comparatively rare occasions that customers actually enter banks to do business, they demand and deserve a higher quality of service then ever before. Frustrated by structure, bureaucracy, and the little things that can go wrong, they are choosing institutions that demonstrate a philosophy that *deserving the customer's business is the very purpose—that is, the only perceived reason—for the bank's existence.*

Quality service demands responsiveness. In many banks, decision-making has become so centralized that the people delivering the services to the customer no longer have responsibility for, or the decision-making power to respond to, even the simplest issues. This fact of operating procedures runs counter to Jan Carlzon's basic concept of inverted pyramids for decision-making in order to maximize each "moment of truth." The banking industry has become much too structured and rigid in its control of employees. In the future, the time and energy currently spent attempting to control employees must be spent training and instilling in them the ability and confidence to make immediate decisions based on a sound knowledge of not only the bank's products and services but the company's policies as well. During these moments of truth, the contemporary bank will truly differentiate itself from the competition.

There are a multitude of positive arguments that can be made for the case or improved productivity. Perhaps the most important consideration for the bank is that productivity improvements generate a better overall attitude among the bank's management and staff. High performance and productivity contribute significantly to the bank's bottom-line. Repeating the contribution every year creates new opportunities that simply are not affordable without instituting productivity improvements. All in all, it is difficult to imagine why a bank would choose to ignore the benefits of improved productivity. With tools readily available to finance the organization beyond survival, it makes sense to step up and meet the challenge.

Management cannot just pursue a "scorched earth" policy to improve earnings. A single-minded pursuit of profit improvement for the sake of profitability will prove short-sighted. The idea is to parlay profit improvements into expanded opportunities for additional profitability through targeted growth. The concept must be driven by the multidimensional need to finance the acquisition of professional skills, provide people with tools to be more productive, invest in state-of-the-art management systems, and acquire contemporary delivery systems. This multidimensional approach will allow bank management to create an efficient marketing machine that is responsive to the marketplace and able to shift gears to differentiate itself from the bank's competitors by projecting a new understanding of service quality and quality service.

SCHEDULING SUCCESS

The resources necessary to achieve success are readily available to financial institutions and are awaiting the commitment. Implementing the necessary infrastructure typically takes 2 years (see Appendix H and I) for a systematic approach to comprehensive action plans and implementation to create a successful sales/service culture. Success must be defined by each day's achievement.

Before undertaking a campaign to improve an organization's sales and service quality performance, we must be realistic. First, forget about periodic, isolated efforts to motivate people; their motivation must come from within. The leader-manager's job is to see that each employee understands what the organization is trying to accomplish and what each person's role is in the overall scheme of things. Next, find out what each person will need to maximize his or her potential.

Second, break down the tasks at hand into realistic action steps to allow people to experience and to become energized by success. There are no panaceas. Small wins will create a momentum for success never before experienced by the traditional banking institution.

The opportunistic forces of change have meant that the bank or thrift of today will bear little resemblance to the financial services institution of the 1990s. Regulatory changes, together with the ever-increasing financial sophistication and technology available to consumer, commercial, institutional and other public sectors, are responsible for the movement of banking into the mainstream of total financial services where competition from nonbank institutions will put even greater pressure on profitability than heretofore experienced.

Changing the way banks do business is not only inevitable, it is critical to the banking industry's future because it provides such great opportunity. The new environment demands diversification. It requires innovative ways to create competitive differences. Bank management must begin to deal solely with decision-making relative to customer priorities. This will provide the direction for the future.

The need for creative managerial leadership has never been greater. We must leave very little to chance. Professional market planning and meticulous execution can prevent costly mistakes and reduce the incidence of poor performance. It will also maximize unlimited opportunity for growth and profit.

The U.S. Comptroller of the Currency recently responded to questions about his observations concerning the current marketing environment for financial services. He said, "The public wants financial services, but it could care less whether it gets them from banks."

This, then, is the challenge for managerial leadership in pursuing its commitment to survive and prosper in the 1990s and beyond: to deserve the public's preference. The only difference between those who will compete successfully and those who will not is the CEO's decision that the issue is important enough to do something about it. The only reason the issue will become so important is because the cost (pain) of not making the necessary commitment is too great.

> The needs of an organization have to be satisfied by common people achieving uncommon performance.
>
> —Peter F. Drucker
> *The Effective Executive*

APPENDIX A*

MARKET-DRIVEN SALES CULTURE: SENIOR MANAGEMENT SURVEY

Rate your organizations' status relative to a market-driven sales culture. In the right hand column assess your organization's position with scores between 1 and 10, with 10 representing a totally prepared position.

A. *Strategic Market Planning*

1. Evaluate your organization's state of completion relative to defining:
   - a. Mission statement ________
   - b. Primary goals ________
   - c. Market opportunities and limitations ________
   - d. Strengths and weaknesses relative to:
     - (1) Planning ________
     - (2) Communications, internal ________
     - (3) Personnel ________
     - (4) Training ________
     - (5) Business development ________
     - (6) Sales tools ________
     - (7) Advertising ________
     - (8) Operations ________
     - (9) Facilities ________
     - (10) Equipment ________
   - e. Competitors' strengths and weaknesses ________
   - f. Your competitive advantage over primary competitors ________

*Material covered in this appendix was first discussed in Chapter 5.

2. Conducted internal and/or external market research to identify the needs and wants of your:
   a. Priority customers ________
   b. Priority prospects ________
   c. Customer satisfaction with existing services ________
3. Evaluated whether or not your clients' and prospects' needs and wants are compatible with your:
   a. Personnel skills ________
   b. Current product/services line ________
4. Developed action plans to resolve the weaknesses and take advantage of your strengths and market opportunities that have a primary influence on goal achievement? ________
5. Assigned officers responsible for each action plan? ________
6. Established an implementation or completion time frame for each action step? ________

B. *People*

Do you or does your senior management have

1. A commitment to securing, either by training or recruitment, the most technically qualified, customer-oriented personnel in your market area for each position in the bank? ________
2. A plan to identify your human resources needs for the next three to five years with a program to ensure that you fill existing voids and provide for productive, goal-oriented, successful management? ________
3. A selection system in place to ensure that you have the most qualified people with the appropriate aptitudes in every position throughout the bank? ________
4. A system in place to evaluate attitudes, encourage participatory management, and reward people for exemplary contribution? ________
5. A personnel administration program in place with position responsibilities by priority and career path and reward programs for exceptional productivity? ________
6. An in-house training coordinator, adequate training equipment, and space? ________
7. A communications plan in operation to ensure that your people are totally informed of corporate and departmental goals, goal achievement, and recognition for exceptional performance? ________

C. *Management Commitment to Sales Culture*

1. Does senior management have a specific plan in operation with quantitative goals for the following:
   a. Officers' involvement in business development ________
   b. Directors' participation in business development ________
   c. A bankwide cross-selling program to integrate retail, commercial, and trust services ________
   d. Measurement systems in place to track bankwide sales performance, bankwide cross-sell as well as referrals throughout the entire organization ________
   e. Incentive programs for business development goal achievement ________
2. Are senior officers and departmental managers measured for sales results against specific goals? ________
3. Are individuals held accountable for goal achievement relative to sales accomplishments? ________
4. Are sales responsibilities defined in every customer contact job description? ________
5. Are sales results a major consideration in annual reviews? ________
6. Is sales performance a major influence on salary adjustments? ________
7. Do you hold weekly bankwide, divisional, or departmental sales meetings with prepared agendas? ________
8. Do you have a central information file (CIF) capability in place providing total customer relationship analysis? ________
9. Is there a senior officer responsible for overall consumer services and another responsible for coordinating all commercial services? ________
10. Is there a commitment made to convert the bank to a professional sales organization? ________
11. Has your organization produced, trained for use of, and distributed a product/services manual that defines each bank product by features, benefits, how to identify a customer, pricing, and referral instructions? ________
12. Has your senior management committed to provide bankwide sales training to resolve the fear of selling, the need to manage change, business development call preparation, customer relations, how to listen, how to handle objections, and how to close? ________

D. *Market Segments/Services*
Has your organization identified the following:
1. The market segments that provide the greatest potential relative to the mission statement, position in the marketplace, goals, and objectives for the next three years ________
2. Priority list of existing and prospective customers ________
3. Specific officer assignment to total account responsibility for all existing and prospective accounts ________
4. Services currently used by your priority clients and complete analysis for each customer to identify additional services needed ________

E. *Trust Services*
1. Is the bank's senior management team committed to manage profit levels commensurate with the investment in the trust area and return on equity as compared with other areas of the bank? ________
2. Have you integrated trust services throughout the bank starting with explicit goals for trust referrals from other than trust officers? ________

F. *Rewards for Performance*
1. Does your organization have measurement systems in place to evaluate divisional, departmental, and individual contribution toward goal achievement? ________
2. Are there financial and recognition incentive programs in place to reward for productivity and goal achievement in the retention and acquisition of:
   a. Quality assets ________
   b. Stable deposits ________
   c. Assets and deposit mix ________
   d. Fee income ________

G. *Profit Management*
Has senior management
1. Incorporated a written asset/liability management policy? ________
2. Organized asset/liability committee? ________
3. Introduced microcomputer asset/liability management systems? ________
4. Reviewed funds management pricing strategies weekly? ________

5. Introduced product cost accounting and departmental profitability centers? ________
6. Identified every area of the bank to maximize performance and productivity to include:
   a. Work flow ________
   b. Personnel ________
   c. Float ________
   d. Noninterest expense ________

APPENDIX B*

MANAGEMENT SKILLS REQUIRED

	Regulated Environment: Product-Driven	*Deregulated Environment: Market-Driven*
Management emphasis on:		
Objectives	General	Specific
Goals	Growth	Profitability
Profitability	Volume	Spread + fees
Communications	Volume	Efficiency
Planning	Top down	Participatory
Direction	Budgeting	Strategic
	"Let things happen"	"Make things happen"
Marketing perception of:		
Market potential	Customers	Clients
Market will buy	Products	Solutions/needs
Product	Promote product	Integrate services
Strategy	Growth	Relationship management
Results	Profit from volume	Profit from customer satisfaction
Marketing emphasis and promotion:		
	"All things to all people"	Specialize for niche Segmentation
	Advertise	Quality
	Price	

(*continued*)

*Material covered in this appendix was first discussed in Chapter 6.

	Regulated Environment: Product-Driven	*Deregulated Environment: Market-Driven*
Product:		
Design/development	Regulators	Entrepreneurs
Pricing	Volume will carry unprofitable area "Haves" subsidize "have nots"	Profit centers Market segments pay their own way
Selling emphasis:		
	Product	Needs and solutions
	Order takers	Counselors
	Volume	Establish relationships
Organization leadership:		
	Product managers	Client managers
	Loans	Consumer services
	Deposits	Commercial services
	Fees	
Personnel:		
Recruit	Numbers	Potential/skills
Emphasize	Security	Opportunity
Train	Technical skills	People skills
Evaluate	Tenure	Productivity
Reward based on	Equal share	Performance
Orientations:		
Orientation	Project	Service
Emphasis	Volume	Productivity
Results	Volume	Measurement
Direction	Operations informs management as to what can be accomplished	Management directs operations as to what will be accomplished

MANAGEMENT EMPHASIS

In the regulated environment of the past, management emphasized growth. With product pricing essentially predetermined, management turned to high volume as the means of increasing profitability. Planning was done through budgeting, and management was content to "let things happen."

In a competitive environment, managers have to increase efficiency and develop fee income from professional services if their bank is to prosper. The complexities of the new financial marketplace mandate a participatory style of management that concentrates on strategic planning and a focus to "make things happen" rather than "let things happen."

MARKETING PERCEPTION

The banking and thrift industries have long viewed their market as consisting of customers who seek services. Therefore, their attitude was one of "let the customer come to us rather than we go to them." Banks used to think in terms of "customers." Today, it is "clients." The distinction is that customers seek services, whereas clients are sought to be served. It is a critical perception.

To retain and satisfactorily serve clients, banks must tailor products to meet specific needs; they can no longer rely on a few products that are made to fit everyone. They must develop integrated packages of services. It is rapidly becoming apparent that profits are being realized from client satisfaction, not volume. Relationship management—in which client satisfaction is paramount—is replacing the emphasis on growth.

MARKETING EMPHASIS/PROMOTION

The days of full-service banks trying to be "all things to all people" are over. To be among the survivors in the financial services industry shakeout, banks must be able to identify and serve specific market segments. Regardless of how large or small the financial institution or marketplace may be, managers should position their bank to specialize and then emphasize professional selling and quality service. Promoting price and "full service" will be unsuccessful in tomorrow's marketplace.

PRODUCT DEVELOPMENT AND PRICING

Managers once looked to regulators to design, size, fabricate, and price bank products. Now, with deregulation, entrepreneurs are performing this function, and, consequently, new products are flooding the market. In this competitive atmosphere, products have life cycles, forcing banks and thrift institutions to periodically evaluate and streamline existing services, introduce new ones, and discontinue outdated ones.

For the most part, managers are now responsible for taking new products and applying them to meet specific market needs rather than expending resources for research and development. Product pricing is also changing, as managers are finding it financially impractical to carry unprofitable products in the hope of attracting high volume elsewhere. In other words, the "haves" can no longer be expected to subsidize the "have-nots." Instead, each market segment has to pay its own way. To determine whether each market segment is, in fact, cost effective, managers must have true central information files (CIFs) for total relationship analysis. Furthermore, profit center accounting must be applied throughout the organization.

SELLING EMPHASIS

Deregulation has had a profound effect on selling, shifting the emphasis from order-takers, who strive to open as many accounts as possible, to professional sales counselors, who attempt to identify client needs and offer solutions to very specific problems.

Establishing bank/client relationships, in which a whole array of products and services are cross-sold to an individual client, is a special skill that requires a well-trained sales force. It is also a critical skill that demands an understanding of account relationships and the rewards for being able to manage relationships. A recent study found that, depending on the market area, 30 to 70 percent of executives, professionals, and small business owners—the primary customers of most banks—are dissatisfied with their current banking relationship. Of those dissatisfied, 30 to 40 percent would change to another financial institution if assured that someone would take responsibility for their account as a relationship rather than as a source to borrow or invest.

Technological advances now allow financial institutions to extend even greater personalized attention. The reliance on high-technology capabilities and the wide selection of financial products on the market necessitates a well-trained staff. There is a definite need to incorporate relationship management skills throughout the organization, a skill heretofore not called for in the traditional financial service environment.

APPENDIX C*

SALES MEASUREMENT SYSTEMS: CRITICAL COMPONENT ANALYSIS

Overall System

Systems Evaluated

Priority Ranking	Tracking System Component	A	B	C	D
	1. In-house data entry and management				
	2. Capacity to run on both a microcomputer and multi-user network				
	3. Ability to read (input) and produce (output) standard files (e.g. ASCII, Lotus)				
	4. Customizable system that fits bank, staff and products				
	5. Ability to establish and easily update staff and group sales goals				
	6. Optional multi dimensional incentive compensation based on sales results profitable to bank				
	7. Calculate incentives earned and produce payroll report				
	8. Quick turn around on reports (2 days or less)				
	9. Flexibility to print specific reports in desired sequence				
	10. User friendly system (pop up menus)				
	11. User flexibility to update/change branches employees, products, referral and marketing codes				
	12. Capacity to store 1 million records				
	13. Capacity to store and print cumulative YTD history				
	14. Built-in error checking and field verification				
	15. Print transaction report of entries at any time				
	16. Optional graphics reports				

*Material covered in this appendix was first discussed in Chapter 8.

APPENDIX D*

SALES MEASUREMENT SYSTEMS: CRITICAL COMPONENT ANALYSIS

Officer Call/Business Development

Systems Evaluated

Priority Ranking	Tracking System Component	A	B	C	D
	1. Track both effort (calls) and results (business) actually developed				
	2. Analyze portfolio profitability (net income contribution) by customer, officer & sales team				
	3. Track customer and officer portfolio growth and profitability over time				
	4. Establish key customer/prospect account portfolio by officer				
	5. Ability to establish inter-department sales teams				
	6. Establish and track individual call goals and results by individual officer and sales team				
	7. Track call status and calls made in relation to goals				
	8. Tickler system to schedule and track future calls				
	9. Ability to analyze results as a function of calls made				
	10. Customized telemarketing/follow-up mail options				

*Material covered in this appendix was first discussed in Chapter 8.

APPENDIX E*

SALES MEASUREMENT SYSTEMS: CRITICAL COMPONENT ANALYSIS

Cross-Sell System

Systems Evaluated

Priority Ranking	Tracking System Component	A	B	C	D
	1. Track sales bankwide (New Accounts to Commercial Loan)				
	2. Establish bankwide norms by job sales function (e.g. new accounts as peer group)				
	3. Establish and track individualized sales goals by region, department, branch, individual				
	4. Measure sales productivity as well as sales volume				
	5. Track deposit/loan cross sell performance separately from total cross sell ratios				
	6. Ability to consolidate data for "floating" staff that work at different branches				
	7. Calculate and accumulate year-to-date averages as well as YTD totals				
	8. Capacity to track insurance sales penetration and premium $ generated				
	9. Track new money deposited and sources of all deposits				
	10. Optional demographic market reports (e.g. sales by age, zip, customer type)				
	11. User flexibility to change products, staff branches, marketing codes at anytime				
	12. Ability to process data independently (e.g. at night) from report printing				
	13. Flexibility to print specific reports in desired sequence				
	14. Flexibility to print optional graphic reports				
	15. Capacity to input or output standard format files (e.g. ASCII, Lotus)				

*Material covered in this appendix was first discussed in Chapter 8.

APPENDIX F*

SALES MEASUREMENT SYSTEMS: CRITICAL COMPONENT ANALYSIS

Referral System

Systems Evaluated

Priority Ranking	Tracking System Component	A	B	C	D
	1. Referral transmission NOT dependent on Customer				
	2. Ability to track and report status of each referral made				
	3. Establish department and individual accountability for each referral received				
	4. Measure referral quality as well as quantity				
	5. Track sales and dollars produced as a result of referrals sold				
	6. Track referrals made and sold bankwide, across all branches and departments				
	7. Establish bankwide norms to referral performance by job function (e.g. tellers as a peer group)				
	8. Establish and measure both individual and group goals for referrals made, sold, and results				
	9. Ability to cancel referrals and report reasons why				
	10. Integrate referrals with officer call/business development				
	11. Optional telemarketing follow-up for referral leads				
	12. Referrals and sales automatically linked by computer				
	13. Flexibility to change referral categories tracked				
	14. User can update/change employee, branch, department information at any time				
	15. Flexibility to print specific reports in desired sequence				

*Material covered in this appendix was first discussed in Chapter 8.

APPENDIX G*

IDENTIFYING THE NEEDS OF SMALL BUSINESSES

The following can serve as an action plan to identify the unmet needs and opportunities within the small business and professional market, as well as to identify the relative competitive strengths and weaknesses of banks in serving this market segment.

ASSUMPTIONS

National research has revealed some interesting facts about small businesses and professionals. For example:

- They are net suppliers of demand deposit account (DDA) balances.
- This market is the fastest growing segment of the total commercial market. Some companies will become "emerging middle market" companies.
- Most money center banks and large regional banks are not effectively capitalizing on the opportunities this market represents.

Previous research also reveals that the emerging small business market consists of three segments. Each segment has unique psychographic and demographic characteristics that translate into distinct banking opportunities.

1. The "family business" is typically stable, conservative, deposit-rich, and loyal in its banking relationship.
2. Steady growth companies are typified by the professional corpora-

*Material covered in this appendix was first discussed in Chapter 11.

tion. Principals in these companies usually use their lead bank for personal banking.

3. Emerging growth companies are often highly leveraged. They are the middle-market businesses of tomorrow.

Unmet needs offer opportunities. Regional and community banks have the potential to establish a competitive advantage by capitalizing on the many opportunities this market represents.

- Thirteen percent of these companies change lead banks each year.
- Personalized service is most important in choosing *and* retaining a bank. However, one-third of small businessmen say they do not have a specific account officer assigned to their company.
- Forty-seven to 57 percent of these companies' financial decision-makers would change banks if they could be assured of knowing who was responsible for their account relationship.
- Seventy percent of small company presidents and 90 percent of professionals use their lead bank for personal banking needs.

BANK CHALLENGES

A number of challenges face all banks serving the commercial customer.

1. *The banking needs of this market are changing rapidly.* Developments in serving the corporate client are affecting the marketing and profit performance of all banks. Changes in the attitudes of company presidents and treasurers relative to service needs, new pricing strategies, product introductions, changing distribution methods, and evolving competitive strategies require bankers to introduce contemporary strategic market planning. To remain competitive, bank management must set directions based on timely, accurate marketing information and strategic analysis. Competitive intrusions of loan production offices, heightened regional competition, and nonbank financial expansion are all formidable competitors.

2. *Small business banking is a rapidly growing market segment.* Small business growth rates and emerging company formations are the most powerful trends driving economic expansion in the United States. The needs of small business as they relate to banking relationships are unique. The opportunities for banks to serve this market are unlimited.

3. *Small businesses and professionals are the banks' most important and most profitable market segment.* Competition is intensifying. Comprehensive marketing research is required for banks to have the necessary information to develop appropriate marketing strategies in order to execute productive business and to capitalize on the unlimited opportunities this market segment represents.

4. *New strategies are needed.* Previous research confirms that bankers are currently competing effectively against the array of competition. Market research is required to establish necessary strategies in order to respond to the inevitable improvement and effort by various competitors as well as to maximize opportunities.

DECISION IMPLICATIONS

A study must be designed to provide bankers with additional insight relative to their competitive position. It should guide both product development and marketing decisions. The study also should include the banking perception of small business and professionals as it relates to:

- What is the bank's competitive position relative to:

  Market share?
  Customer satisfaction?
  Strengths and weaknesses?
  Service delivery and quality?
  Officer contact frequency?
  Officer performance?

- What factors most influence the choice of a small business banking relationship?

  Services.
  Lending policies.
  Location.
  Account officers' professionalism.
  Knowledge
  Personal relationships.
  Friendliness.
  Accuracy.
  Call frequency.

- What are the key small business market segments?
  Company size.
  Industry growth.
  Growth and stability.
  Business style.
  Loan and deposit potential.
- What are the most profitable product and service opportunities?
  Business checking and transaction services.
  Lending.
  Investment services.
  Financial planning and investment services.
  Cash management.
  Computer banking services.
  Pension and profit-sharing services.
  Planning and consulting services.
- What is the ideal prototype for account and service personnel?
- How should products and services be packaged and priced?
- What level of resources should bankers commit to profitably serve the small business market?

The study should be designed to provide information and knowledge that will enable bankers more profitably to serve the small business market.

APPROACH

To completely develop a strategic marketing plan to market small business banking services, four inputs are essential:

1. Emerging small business market.
2. Calling and supporting business banker interviews.
3. Shopping small business bankers.
4. Competitive analysis/marketing plan.

Small Business Market

The study of small businesses should provide a concise and detailed analysis of the bank's position in this important market segment. Some of the questions answered in this phase are:

- What is the bank's share of the market?
- What is the bank's share by sales size?
- Is the bank's market share improving or declining?
- Is the bank strengthening relationships with existing customers?
- How about competitors?
- What do business decision-makers and professionals say are the bank's strengths? Weaknesses?
- What do noncustomers say about the bank's strengths and weaknesses?
- What about saturation? How frequently are bank officers soliciting new business from customers? Noncustomers?
- How frequently do bank competitors solicit our customers? Our prospects?
- How does bank service performance compare?

Calling and Support Business Banker Interviews

The purpose of this exercise is not to identify and qualify the banking officer. Rather, this series of interviews will quantify bankers' perceptions of customer needs, services provided, and customer satisfaction. This data, then, can be compared with the client data to determine whether bank officers leave an accurate perception of the priority clientele they serve.

The first step provides a good view of how these markets profile banks as well as bank competitors in satisfying banking needs. Next, we need to know how the bank's calling personnel view the markets and their competitors and what their opinions are on strategies to acquire new, profitable business and perceived customer satisfaction.

The objective of this phase is also to elicit experiences and ideas of those closest to the customer and prospect.

Shopping Small Business Bankers

Personnel from banks and competitive personnel have recently been shopped at random by legitimate business people with legitimate banking needs. Eleven specific cities with approximately 25 visits per city have been completed.

The purpose of the local shopping visits is not intended to assess an individual calling officer's performance. Thus, names should be maintained anonymously. Instead, shopping visits of the bank and selected competitors are intended to provide information in the following areas:

- Product knowledge.
- Professionalism.
- Sales approach.
- Sales materials and usage.
- Sales effectiveness.
- Support staff usage.
- Pricing accommodations.
- Promotional knowledge.

Developing the Strategic Marketing Plan

The ultimate product of the study is in facilitating implementation of the findings. Focus will begin by conducting quality marketing research and is followed by making recommendations to implement necessary strategies in order to take advantage of the local market dynamics.

Two products are specifically derived from the interaction: (1) *competitive analysis and spelcific positioning* and (2) *the strategic marketing plan.*

A competitor's profile of marketing strenghts and weaknesses is developed from each of the previous three phases of the research. Recommendations should include action plans to counter competitive threats and to take advantage of specific weaknesses.

A similar but more in-depth process is used to develop the overall strategic plan. We recommend an interactive approach as the most effective and efficient method to achieve our objectives. The findings are communicated in an attractive, action-oriented audiovisual presentation as well as through in-depth reports that can be shared with the membership.

APPENDIX H*

IMPLEMENTING SALES/SERVICE QUALITY CULTURE

(See Appendix I for implementation schedule.)

ACTION PLAN

1. Planning
   a. Creative Vision and Master Strategy
   b. Design and/or update Strategic Plan
   c. Market Segmentation Plans
      (1) Identify needs of priority market segments
      (2) Design game plans for each segment
   d. Finalize Market Plan
2. Commitment
   a. Assign sales leadership/sales management responsibilities
   b. Assign organizational responsibilities
   c. Communicate focus, priorities, and commitment bankwide
3. Training and/or reinforcement
   a. Officer call and cross-sell/referral
   b. Product knowledge/testing
   c. Sales management skills
   d. Service quality
4. Set goals for sales, cross-sell, and referrals for individuals, teams, and market segments to reinforce bankwide goals.
5. Introduce sales management, structure, and administration procedures.

*Material covered in this appendix was first discussed in Chapter 12.

6. Implement bankwide sales performance measurement systems.
   a. Officer call (manual before micro)
   b. Cross-sell and referral (micro)
7. Design and implement reward for performance to include recognition for:
   a. Bankwide goal achievement
      (1) Bonus
      (2) Pension and/or profit sharing
   b. Division, departmental, team, and/or individual
      (1) Sales, cross-sales, and referrals
      (2) Work flow
      (3) SPIFs
8. Introduce annual review instruments to include performance analysis of each participant involved directly and indirectly in sales.
9. Appoint a task force for both commercial and consumer product development and enhancement responsibilities.
10. Implement a total CIF with total relationship analysis.

APPENDIX I†

SALES/SERVICE QUALITY IMPLEMENTATION SCHEDULE

		Months																		Quarter			
ACTION PLANS	Off. Resp	1	2	3	4	5	6	7	8	9	10	11	12	13	14	15	16	17	18	7	8	9	10
1. Planning																							
a. Vision/Master Strategy	CEO	P	D																				
b. Strategic Plan	Sr Mgr		P	S	R-D	I	*	*	Rv	Rv	Rv	S	R	I									
c. Market Segmentation	MD				P	P	N	N	N	R	D	B	*	I	*	*	Rv	*	*	P	*	*	P
d. Market Plan	MD								P	P	P	B	*	I	*	*	Rv	*	*	P	*	*	P
2. Commitment	CEO																						
a. Sales Leadership/Mgmt	CEO		AR	*	*							Rv			*	*			*		Rv		*
b. Organizational Responsibilities	CEO					AR	*	*	*			Rv			*	*			*		Rv		*
3. Training	MD HR									P	P	B								P	B		
a. Sales/Cross Sale/Ref	MD				P	E	R	D	T	T	T	T	T	Rf	Rf	Rf	Rf	Rf	Rf	Rf	Rf	Rf	Rf
b. Product Testing	HR				P	P	I	T	T	T	T	T	T	T	T	T	T	T	T	T	T	T	T
c. Sales Managment	MD		AR	T	T	T	Rf	Rf	Rf	Rf	Rf	Rf	Rf	Rf	Rf	Rf	Rf	Rf	Rf	Rf	Rf	Rf	Rf
d. Service Quality	HR					P	E	R	D	T	T	T	T	T	Rf	Rf	Rf	Rf	Rf	Rf	Rf	Rf	Rf
4. Set Goals	EA							P	P	P	R-D	G	G	*	*	*	*	*	*	P	R-D	G	*
5. Sales Administration	MD								P	P	P	I	*	*	*	*	*	*	*	Rv	*	*	*
6. Sales Performance Measurement	BK			P	P	T	T	I	*	*	Rv			Rv			Rv			Rv	Rv	Rv	Rv
7. Reward for Performance	MR BK			Rv	P	P	R-D	P	P	P	P	B	I	*	*					R-D	B	*	*
8. Annual Reviews	TH				E	P	P	I				Rv				T	T	*	*		Rv		
9. Product TFs	BK			AR	*	*	*	*	*	*	*	*	*	*	*	*	*	*	*	*	*	*	*
10. CIF	KO			P	P	C	C	C	C	C	C	C	C	C	C	C	C	C	C	I	*	*	*

AR= Assign Responsibility B=Budget C=Conversion D=Decision E=Evaluate G=Set Goals I=Implement M=Measure MR=Market Research N=Identify Needs P=Plan R=Recommendation Rv= Review Rf=Reinforce S=Schedule Sem=Seminar T=Train *=Ck Status X=Ongoing

†Material covered in this appendix was first discussed in Chapter 12.

GLOSSARY

driving force The underlying purpose behind the motivation and decision-making of all objectives being pursued.

goals The significant quantitative values leading to the overall success of the mission and its objectives.

major objectives Specific quantitative values leading to the overall success of the mission and its objectives.

mission The future direction of the organization. In broad terms, its effort and activities. Does not include profitability, which is a goal of an organization.

professional selling The enthusiastic transfer of belief in the product or service required to fulfill a need.

strategic marketing Targeting high-level leverageable businesses through accurate repositioning of the company's image, its products, and its support services. Traditional marketing attracts the customer through the appropriate adoption of product price packaging and promotion of techniques.

strategic planning The deliberate process of organizing and directing the future destiny of an organization as well as the individuals who are part of it.

strategic positioning The creation of a unique and vital niche in either the industry or the marketplace. The niche should be both profitable and defendable. Strategic thinking is the effective balance between both creative and analytical thinking such that an optimum effort is concentrated on precise objectives.

strategy The framework of definitive critical activities resulting from the strategic planning process.

tactics Specific actions directly involved with contact elements inevitably responsible for affecting the final results of a given situation.

vision The verbal expression of a distinct and visible future market position.

SUGGESTED READINGS

Aaker, David A. and George S. Day. *Marketing Research.* New York: John Wiley & Sons, 1983.

Albrecht, Karl. *At America's Service.* Homewood, Illinois: Dow Jones-Irwin, 1988.

Berry, Leonard L., David R. Bennett, and Carter W. Brown. *Service Quality: A Profit Strategy for Financial Institutions.* Homewood, Illinois: Dow Jones-Irwin, 1989.

Berry, Leonard L., Charles M. Futrell, and Michael R. Bowers, *Bankers Who Sell: Improving Selling Effectiveness in Banking.* Homewood Illinois: Dow Jones-Irwin, 1985.

Burns, Thomas J. *Effective Communications and Advertising for Financial Institutions.* Englewood Cliffs, New Jersey: Prentice-Hall, Inc., 1986.

Case Studies in Financial Services Marketing. Chicago, Illinois: Information Services Department, Bank Marketing Association, 1988.

Day, George S. *Analysis for Strategic Market Decisions.* St. Paul, Minnesota: West Publishing Company, 1985.

Donnelly, James H. Jr., Leonard L. Berry, and Thomas W. Thompson. *Marketing Financial Services: A Strategic Vision.* Homewood, Illinois: Dow Jones-Irwin, 1985.

Drucker, Peter F. *The Effective Executive.* New York: Harper & Row, 1966.

Engel, James F., et al. *Promotional Strategy.* Homewood, Illinois: Richard D. Irwin, Inc., 1983.

Hughs, C. David, and Charles H. Singler. *Strategic Sales Management.* Reading, Massachusetts: Addison-Wesley Publishing Company Inc., 1983.

Kinnear, Thomas C., and Kenneth L. Bernhardt. *Principles of Marketing.* Glenview, Illinois: Scott, Foresman & Company, 1986.

Kotler, Philip. *Marketing Management: Analysis, Planning and Control,* Fifth Edition. Englewood Cliffs, New Jersey: Prentice-Hall, Inc., 1984.

Levitt, Theodore. *The Marketing Imagination.* New York: The Free Press, 1983.

Luck, David J. and O. C. Ferrell. *Marketing Strategy and Plans,* Second Edition. Englewood Cliffs, New Jersey: Prentice-Hall, Inc., 1985.

Macdonald, Charles R. *The Marketing Audit Workbook.* Englewood Cliffs, New Jersey: Institute for Business Planning, a Prentice-Hall Company, 1982.

Magrath, Allan J. *Market Smarts: Proven Strategies to Outfox and Outflank Your Competition.* New York: John Wiley & Sons, 1988.

Measuring and Monitoring Service Quality. Chicago, Illinois: The Research and Planning Department, Bank Marketing Association, 1988.

Miller, Robert B. and Stephen E. Heiman (with Tad Tuleja). *Strategic Selling: The Unique Sales System Proven Successful by America's Best Companies.* New York: William Morrow & Company, Inc., 1985.

Nation's Premier Small Business Banking Programs, Volume II: Preview of New Products and Services. Chicago, Illinois: Council on Financial Competition, 1987.

Porter, Michael E. *Competitive Advantage: Creating and Sustaining Superior Performance.* New York: Free Press, 1985.

Richardson, Linda. *Winning Negotiation Strategies for Bankers.* Homewood, Illinois: Dow Jones-Irwin, 1987.

Richardson, Linda. *Bankers in the Selling Role: A Consultative Guide to Cross-Selling Financial Services.* New York: John Wiley & Sons, 1981.

Seglin, Jeffrey and Jeffrey Lauterbach. *Personal Financial Planning in Banks: A Handbook for Decision Making.* Boston, Massachusetts: Bankers Publishing Company, 1986.

Shaw, Roy and Richard J. Semenik. *Marketing,* Fifth Edition. Cincinnati, Ohio: South-Western Publishing Company, 1985.

Sinkey, Joseph F. Jr. *Commercial Bank Financial Management,* Second Edition. New York: Macmillan Publishing Company Inc., 1986.

Thamara, Thomas. *Banker's Guide to New Growth Opportunities.* Englewood Cliffs, New Jersey: Prentice-Hall, Inc., 1988.

INDEX

O